Prentice-Hall
WORKBOOK
FOR WRITERS
FOURTH EDITION

Prentice-Hall
WORKBOOK
FOR WRITERS
FOURTH EDITION

Melinda G. Kramer
Purdue University

John W. Presley
Augusta College

Donald C. Rigg
Broward Community College

Prentice-Hall, Inc., Englewood Cliffs, New Jersey 07632

Editorial/production supervision
  and interior design: Sylvia Moore
Manufacturing buyer: Harry P. Baisley

Cover:
Blackish Green Tone on Blue, 1957
Oil on canvas. 103 × 116¾"
© Estate of Mark Rothko, 1984

Printed in the United States of America

10 9 8 7 6 5 4 3 2

ISBN 0-13-696055-3 01

Prentice-Hall International, Inc., *London*
Prentice-Hall of Australia Pty. Limited, *Sydney*
Editora Prentice-Hall do Brasil, Ltda., *Rio de Janeiro*
Prentice-Hall Canada Inc., *Toronto*
Prentice-Hall Hispanoamericana, S.A., *Mexico*
Prentice-Hall of India Private Limited, *New Delhi*
Prentice-Hall of Japan, Inc., *Tokyo*
Prentice-Hall of Southeast Asia Pte. Ltd., *Singapore*
Whitehall Books Limited, *Wellington, New Zealand*

CONTENTS

*Corresponding sections of *Prentice-Hall Handbook for Writers*, 9th Edition, indicated in parentheses.

SENTENCE FAULTS

MANUSCRIPT MECHANICS

PUNCTUATION

EFFECTIVE SENTENCES

PREFACE

The *Prentice-Hall Workbook for Writers,* 4th Edition, provides what users want most in a workbook. It contains new exercises in almost every section. In addition, the fourth edition preserves those teaching and learning aids from previous editions that suit the workbook for either classroom use or successful self-study.

The reason behind the new exercises is fairly simple: students learn better if the material is fresh and engaging. Since the ethnic heritage theme that proved so popular in the third edition offers an almost limitless store of rich material for exercises and examples, we were delighted to continue that theme in this edition. As before, we have included a wide range of types of exercises and a large number of them. In areas where students frequently need extra work, the number of exercise sentences is especially plentiful.

Second, the *Workbook* has an extremely useful format. So that students will not lose the instructional material when they tear out the exercise pages, the exercises and the "teaching" portions are separated. This format allows for expanded instructional sections as well; students receive more complete explanations and examples before they work the exercises.

Also, a number of sections contain short "practices" to which answers are given at the end of the section. Thus, students can check their understanding of the subject matter and receive immediate feedback. Used in class, the practices enable instructors to identify and address problems that need further attention *before* students work the exercises rather than after the fact.

The *Workbook* has always had a dual purpose. It was conceived as a companion to the *Prentice-Hall Handbook for Writers,* providing explanations and exercises to complement those in the *Handbook.* But it has also been effectively used alone in composition courses and is written as a totally self-sufficient text. The fourth edition continues to fulfill those two aims.

The fourth edition of the *Workbook* and the ninth edition of the *Handbook* follow the same order of presentation. Teachers wishing to refer students to the *Workbook* for supplementary exercises will have no trouble finding appropriately sequenced, matching material. References to corresponding *Handbook* sections are given in parentheses in the *Workbook's* section headings and in the table of contents.

Classes using the *Prentice-Hall Diagnostic Test for Writers* will also find the *Workbook* to be a valuable aid. Its explanatory sections and exercises can give students additional instruction and practice in problem areas. The *Workbook* also contains review sections intended to familiarize students with the kinds of material in, and the format of, the *Diagnostic Test.*

Because we recognize that there are as many methods for teaching writing as there are writing teachers, we have used a variety of approaches in the *Workbook's* exercises while striving to keep the majority of them key-gradable. We advocate no one theory but acknowledge the best of our profession's pedagogy. We understand the concerns of traditionalists; at the same time, we value the innovations derived from recent research. Our constant goal has been to present what colleagues and students tell us is sensible—and what works.

We gratefully acknowledge the guidance and assistance of our acquisitions editor at Prentice-Hall, Phillip Miller, and our production editor, Sylvia Moore. The worthiness of a book is due in no small part to the quality of the team supporting the authors; our support from Prentice-Hall has been outstanding.

Finally, we wish to thank the students at Purdue University, Augusta College, and Broward Community College. It is our students, as always, who provide the essential challenge and inspiration.

MELINDA G. KRAMER

JOHN W. PRESLEY

DONALD C. RIGG

Prentice-Hall

WORKBOOK
FOR WRITERS
FOURTH EDITION

OUR COMMON LANGUAGE

This book is about language, particularly written English and specifically *standard* written English. Few of us always speak standard English; we frequently use slang, jargon, or dialects easily recognized by our families, friends, and coworkers. But when we pick up popular magazines or newspapers, open textbooks, or look at notices on bulletin boards, what we see—and *expect* to see—is standard English.

Because they are widely accepted and generally followed, the rules and conventions governing standard English ensure that the greatest number of people will understand a written message. We use standard English not necessarily because it is "good" or "right," but because it is the accepted norm; in fact, *standard* means "the norm." Of course that's the purpose of communication—to get the message across, to be easily understood by as many readers as possible.

Having a standard language is important to the development of a society. It enables people from different backgrounds and ethnic origins to communicate with one another. In a society as culturally mixed as the United States', standard English has been crucial. We are a nation of immigrants. You and I, or our relatives, came to this country from some place else. Even native Americans, the American Indians, immigrated to this continent from another land—from Asia, across the Bering Strait, so anthropologists tell us. The fact that our common language is English rather than Spanish, Swahili, French, or Vietnamese is much less important than the fact that we have a common language for communicating our present ideas and sharing our richly diverse pasts.

This book is also about sharing the past. Many of the exercises contain information about America's ethnic roots. Since we or our ancestors originally came from some place else, a book devoted to our common language is an appropriate place to learn a little about what we immigrants have contributed to American society.

*   *   *   *   *

My grandmother's family immigrated to America from Switzerland. As a child, Grandmother spoke only German. I remember asking her what she had wanted most when she was a little girl—assuming that, like me, she had wanted a pony or a new doll. I have never forgotten her answer: "I wanted most," she said, "to know English."

Melinda G. Kramer, *coauthor*

A WORKING VOCABULARY

One way people analyze a subject to find out how it works is to break that subject into categories, into its various parts, so they can more easily examine how the individual parts work together as a whole. They may also develop a special vocabulary or set of terms for naming the parts and their functions.

You have performed this kind of analysis and naming many times during your life. In order to know how to improve your car's performance, you must learn how the engine works. To do that, you have to learn the names for the parts: the carburetor, the pistons, the distributor. In order to understand the way the human body functions, you learn about its various systems—the cardiovascular system, the nervous system, the digestive system—and their parts, such as the heart, the brain, the stomach.

Learning about language is no different. It too is a system with parts and functions described by a vocabulary of terms. Just as you breathe without analyzing how to do it, so you write and speak without worrying much about the system or the terms for explaining how language is used. But in order to talk *about* language, about writing, important first steps are understanding the system and knowing the vocabulary.

The following paragraphs introduce some of the basic vocabulary used to describe how written language works, how individual words come together in larger groups that convey meaning. **Part** and **function** are key terms describing how English works. Both words and sentences can be classified by part (what they are called) and function (what they do).

We can categorize words by the parts of speech to which they belong—such as nouns or verbs. We can also categorize sentences by their parts—such as subjects, predicates, or objects. Word functions are naming, predicating, modifying, or connecting. Sentence functions are asserting (stating), interrogating (questioning), or exclaiming. For now we'll concern ourselves just with the categories for words.

TYPICAL WORD FUNCTIONS	PARTS OF SPEECH	EXAMPLES
naming	nouns, pronouns	grandmother, German, home, my
predicating (stating, asserting)	verbs	spoke, was
modifying	adjectives, adverbs	rapid, fluent, always
connecting	prepositions, conjunctions	at, and

That parts of speech can change their functions from sentence to sentence can sometimes be confusing. For example, a noun is always a noun, but it can modify as well as name.

NAMING NOUN	My *grandmother* always spoke rapid, fluent German at home.
MODIFYING NOUN	My *grandmother's* German was always rapid and fluent.

In the first sentence, *grandmother* is a straightforward noun telling us who spoke German. In the second sentence, however, *grandmother's* takes the possessive form and tells us whose German was rapid and fluent. In the second case, we say *grandmother's* is a noun functioning as a modifier. In fact, we can say that the noun functions as an adjective, describing or qualifying *German*, another noun.

Now you know why the preceding list used the heading ***Typical** Word Functions*. First you learn how a part of speech usually functions. In time, as you become familiar with the way language works, you will learn to recognize and become able to explain the variations.

1

NOUNS AND PRONOUNS (1a)

NOUNS

A **noun** names a person, place, or thing. A **concrete noun** names something that can be seen, heard, touched, smelled, or tasted, something that can be perceived by the senses; an **abstract noun** names an idea, quality, or concept, not a substance. A **proper noun** names a particular person, place, or thing and should be capitalized; a **common noun** is the general name of a person, place, or thing and is not capitalized. A **collective noun** uses the singular form to name a group of individuals in a unit.

CONCRETE NOUN	America is a *land* of *immigrants.*
ABSTRACT NOUN	Some people came here to escape *oppression.*
PROPER NOUN	Others, like my *Great-grandfather Kelly,* came to escape the famine in *Ireland.*
COMMON NOUN	Before 1820, no official immigration *records* were kept.
COLLECTIVE NOUN	But since 1820, the *population* has increased by nearly 50 million foreign-born men and women.

Practice A: Identifying nouns   *Underline all the words functioning as nouns in the following sentences. The answers are listed at the end of this section.*

[1] The nations in North America, Canada and the United States, are probably the most ethnically diverse countries in the world. [2] Other large nations, such as China or the Soviet Union, have many ethnic groups living within their borders, but North America was uniquely populated by immigrants who began arriving in the seventeenth century and are still arriving today. [3] Even the original native population, the American Indians, may well have immigrated from Asia into North America by crossing the Bering Strait into Alaska. [4] Their numbers were eventually combined with people from almost every other country in the world.

PRONOUNS

A **pronoun** is a word used in place of a noun. Pronouns (and other words that substitute for nouns) are sometimes called **substantives.** There are several types of pronouns:

PERSONAL	I, we, you, he, she, it, they, me, us, him, her, them, mine, our(s), your(s), his, hers, its, their(s)
RELATIVE	who, which, that
INTERROGATIVE	who, which, that
DEMONSTRATIVE	this, that, these, those
INDEFINITE	one, any, each, anyone, somebody, all, etc.
RECIPROCAL	each other, one another

3

| INTENSIVE | myself, yourself, himself, etc. |
| REFLEXIVE | myself, yourself, herself, etc. |

PERSONAL   RELATIVE   INTERROGATIVE
We   are a nation of immigrants *who* assumed (and *who* has

       DEMONSTRATIVE   INDEFINITE
not?) in   *this*   country new identities,   *each*   learning to call

RECIPROCAL   INTENSIVE   REFLEXIVE
one another American, just as we *ourselves* finally learned to think of *ourselves*

as Americans.

Practice B: Identifying pronouns   *Underline all the pronouns in the following sentences. The answers are listed at the end of this section.*

[1] The continent of North America was "discovered" and claimed by many different ethnic groups. [2] We all know the story of its discovery by Christopher Columbus, who claimed it in the name of Queen Isabella. [3] He was followed by English and Portuguese explorers, each of whom claimed an area for his country. [4] All these explorers may have been preceded by others, though. [5] It is generally accepted that Leif Ericson and his Viking sailors were in North America before Columbus. [6] Even the Vikings may have discovered America after someone else, however, since there is evidence that this country was visited centuries earlier by Chinese sailors. [7] Who knows what evidence we may eventually discover ourselves about early "discoverers" of America?

Answers to Practice A   [1] nations, North America, Canada, United States, countries, world   [2] nations, China, Soviet Union, groups, borders, North America, immigrants, century   [3] population, American Indians, Asia, North America, Bering Strait, Alaska   [4] numbers, people, country, world

Answers to Practice B   [2] we, all, its, who, it   [3] He, each, whom, his   [4] All, these, others   [5] It, that, his   [6] someone, that, this   [7] Who, what, we, ourselves

EXERCISE 1, NOUNS AND PRONOUNS   (1a)

In the blanks, copy all the nouns and pronouns from the following sentences. If a noun or pronoun is repeated in a sentence, write it out each time it appears.

Example   Many early settlers in America were Polish.

_____ *settlers, America* _____

1. There are legends that Columbus had Polish sailors aboard his ships.

_____

2. Pulaski and Kosciuszko were both heroes of the American Revolution.

_____

3. Count Pulaski was an idealist who volunteered to fight.

_____

4. He created an American cavalry force that won many battles.

_____

5. His cavalry was created just at the time when Washington himself was becoming discouraged.

_____

6. Pulaski may have been Washington's major military strategist.

_____

7. General Kosciuszko helped Washington and his army in different ways.

_____

8. He was an engineer who built forts and fortifications.

_____

9. Kosciuszko was a genius at using natural terrain as a defense.

_____

10. He dug trenches, cut trees, and used natural barriers to fortify all of Washington's camps.

_____

11. His use of the terrain at Saratoga probably won this battle for Washington.

_____

12. That victory convinced the French that they should enter the war as American allies.

_____

13. During the nineteenth century, a steady stream of Poles immigrated to America.

_____

14. By the early years of this century, almost three million Polish peasants had come to America.

_____

15. Because of their numbers, they were often a source of cheap labor, and they were forced to live in ethnic "neighborhoods."

_____

16. Within a generation, Poles began to excel in the professions, the arts, and the sciences.

_____

17. Helena Modjeska was probably the finest Shakespearean actress in the world at the turn of this century.

_____

18. Madame Curie, who discovered radium, was actually Marie Curie-Sklodowska.

_____

19. She was originally Polish, and she had married a French physicist.

_____

20. The Curies traveled to America to help establish Polish-American schools.

_____

21. Polish names are familiar in almost every walk of life in America today.

_____

22. Arthur Rubenstein, Charles Bronson, and Jack Palance are all creative artists of Polish lineage.

_____

23. Matuszak, Yastrzemski, and Strain are some Polish names familiar to sports fans.

_____

24. Goldwater, Muskie, and Brzezinski are names that illustrate the continuing influence of Poles in American politics.

_____

25. The intermingling of Polish and American history is still as thorough as ever.

_____

2
VERBS AND VERBALS (1a–b)

VERBS

A **verb** provides the energy in a sentence. It usually expresses action, occurrence, or condition and indicates time relationships by its tense. For example, "My grandmother *spoke* German" expresses the action of speaking and places that action in the past. "My grandmother's English *improved* slowly" expresses an occurrence that took place in the past. "My grandmother's German *was* fluent" expresses a condition (fluency) that existed in the past.

Verbs may appear as single words or in groups called **verb phrases**. Verb phrases are composed of main verbs and auxiliaries, also known as helping verbs. The most common helping verbs are *have, had, is (am, are), was (were), does (do), did, will, would, can, could, shall, should, may, might,* and *must.*

We look at verbs in more detail in Sections 11 through 14.

VERB PHRASE	VERB

Although I *might have   learned* German from my grandmother, I *learned* it at
     AUXILIARIES MAIN
                  VERB

school instead.

VERBALS

Verbals is the term used for verb forms that are not functioning as **predicators**. In other words, verbals do not assert, ask questions, or otherwise work like verbs. Instead, they name or modify. Verbals act as noun substitutes, adjectives, or adverbs. The forms of the three types of verbals can help you distinguish them from verbs functioning as predicates.

TYPE OF VERBAL	FORM OF VERBAL	FUNCTION OF VERBAL
Infinitive	*to* + verb	naming or modifying: noun substitute, adjective, adverb
	to win	*To win* was very important. [Used as noun]
Participle	verb + *ing* (present form)	modifying: adjective only
	cooking	The soup smelled good *cooking.* [The participle *cooking* modifies *soup.*]
	verb + *ed* or *en* or internal vowel change (past form)	
	cooked, eaten, gone	*Cooked, eaten,* and *gone,* the soup had satisfied their hunger. [The participles modify *soup.*]
Gerund	verb + *ing*	naming: noun substitute only
	cooking	*Cooking* is hard work. [*Cooking* functions as a noun.]

Some predicating verb phrases are composed of participles and helping verbs (as in *Max was running*). To further add to the confusion, of the three types of verbals, both participles and gerunds can have the *-ing* form. You have to check the function of an *-ing* word to know which it is. Participles used alone (without helping verbs) function only as adjectives. Gerunds serve only as nouns. All verbals, however, use adverbs as modifiers, as do true verbs. For more practice with verbals, see Section 6, *Phrases.*

Practice: Identifying verbs   Underline all the verbs and verb phrases in the following sentences. The answers are listed next.

[1] Ralph Bunche was born in Detroit and educated at UCLA and Harvard. [2] He is mainly remembered for his part in the civil rights struggle, but he also served at very high levels in government. [3] After teaching at Howard University and working for the War Department as an African and Far East specialist, Bunche went to work as a department head at the State Department. [4] He later helped to plan the United Nations; in 1950 he was awarded the Nobel Peace Prize. [5] He had taken part in the armistice talks after World War II; he received the country's highest civilian award, the Medal of Freedom, for this service.

Answers to the Practice   [1] was born, educated   [2] is remembered, served
[3] went   [4] helped, was awarded   [5] had taken, received

EXERCISE 2, VERBS (1a)

In the blanks, copy all the verbs and verb phrases from the following sentences. Circle the main verb in each verb phrase you write.

Example   There are many Black American military heroes.

_____ *are* _____

1.   Black Americans have served in every American military action.

_____

2.   History books often omit the military contributions of Blacks.

_____

3.   In early military actions like the Revolutionary War, the role of Blacks was admittedly small.

_____

4.   The number of free Blacks in America at that time was small.

_____

5.   Even though they almost begged to be allowed to fight, Blacks served with great honor.

_____

6.   Two Black men, Oliver Cromwell and Prince Whipple, crossed the Delaware River with Washington.

_____

7.   General Newport, of the Royal Army, was captured by Prince Estabrook, a Black soldier in the Continental Army.

_____

8.   Another Black hero, Peter Salem, killed Major Pitcairn as he was savoring his expected victory at Bunker Hill.

_____

9.   Black soldiers were often forced to serve in segregated units.

_____

10. Whites had long believed that Blacks could not command well or use firearms accurately.

_____

11. Despite these bigoted views of their abilities, Blacks distinguished themselves in combat.

12. The Medal of Honor was awarded in 1863 to William Carney.

13. Carney fought against the Plains Indians with the Massachusetts Colored Infantry.

14. Isaiah Dorman, a Black scout, served and died at the Little Big Horn with Custer in 1876.

15. In 1877, Henry Flippes was the first Black to graduate from West Point.

16. By World War I, 40,000 Black combat soldiers were serving with the French command.

17. Neither U.S. nor British commanders wished to use these men.

18. The *Croix de Guerre* had never been awarded to Americans before World War I.

19. The French government awarded it to Henry Johnson and Needham Roberts at the close of World War I.

20. Both men had served in the 369th Infantry's Black "Hellfighters" group.

21. During World War II, over 1.4 million Black men and women were drafted or volunteered for military service.

22. At Pearl Harbor, four enemy planes were brought down by a Black mess attendant who manned a machine gun.

23. The attendant, Dorie Miller, was acclaimed as a hero very quickly.

24. The Black fighter pilots of Benjamin Davis, Jr. proved courageous and valuable during the Italian campaign.

25. American military history has been made, in large part, by Black Americans who served their country capably.

3
ADJECTIVE AND ADVERB FUNCTIONS   (1b)

ADJECTIVES

An **adjective** modifies a noun or pronoun. It describes, limits, or qualifies the meaning of the word it modifies, often telling *what kind, how many,* or *which one.* An adjective cannot modify an adverb or another adjective. There are several types of adjectives:

DESCRIPTIVE	English is the *common* language in America.
POSSESSIVE	*Our* brand of English is somewhat different from the English in Great Britain.
DEMONSTRATIVE	*That* variety of English is now called British English, whereas our language is called American English.
INTERROGATIVE	*What* differences are there between the two?
NUMERICAL	To cite just *one* example, Americans say a car has a "hood," but the British say it has a "bonnet."
ARTICLES	Whereas we refer to *a* car's "trunk," *an* English person calls *the* trunk a "boot."

Several words in the preceding examples also appeared in the previous list of pronouns. *That* is listed both as a demonstrative pronoun and as a demonstrative adjective. *What* shows up twice: once as an interrogative pronoun and once as an interrogative adjective. Remember that classifying a word by its part of speech sometimes depends on its function in a sentence. The appearance of *that* and *what* in two categories illustrates this point very well. In the examples here, *that* and *what* could be described as pronouns functioning as modifiers—that is, pronouns performing the function of adjectives.

Practice A: Identifying adjectives   Underline all the words (including the articles) that function as adjectives in the following sentences. The answers are listed at the end of this section.

[1] A short history of one textile town in New England helps illustrate America's lure for immigrants. [2] When the mill first opened, young girls from Scotland, skilled weavers, were brought to America to teach weaving skills to local workers. [3] Later, the Scots workers often brought over their relatives. [4] By 1860, Irish families were becoming the basis of the work force as their work as canal builders and railroad workers led them to more New England towns. [5] By this time, over one-fourth of the town's citizens were of foreign birth. [6] German and Swedish immigrants took jobs in the mill as skilled craftspeople. [7] In the 1870s, scarce land and depleted farms in Canada sent many French-Canadians, drawn by the mill's agents who traveled through Canada recruiting unskilled labor, into New England mill towns in search of work.
[8] Later immigrants, particularly Greeks and Poles, arrived in smaller numbers, but as long as it was thriving, the textile industry and its steady wages continued to draw immigrants.

ADVERBS

An **adverb** modifies, describes, limits, or qualifies the meaning of a verb, an adjective, or another adverb. Besides modifying single words, adverbs can also modify whole sentences or parts of sentences. Adverbs frequently indicate time, place, manner, or degree, telling *when*, *where*, or *how*. Negatives such as *no, never,* and *not* may be used as adverbs. Some adverbs have a distinctive *-ly* ending, making them easy to spot in sentences. The following examples show the use of adverbs:

TIME   American English began to develop *soon* after English settlers arrived in the New World. [*Soon* modifies the verb phrase *began to develop*, telling when.]

PLACE   The settlers needed new words to describe the new experiences they found *here*. [*Here* modifies the verb *found*, telling where.]

MANNER   So they invented words or borrowed or adapted *suitably* descriptive words from other languages. [*Suitably* modifies the adjective *descriptive*, telling in what way.]

DEGREE   The settlers' vocabulary *very* quickly began to reflect their new surroundings. [*Very* modifies the adverb *quickly*, telling how.]

NUMBER   A new word spoken *once* or *twice* is just a novelty, but with repeated use it becomes part of the common language. [*Once* and *twice* modify the verb *spoken*, telling how many times.]

Practice B: Identifying adverbs   *Underline all the words functioning as adverbs in the following sentences. The answers are listed at the end of this section.*

[1] Colonial America, while still remaining basically English, was already a melting pot. [2] Germans, who comprised about 6 percent of the population, had settled mainly in Pennsylvania; they were erroneously called the Pennsylvania Dutch, a stubbornly persisting error even today. [3] The Scotch-Irish, who made up 7 percent of the colonial population, were really Scots Lowlanders who had been transplanted to northern Ireland. [4] Their economic life was severely hampered when the English arbitrarily placed restrictions on the linen and wool industries. [5] Early in the 1700's, the embittered Scotch-Irish immigrated to the Colonies, where they found the best land already taken by the previous immigrants; they immediately moved to claim new ground in frontier areas. [6] Another 5 percent of the colonial population was French, Dutch, Swedes, Jews, Irish, Swiss, and Scots Highlanders. [7] Approximately one-fifth of the population was Black, and thus constituted easily the largest non-English element in the Colonies.

Answers to Practice A   [1] A, short, one, textile, America's   [2] the, young, skilled, weaving, local   [3] The, Scots, their   [4] Irish, the, the, work, their, canal, railroad, more, New England   [5] this, the, foreign   [6] German, Swedish, the, skilled [7] the, scarce, depleted, many, the, mill's, unskilled, New England, mill   [8] Later, smaller, thriving, the, textile, its, steady

Answers to Practice B   [1] still, basically, already   [2] mainly, erroneously, stubbornly, even, today   [3] up, really   [4] severely, arbitrarily   [5] Early, already, immediately   [7] Approximately, easily

EXERCISE 3, ADJECTIVE AND ADVERB FUNCTIONS   (1b)

Each of the following sentences contains at least one adjective or adverb. Some sentences contain both. In the blanks, copy the adjectives and adverbs, labeling them *adj* or *adv*. Write the words they modify in parentheses. Do not copy or label the articles *a, an,* or *the.*

Example   The facts about ethnic groups can be really surprising.

ethnic, adj (groups), really, adv (surprising)

1. Which is the richest town in America?

2. High on any list of rich cities will be Palm Springs, California.

3. Few houses in Palm Springs are worth less than half a million dollars.

4. In Palm Springs, people write personal checks for the full price of new Rolls Royces.

5. Rich and famous people come to Palm Springs regularly for relaxation.

6. To keep the city looking wealthy, its appearance is strictly regulated.

7. There are no flashing neon signs and no billboards.

8. There are simply no motels in Palm Springs; all hotels are called "resorts."

9. The height and color of buildings are regulated; everything is a soothing pastel color.

10. If a wealthy homeowner installs a chandelier which is visible from the street, the chandelier must be approved by a committee.

11. The result is a city of beautiful white stucco walls and red Spanish tiled roofs.

12. There is, however, a startling number of empty lots, worth a half million per acre, in the center of Palm Springs.

___

13. These lots are owned by 107 Agua Caliente Indians, the richest minority group in the United States.

___

14. The Aguas originally owned all of Palm Springs.

___

15. President U. S. Grant gave the Aguas 32,000 sandy acres in exchange for allowing a right of way to Southern Pacific Railway.

___

16. A new treaty in 1959 allowed the Aguas to sell or lease the land to white businesspeople and homeowners.

___

17. That's the real reason so many of the Rolls Royces belong to the Agua Calientes.

___

18. The original treaty allowed the Aguas to hold their land "without encumbrance."

___

19. Recent court rulings say taxes and zoning laws are "encumbrances."

___

20. Besides paying no taxes, the Aguas are the only people in Palm Springs who can do whatever they wish with their sandy land.

___

21. The Aguas signed long-term leases with the businesspeople who built hotels and other buildings in Palm Springs.

___

22. Those leases are the source of their vast wealth.

___

23. The Aguas have very intelligently planned for their future security, too.

___

24. While the lots they leased out bring in money, the empty lots are simultaneously increasing in value.

___

25. Meanwhile, the Agua Calientes ride in their expensive cars, too, surrounded by the rich and famous.

___

4
PREPOSITIONS AND CONJUNCTIONS   (1b)

PREPOSITIONS

A preposition is a connecting word that typically indicates time, place, or movement. Some common prepositions are *about, above, across, after, around, at, before, behind, between, by, during, for, from, in, into, of, off, on, out, over, since, through, to, under, up, with.*

A preposition connects its object (a noun, pronoun, or noun substitute) with some other word in a sentence. Together the preposition, its object, and any words modifying the object form a prepositional phrase—for example, *on a sunny morning.*

		PREPOSITIONAL PHRASE
	VERB PHRASE	MODIFYING VERB

The words *succotash* and *skunk* were borrowed   from   the Algonquian Indians.

PREPOSITION   OBJECT OF
PREPOSITION

Prepositions and prepositional phrases can modify nouns, verbs, adjectives, or adverbs; they supply additional information about the words they modify.

USED AS ADJECTIVE	American English has borrowed many words *with Indian origins.* [The prepositional phrase modifies the noun *words*, telling what kind.]
USED AS ADVERB	Algonquian words are alive *in our vocabulary today.* [The prepositional phrase modifies the adjective *alive*, telling where.]
USED AS ADVERB	We still use more than 100 words we owe *to the Algonquians.* [The prepositional phrase modifies the verb *owe*, telling whom.]
USED AS ADVERB	Once *upon a time* Algonquian was America's most widely spoken Indian language. [The prepositional phrase modifies the adverb *once*, telling exactly when.]

Practice A: Identifying prepositions   Underline all the prepositions in the following sentences. The answers are listed at the end of this section.

[1] The Scotch-Irish who settled on frontier lands sometimes found these lands occupied by red or white owners. [2] The pugnacious Scotch-Irish simply "squatted" on these lands, and from necessity became superb scouts and Indian fighters. [3] They brought with them from Scotland and Ireland the secrets of whiskey distilling and quickly established stills wherever they went. [4] In fact, the Scotch-Irish were quite religious; even their detractors said the Scotch-Irish kept the Sabbath, along with anything else they touched. [5] They had no love for the British who had uprooted them twice, so they eagerly joined in the American Revolution. [6] About a dozen Presidents have been of Scotch-Irish descent.

CONJUNCTIONS

A **conjunction** connects words, phrases, or clauses, and thus creates a relationship between sentence elements. Conjunctions can establish the following relationships between words or word groups:

Coordinating conjunctions show equal rank or importance. The coordinating conjunctions are *and, but, for, nor, or, so, yet.*

> Many English words were adopted from their Indian inventors, *but* Indians did not invent "peace pipe" *and* "pale face." [The first half of the sentence tells a fact. The second half challenges a related misconception. The contrast between what is true and not true about Indian contributions to English is given equal grammatical emphasis by *but. And* connects *peace pipe* and *pale face* and establishes their equal status as examples of words Indians did not invent.]

Subordinating conjunctions create unequal rank or dependence. They join words, phrases, or clauses that depend on other parts of the sentence to complete their meanings. The subordinating conjunctions are *after, although, as, if, since, that, unless, until, when, where, whether, while, why.*

> *Although* these words are associated with Indians, white settlers invented them. [The *although* clause depends upon, or is subordinated to, the second clause, because without the second clause the meaning of the first clause is incomplete.]

Practice B: Identifying conjunctions   Underline all the conjunctions in the following sentences. The answers are listed at the end of this section.

[1] Although heavy immigration from Europe occurred during the Colonial period, in 1798 the Federalists and the anti-French elements in Congress passed a set of laws designed to discourage immigration. [2] Because they were penniless, most immigrants were scorned by the Federalists. [3] But the more democratic Jeffersonians welcomed the immigrants as voters. [4] Aliens were suddenly required to reside in America for fourteen years before they could become citizens, and the President was given the power—by a Federalist Congress—to deport or imprison undesirable immigrants. [5] Though these laws may have been partially justified, since hundreds of revolutionaries were leaving Europe for America, the laws were never enforced. [6] Even if the laws were necessary as a war measure, they seemed to be an arbitrary use of power and contrary to the spirit of the Constitution.

Answers to Practice A   [1] on, by   [2] on, from   [3] with, from, of   [4] In, along with   [5] for, in   [6] About, of

Answers to Practice B   [1] Although, and   [2] Because   [3] But   [4] before, and, or   [5] Though, since   [6] Even if, and

EXERCISE 4, PREPOSITIONS AND CONJUNCTIONS (1b)

Prepositional phrases function as modifiers by adding information to sentences. Expand each of the following sentences by supplying prepositional phrases that add modifying information.

Example Professor Smith is an expert.

Professor Smith is an expert in foreign affairs.

1. America has many ethnic groups.

_____

2. Some are very interesting.

_____

3. Each has a culture and tradition.

_____

4. Some maintain their culture.

_____

5. I am interested in studying one.

_____

Conjunctions connect sentence elements, allowing us to combine information and ideas. Combine the following pairs of sentences using coordinating conjunctions, subordinating conjunctions, or both.

Example Many ethnic groups have distinctive dress. They also have distinctive foods.

Many ethnic groups have distinctive dress, and they also have distinctive foods.

6. Geographic patterns of immigration can be discovered. The patterns are not all-inclusive.

_____

7. French-Canadians settled in New England. New England is close to Canada.

_____

8. Cuba and Florida are only 90 miles apart. Many Cuban immigrants settled in Florida.

_____

9. The Southwest has large Hispanic communities. It is close to Mexico. It was once owned by Mexico.

_____

10. California was once ruled by Spain. It has large Asian communities. It is directly east of Asia and the Pacific Islands.

_____

For each of the following sets of sentences, use prepositional phrases, conjunctions, or both to compose one sentence including all the information given. You may have to rearrange or omit words to create a smooth sentence.

Example   I like French cooking. It is elegant. It is sophisticated.

I like French cooking because it is elegant and sophisticated.

11. I enjoy Mexican food. It is usually hot. It is usually spicy.

_____

12. I like tacos. I like burritos. I like chimichangas. I haven't developed a taste for guacamole yet.

_____

13. Some Mexican dishes are surprisingly mild. I enjoy quesadillas. A quesadilla is covered with a mild cheese sauce.

_____

14. Spanish food is milder than Mexican food. Good Spanish restaurants are hard to find.

_____

15. There are many seafood dishes native to Spain. Mexican dishes do not emphasize seafood much. Paella is a mixture of seafood and pimiento-flavored rice.

_____

5
SUBJECTS, PREDICATES, AND SENTENCE PATTERNS   (1a)

All complete sentences have a **subject** and a **predicate**. The **subject** of a sentence is most often a noun, pronoun, or noun substitute that names someone or something. A subject with all its modifiers is called a **complete subject**. A subject without any modifiers is called a **simple subject**. The following sentences show various types of subjects. Each complete subject appears in italics; each simple subject is in boldface italics.

*The largest **group** of immigrants to America* was the Germans. [Noun as subject]

They have accounted for more than 15 percent of the immigrants in the last century and a half. [Pronoun as subject]

Being of German descent is a source of pride for many people. [Verbal phrase substituted for noun subject]

*German **men** and **women*** made up 10 percent of America's total population in 1776. [Two nouns as subjects, called *compound subject*]

The **predicate** of a sentence gives information about the subject by making an assertion or asking a question. The most important part of the predicate is the **verb** or **verb phrase** that makes up the **simple predicate**. The simple predicate expresses action, occurrence, or condition (state of being). Other words in a **complete predicate** either are modifiers or receive the action of the predicate's verb. In the following sentences, the complete predicate is italicized and the simple predicate is in boldface italics.

The first wave of German immigrants ***began** in 1683*. The second wave ***began arriving** in 1825*. [Action]

In both cases, Germany *was **suffering** from bad economic conditions*. [Occurrence]

Most of the seventeenth-century immigrants ***were** happy with their new lives*. [Condition, state of being]

Practice: Identifying subjects and predicates   Underline the simple subject and simple predicate in the following sentences. Be sure not to overlook possible compound subjects or verbs. The answers are listed at the end of this section.

[1] Letters back home from immigrants to America were called "America letters." [2] These letters described and praised life in the new country in glowing terms: America had no taxes, no compulsory military service, and every man, woman, and child ate three "meat meals" a day. [3] With the introduction of transoceanic steamships, the ocean voyage took twelve days instead of twelve weeks. [4] The influx of immigrants tripled by 1850.

SENTENCE PATTERNS

Pattern 1   The simplest sentences contain only a subject and a verb, as in *Immigrants settled.* We can add information to these simple, or **core**, sentences by supplying modifiers: adjectives, adverbs, prepositional phrases.

SUBJECT   VERB
The Dutch immigrants settled quickly in their new homes.

Besides the pattern shown in a core sentence, English sentences can follow four other patterns that provide additional information in the predicate. The pattern variations all occur in the predicate—in the verb and what follows it.

Pattern 2   The predicate may contain a **direct object,** a noun, pronoun, or noun substitute that receives the action of the verb and answers "what" or "whom."

<pre>
          SUBJECT VERB   DIRECT OBJECT
A German immigrant built the Brooklyn Bridge.
</pre>

Pattern 3   The predicate may contain a direct object followed by an **object complement,** a noun or modifier that renames or describes the direct object.

<pre>
SUBJECT VERB   DIRECT OBJECT   OBJECT COMPLEMENT (NOUN)
People   called the Brooklyn Bridge the Eighth Wonder of the World.
</pre>

<pre>
   SUBJECT   VERB   DIRECT OBJECT OBJECT COMPLEMENT (ADJECTIVE)
The   bridge   helped make   Brooklyn   famous.
</pre>

Pattern 4   The predicate may contain a direct object preceded by an **indirect object,** a noun or pronoun that identifies the receiver of whatever is named in the direct object.

<pre>
   SUBJECT VERB   INDIRECT OBJECT   DIRECT OBJECT
A con artist tried to sell   me   the Brooklyn Bridge.
</pre>

Indirect objects function rather like prepositional phrases with the *to* or *for* left out: *A con artist tried to sell [to] me the Brooklyn Bridge.*

Pattern 5   The predicate may contain a linking verb followed by a **complement**—either a **predicate noun** or a **predicate adjective.** Linking verbs are discussed in Section 12. Some common linking verbs are *is, are, was, were, has been, might be, see, appear, become*; sometimes *feel, act, look, taste, smell,* and *sound* function as linking verbs. You will be able to spot predicate nouns if you remember that they rename the subject of the sentence. Predicate adjectives modify the subject.

		COMPLEMENT	
SUBJECT	VERB	PRED. NOUN	PRED. ADJ.
The builder of the Brooklyn Bridge	was	a German.	
His name	was	John Roebling.	
Roebling's death	appears		tragic.
The bridge	may have been		responsible.

These patterns form the basis for all English sentences. All of their elements can be compounded without changing the basic sentence pattern. That is, a sentence may have two or more subjects, verbs, indirect objects, direct objects, and/or complements. *Someone tried to sell my friend and me the Brooklyn Bridge.* has a compound indirect object (*friend, me*), but the basic sentence pattern remains unchanged.

Other sentence variations are created by rearranging or recombining the elements in these patterns. One variation is worth special notice because it can be confusing. Certain sentences use *there* plus a verb as something called an **expletive.** Such a phrase is never the subject of a sentence. For instance, in *There were two deaths in his family last year., there were* is an expletive. The verb makes a statement about *deaths*, not about *there. Deaths* is the subject. The sense of the sentence is "Two deaths occurred in his family last year."

Answers to Practice   [1] Letters, were called   [2] letters, described [and] praised;
America, had; man, woman, [and] child, ate   [3] voyage, took   [4] influx, tripled

EXERCISE 5, SUBJECTS AND PREDICATES   (1a)

Underline and label the subjects (*s*), verbs (*v*), direct objects (*do*), indirect objects (*id*), and complements (*c*) in the following sentences.

Example   The game of darts was brought to America by English colonists.

(with labels: S above "game", V above "was brought")

1.   Darts was a popular game in the early colonies.

2.   Drinkers at taverns and travelers made the game popular.

3.   Gradually, an American version of the classic game was developed.

4.   In the last century the game lost popularity everywhere except the Northeast.

5.   The old English pub game is being reintroduced now, so American players can

compete in international tournaments.

6.   Brass is the favored metal for competition darts.

7.   The dart weighs between 11 and 45 grams.

8.   The competition dartboard is the "English clock" dartboard.

9.   The dartboard is divided, like a pie, into twenty numbered sections.

10.   The English dartboard is constructed by tying bristle into the correct shape.

11.   Bristle doesn't deteriorate as quickly as a cardboard surface will.

12.   The classic English pub game is called "301."

13.   Each player starts with a score of 301 points.

14.   Each player takes three throws at the board from eight feet away.

15.   Darts that hit within the scoring area earn a score equal to the number of the section.

16.   There are also double and triple zones which double or triple the score earned.

17.   In 301, the score earned is subtracted from 301.

18.   The first player to reach zero wins the game.

19. In addition, each player must begin and end the game by hitting a double zone.

20. The English version of darts makes the American version, in which points are simply added up, seem awfully simple.

21. Other English variations on the game are 501, 801, 1001, "cricket," "baseball," and "killer."

22. Almost 4 million people in America play darts seriously, at the tournament level.

23. Some of the top tournaments are the U.S. Open and the World Masters Tournament.

24. In world play, the English still dominate the game.

25. Twenty million players make the British the leading power in darts.

6
PHRASES (1c)

If you have read the sections in this book on verbs and prepositions, you already have a working knowledge of phrases. A **phrase** is a group of related words that differs from a clause in that a phrase lacks either a subject or a verb. A phrase may contain a subject or a verb but never both. For example, the following sentence is constructed of a **noun phrase** containing a subject and a **verb phrase** composed of a finite verb and its auxiliary:

The old man   has died.

The sentence *The old man has lived a long life.* contains two noun phrases (*the old man* and *a long life*), each having its own subject (*man* and *life*) and a verb phrase (*has lived*).

Keep in mind that even though a phrase may contain its own subject or verb, these do not necessarily function as the subject or predicate of the entire sentence. For example, although *life* is the subject of its noun phrase in the example sentence, it is also the direct object of the verb and is thus a part of the predicate in the sentence as a whole.

Other types of phrases usually consist of a **preposition** and its object or a **verbal** and its object.

PREPOSITIONAL PHRASES	*In the forest, down the road*
PARTICIPIAL PHRASE	The man *picking the flowers* was in love.
GERUND PHRASE	*Driving the stake* caused her to sweat.
INFINITIVE PHRASE	He wanted *to leave home.*

You also know, if you have read about verbals (Section 2) and prepositions (Section 4), that phrases frequently function as modifiers. They act as adjectives when they modify nouns or noun substitutes. They act as adverbs when they modify verbs, adjectives, or other adverbs. Some verbal phrases and, occasionally, prepositional phrases can also function as nouns. The following examples show how phrases (in this case, prepositional phrases) can function as adjectives, adverbs, and nouns:

ADJECTIVE MODIFYING NOUN	She likes pastry *with cherry filling.* [Modifies *pastry*]
ADVERB MODIFYING VERB	The recipe came *from Vienna.* [Modifies *came*]
ADVERB MODIFYING ADJECTIVE	Viennese pastries are full *of calories.* [Modifies *full*]
ADVERB MODIFYING ADVERB	Viennese pastries should be eaten slowly *for the most satisfaction.* [Modifies *slowly*]
NOUN SUBSTITUTE	*"Without guilt"* is my motto when eating fattening, luscious pastry. [Acts as subject of sentence]

Phrases are among a writer's most versatile tools. They enable you, as a writer, to elaborate, to amplify, and to qualify the core of a sentence—its subject and its verb. With a few well-chosen phrases, you can give your readers a wealth of information and thus add substantially to their understanding of a sentence's meaning.

For example, suppose you have written the simple sentence *Pastries tempt me.* Most people will read the sentence sympathetically and will agree, "Me too." Each reader will also supply his or her own mental picture of a tempting pastry. Perhaps this is the reaction you want, but you've left a lot of "detail work" up to each reader's imagination. In fact, you haven't really exerted very much control over the writer-reader relationship because the sentence is so bare. Chances are that you, too, have a specific mental image of a tempting pastry, and chances are that you really want the reader to see *your* image. Using phrases to expand the core sentence is an appropriate means for providing the reader with a more complete understanding of just what *you* mean.

PARTICIPIAL PHRASE
    PREPOSITIONAL PHRASE
Covered   in thick, sugar icing,

    PARTICIPIAL PHRASE
        PREPOSITIONAL PHRASES   CORE
scenting the bakery shop with their aroma of yeast and fruit filling, pastries tempt me

  INFINITIVE PHRASE   PREPOSITIONAL PHRASE
to stop and spend my money on short-lived delights but long-lived pounds.

Two participial phrases, an infinitive phrase, and four prepositional phrases have expanded the three-word core sentence *Pastries tempt me.* into a richly detailed sensory experience for the reader. Of course, you will not always need so much information in your sentences, but phrases do give you the tools for building detail and adding information when you want it.

Practice: Expanding a sentence with phrases   *Write a brief core sentence; then expand your sentence with details, using at least one participial or gerund phrase, at least one infinitive phrase, and at least two prepositional phrases. Be sure that the final sentence is grammatically correct and that it is logical. Revise your sentence until you feel satisfied with it.*

EXERCISE 6, PHRASES   (1c)

Write sentences with prepositional phrases using the given prepositions.

Example   with *Pizza with anchovies is my favorite.*

1. *in* _____

2. *of* _____

3. *behind* _____

4. *for* _____

5. *by* _____

6. *between* _____

7. *on* _____

8. *under* _____

9. *above* _____

10. *with* _____

11. *through* _____

12. *before* _____

13. *upon* _____

14. *across* _____

15. *during* _____

Form participles, gerunds, and infinitives from the following verbs; then write sentences using your results as participial, gerund, and infinitive phrases. Review the end of Section 2 on verbals if you need a refresher.

Example   *search*

(participial) *We were searching the stands for our friends.*

(gerund) *Searching the stands was a waste of time.*

(infinitive) *It was pointless to search the stands because our friends had gone.*

25

16. *travel*

(participial) _____

(gerund) _____

(infinitive) _____

17. *hope*

(participial) _____

(gerund) _____

(infinitive) _____

18. *lament*

(participial) _____

(gerund) _____

(infinitive) _____

For each of the following sentences, indicate whether the italicized phrase functions as a noun (*n*), an adjective (*adj*), or an adverb (*adv*) by writing the appropriate abbreviation over it.

adv

Example   The Civil War was won *with the aid* of immigrants.

19. *Between 1861 and 1865,* the number of immigrants flowing to the North more than equaled the number of war casualties.

20. The majority of these immigrants were *of British, Irish, or German birth.*

21. Thousands of them, *inspired by gratitude to their new land,* enlisted in the Union Army.

22. One-fifth of the men *to fight* on the Union side were foreign born.

23. *Commanding such forces* was difficult; in one division, commands had to be given in four different languages.

7
CLAUSES (1d)

INDEPENDENT CLAUSES

An **independent clause**, often called a **main clause**, has both a subject and a verb. It makes a complete, independent statement, and it is not introduced by a subordinating word.

A sentence may have one main clause, or it may have several. When two or more main clauses are present in a sentence, they are usually joined by **coordinating conjunctions.** The most common coordinating conjunctions are *and, but, or, nor, for,* and sometimes *so* and *yet.* Ordinarily, a comma is used before a coordinating conjunction that joins independent clauses.

My Danish mother is a fantastic cook, *and* she is proud of it.
She prepares delicious meals, *yet* she makes it look easy.

Conjunctive adverbs are another group of words used to connect independent clauses. When a conjunctive adverb is used between independent clauses, it is preceded by a semicolon and followed by a comma. The principal conjunctive adverbs are these:

accordingly	consequently	hence	moreover	then
also	else	however	nevertheless	therefore
besides	furthermore	likewise	otherwise	thus

The following sentences use conjunctive adverbs between independent clauses:

The Danes love Danish bacon; *however,* they cannot buy it in Denmark.
Danish bacon is exported only; *consequently,* Danes buy it abroad when they travel and bring it home.

SUBORDINATE CLAUSES

A **subordinate** or **dependent clause,** like an independent clause, has both a subject and a verb. However, it functions as an adjective, adverb, or noun and thus cannot stand alone as a complete sentence. Whenever a group of words contains a subordinate clause, the group must also contain an independent clause in order to qualify as a sentence.

When I arrived [Subordinate clause is not a sentence; the meaning is incomplete.]
When I arrived in Denmark, my mother asked if I had brought home any bacon.
[Subordinate clause is joined to an independent clause which completes its meaning; the construction is a sentence.]

A subordinate clause is always preceded by a **subordinating conjunction** or a **relative pronoun.** Some of the most widely used subordinating conjunctions follow:

after	how	though	when
although	if	unless	where
as	since	until	whether
because	then	whatever	why

Relative pronouns often introduce subordinate clauses. When used in this way, a relative pronoun may also be referred to as a conjunctive pronoun. Common relative pronouns are the following:

that which who whom whose

A subordinate clause can function as an adjective, an adverb, or a noun. An **adjective clause** modifies either a noun or a noun substitute.

> Anyone who has seen Victor Borge loves this humorous Danish immigrant. [The subordinate clause *who has seen Victor Borge* modifies the pronoun *anyone.*]

The **adverb clause** modifies either a verb, an adjective, or an adverb.

> People laugh when he plays the piano. [The subordinate clause *when he plays the piano* modifies the verb *laugh.*]
>
> Borge is especially funny because he mixes jokes and music. [The subordinate clause *because he mixes jokes and music* modifies the adjective *funny.*]
>
> He can play seriously if he wants to. [The subordinate clause *if he wants to* modifies the adverb *seriously.*]

The **noun clause** may serve as either a subject, a complement renaming the subject, an indirect object, a direct object of a verb, or an object of a preposition.

> Whoever Borge entertains is made happier. [The subordinate clause *Whoever Borge entertains* serves as the subject.]
>
> His infectious humor is what audiences like. [The subordinate clause *what audiences like* serves as the complement, the predicate noun, of the sentence.]
>
> Borge brings whoever listens moments of delight. [The subordinate clause *whoever listens* serves as the indirect object of the verb *brings.*]
>
> Audiences frequently request that he play certain songs. [The subordinate clause *that he play certain songs* serves as the direct object of the verb *request.*]
>
> They are always curious about when he will give another concert. [The subordinate clause *when he will give another concert* serves as the object of the preposition *about.*]

USING CLAUSES TO COMBINE IDEAS

Clauses enable a writer to combine several related ideas into a single sentence, instead of having to use a separate sentence for each thought. In elementary school you may have learned this definition of a sentence: A sentence is a complete statement expressing a single thought. Although that definition is true in a very general way, sentences containing several clauses allow for the expression of complex, or multifaceted thoughts.

Consider, for example, the following sentences:

> Lego toys are plastic bricks. They interlock. Children build houses, cars, and towers with them. Lego toys were invented by Ole Christiansen during the Depression. Christiansen was a Danish cabinetmaker. He could not find work. He made the Lego toys from wood. He then exchanged them for food.

Notice how short and choppy many of these sentences sound. As you read them, you probably began combining some of the related thoughts in your mind to smooth out the bumps. The practice with phrases in Section 6 gave you some tools for expanding sentences with details. By using clauses to form additional relationships, you can also coordinate and subordinate ideas:

                                    INDEPENDENT
                SUBORDINATE CLAUSE
    The Lego toys that children use to build houses, cars,

    CLAUSE

                                                        INDEPENDENT
    and towers are interlocking, plastic bricks. They were invented by Ole Christiansen

                                                INDEPENDENT
    CLAUSE   SUBORDINATE CLAUSE
    during the Depression. Christiansen, who was a Danish cabinetmaker, could not

    CLAUSE
            INDEPENDENT CLAUSE   SUBORDINATE CLAUSE
    find work, so he made wooden Lego toys which he then exchanged for food.

In place of the choppy statements, we now have three sentences that combine ideas from the original eight. Besides being smoother, these three sentences establish relationships between ideas by means of their interlocking clauses.

CONFUSING PHRASE AND CLAUSE CONNECTIVES

Certain words that can be either prepositions or conjunctions sometimes cause students to confuse phrases with clauses. This confusion can occur if you try to identify a word group on the basis of the connective alone instead of examining the entire word group. For example, the following sentences use the same connective; but in the first sentence the connective introduces a phrase, and in the second it introduces a clause:

    George has not practiced the piano *since* his accident.
    Since he broke his arm, he has been unable to play.

Rather than rely on the connective alone, examine the entire word group it introduces. Remember that a preposition introduces a phrase—the noun, pronoun, or substantive that is the object of the preposition, and any words that modify that object. A conjunction, on the other hand, introduces a clause—a group of words containing a subject and a verb. A phrase never contains both a subject and a verb.

Some of the words that may be either prepositions or conjunctions are *after, before, for, until,* and *since.*

Practice: Using clauses to combine ideas   Revise the following sentences, using subordinate clauses to combine the original ten sentences into no more than five sentences expressing the same ideas. One possible answer is listed at the end of this section.

A significant number of early colonists were indentured servants. The indentured servants were frequently from England, Wales, or Germany. An indentured servant could not pay his or her own passage to the Colonies. Indentured servants sold their labor to a wealthier colonist in return for passage to America. In Georgia, for example, the period of service lasted from four to fourteen years. At the end of his or her service, the Trustees of the Georgia Colony gave the freed servant land. The former master was required to give the freed servant farming implements. Ship captains were allowed to provide passage for such servants and then to offer them for sale to the highest bidder. There were always people willing to obtain passage to the Colonies in such a manner. The system was a failure. Indentured servants were discontented and anxious to get started on their own.

Answer to the Practice: Many answers are possible; the following revision shows one representative type.

A significant number of early colonists were indentured servants who were from England, Wales, or Germany and were unable to pay their own passage to the Colonies. Indentured servants sold their labor for a period which ranged in Georgia, for example, from four to fourteen years, at the end of which the servant was given land by the Trustees of the Georgia Colony and farming implements by his or her former master. Ship captains were allowed to provide passage for such servants and then to offer them for sale to the highest bidder. Even though there were always people willing to obtain passage to the Colonies in such a manner, the system was a failure since the indentured servants were discontented and anxious to get started on their own.

Name _____ Date _____ Score _____

EXERCISE 7–1, INDEPENDENT AND SUBORDINATE CLAUSES **(1d)**

Write sentences with two independent clauses joined by the listed coordinating
conjunctions and conjunctive adverbs. Be sure to punctuate your sentences correctly.

Example *accordingly* She studied hard; accordingly, she passed the test.

thus We brought raincoats; thus, we were prepared for the storm.

1. *meanwhile* _____
2. *nor* _____
3. *furthermore* _____
4. *hence* _____
5. *or* _____
6. *moreover* _____
7. *otherwise* _____
8. *for* _____
9. *likewise* _____
10. *and* _____
11. *consequently* _____
12. *but* _____
13. *then* _____
14. *so* _____
15. *also* _____
16. *besides* _____
17. *nevertheless* _____
18. *however* _____

19. *therefore* _____

20. *else* _____

Write sentences, each with an independent clause and a subordinate clause. Begin the subordinate clause with the given subordinating conjunction or relative pronoun.

Example   *until* *Until you cooperate, we can do little for you.*

                that *They knew that the time was right.*

21. *since* _____

22. *then* _____

23. *whatever* _____

24. *why* _____

25. *whoever* _____

26. *whether* _____

27. *whose* _____

28. *where* _____

29. *when* _____

30. *until* _____

31. *who* _____

32. *unless* _____

33. *which* _____

34. *though* _____

35. *if* _____

36. *how* _____

37. *because* _____

38. *after* _____

39. *as* _____

40. *although* _____

EXERCISE 7-2, FUNCTIONS OF SUBORDINATE CLAUSES (1d)

In the following sentences, underline main clauses once and subordinate clauses twice. Indicate whether a subordinate clause functions as an adjective (*adj*), adverb (*adv*), or noun (*n*) by writing the appropriate abbreviation above the clause.

Example   Immigration substantially stopped in the Great Depression, except for
adj
a few refugees who were fleeing from fascism.

1. Though the last wave of immigrants had not achieved full social equality, the Great Depression gave them their first opportunities.

2. The economic upheaval that caused the Depression gave Italians, Poles, South Slavs, and Jews the chances for better lives.

3. Whereas craft unions had discriminated against the newcomers, the industrial unions now welcomed them.

4. The New Deal, which was President Roosevelt's sweeping political reform, gave them their first chances at politics and public service.

5. Roosevelt once reminded the Daughters of the American Revolution that all of us are descended from immigrants and revolutionists.

Underline the subordinate clause in each of the following sentences twice. Indicate whether it functions as an adjective clause, an adverb clause, or a noun clause by writing *adj, adv,* or *n* above it. Then underline once the word that the clause modifies or complements, or that serves as subject or object.

adj
Example   Fifty-one judges who were appointed by Roosevelt were Catholic.

6. Roosevelt had no respect for the old attitude that recent immigrants were somehow inferior.

7. Whether an appointee was competent or incompetent was all that interested Roosevelt.

8. When he had finished building the new agencies of his administration, Roosevelt staffed them with many people from ethnic minorities.

9. Political brokers in the cities, like Mayor LaGuardia of New York, gave recognition to groups that had been shut out of politics.

10. Though the Depression was cruel to many, it helped assimilate various ethnic groups into American politics.

Write sentences containing subordinate clauses that perform the stated functions.

Example   (adverb clause modifying verb)

I jumped when the firecracker exploded.

11. (subordinate adjective clause modifying noun)

12. (subordinate adjective clause modifying pronoun)

13. (subordinate adverb clause modifying verb)

14. (subordinate adverb clause modifying adjective)

15. (subordinate adverb clause modifying adverb)

16. (subordinate noun clause, subject)

17. (subordinate noun clause, complement)

18. (subordinate noun clause, direct object)

19. (subordinate noun clause, object of verb)

20. (subordinate noun clause, object of preposition)

Name _____ Date _____ Score _____

EXERCISE 7–3, CONFUSING PHRASE AND CLAUSE CONNECTIVES   (1d)

A few connectives may be either prepositions or conjunctions and can thus introduce both phrases or clauses. These collectives are *after, before, until, for,* and *since.* In the following sentences, carefully examine the word groups introduced by the italicized connectives. Then write *P* above the connective if it is a preposition (introducing a phrase) or *C* if it is a conjunction (introducing a clause).

Example   <u>*Until*</u> the Depression, Blacks had been largely neglected by politicians.

1. *Since* Blacks traditionally voted for Republicans, even Republican politicians ignored them.

2. *Since* the days of Reconstruction, Blacks had been victims of economic neglect.

3. The Black was, *until* Roosevelt's New Deal, "the last hired and the first fired."

4. *Before* Roosevelt, Black leaders had referred to "the lily-White House."

5. *After* Roosevelt took office, Washington began to demonstrate sympathy for the problems of Blacks.

6. New Deal agencies like the CCC created new opportunities *for* Blacks.

7. Many able Blacks were nominated *for* senior jobs in these agencies.

8. *After* taking office these Blacks initiated programs that helped their fellow Blacks.

9. Of course, these agency administrators symbolized new opportunities *for* their race.

10. By 1936, Black voters were shifting support to Democratic candidates, *since* these opportunities were considered to be Roosevelt's creation.

In each of the following sentences, word groups are italicized. Write *P* above it if the group is a phrase or *C* if it is a clause.

Example   The Depression continued <u>*until the industrial boom needed for*</u>
<u>*World War II gained strength.*</u>

11. *Since the country was fighting fascism in Europe,* it could hardly continue segregationist policies at home.

12. The income gap between whites and Blacks narrowed *after industrial production speeded up.*

13. Blacks became bitter *for they were assigned menial tasks in the segregated army or defense industries.*

14. *Until June 1941,* this policy conflicted with all the war idealism abroad in the country.

15. A. Philip Randolph, a union president, planned a march on Washington *until Roosevelt issued Executive Order 8802.*

16. *After this order took effect,* all discrimination in hiring by defense industries was illegal.

17. The Fair Employment Practices Commission worked constantly *for greater job opportunities for Blacks.*

18. The Commission's work was easier than it might have been *before labor came into short supply during the war.*

19. *Since the military needed personnel equally desperately,* the desegregation of the armed services was rapid.

20. Not *until the 1960's,* however, were civilian facilities desegregated to any great extent.

Write sentences using the listed connectives to head phrases or clauses, as indicated.

21. (*before,* phrase) _____

22. (*before,* clause) _____

23. (*until,* phrase) _____

24. (*until,* clause) _____

25. (*after,* phrase) _____

26. (*after,* clause) _____

27. (*since,* phrase) _____

28. (*since,* clause) _____

29. (*for,* phrase) _____

30. (*for,* clause) _____

8
SENTENCE TYPES   (1d)

Since you began studying the parts of speech in the first section of this book, you have been increasing your knowledge of the way words function individually and in groups. You have been learning to analyze sentences and to describe how their components work together. Beginning with words and progressing through phrases to clauses, the relationships of the components have grown more and more complex.

Being able to analyze the components in a sentence is likely to make you a better writer. When you understand how sentences work, you have better control over the ones you write. When things go wrong, you can figure out why. When you want to achieve a certain effect, you can take sentence structures apart and put them back together in new, planned ways.

For example, if a paragraph you have written sounds monotonous because all the sentences seem the same, you have probably used only one or two sentence patterns. Your knowledge of sentence patterns, clauses, and phrases will enable you to vary those sentences, creating a much more pleasing paragraph.

Now we are ready to examine the broadest category in our analysis of word groups: sentence types. There are four. **A simple sentence** is composed of a single independent clause. **A compound sentence** is composed of two or more independent clauses. A **complex sentence** has an independent clause and one or more subordinate clauses. A **compound-complex sentence** contains two or more independent clauses and one or more subordinate clauses. Examples of each type of sentence follow:

SIMPLE SENTENCE

INDEPENDENT CLAUSE
It is raining outside.

COMPOUND SENTENCE

INDEPENDENT CLAUSE   INDEPENDENT CLAUSE
It is raining outside,   and it is quite chilly.

COMPLEX SENTENCE

SUBORDINATE CLAUSE
The bike trip   that we planned

SUBORDINATE CLAUSE
will have to be postponed because we'll get soaked

SUBORDINATE CLAUSE
if we go now.   [*The bike trip will have to be postponed* is the independent clause.]

COMPOUND-COMPLEX
SENTENCE

SUBORDINATE CLAUSE
Although I was looking forward to the trip,

INDEPENDENT CLAUSE
the rain will make my cold worse, so

INDEPENDENT CLAUSE
I'd better stay home.

Practice: Identifying sentence types   *Examine the following sentences and decide whether each is a simple, compound, complex, or compound-complex sentence. The answers are listed next.*

[1] Interestingly, most ethnic groups do not name themselves. [2] The Pima Indians, for example, call themselves Ootham; "Pima" was a derogatory name given to them by another tribe. [3] When an ethnic group consciously attempts to create a name for itself, disagreement is almost inevitable, but a name can often unify ethnic groups politically. [4] Hispano, Latino, Chicano, Hispanic-American, or Mexican-American are all names that have been used in the attempt to name Americans of Mexican descent, but all of the names have been objectionable to one group or another. [5] For example, all Chicanos are Mexican-Americans, but not all Mexican-Americans are Chicanos. [6] This is, in fact, a serious issue, since a single name would create the impression of political and economic unity. [7] Recently, the term "Hispanic" has been promoted as a way to solve this problem, and this name seems to be acceptable to everyone.

Answers to the Practice   [1] simple   [2] compound   [3] compound-complex
[4] compound-complex   [5] compound   [6] complex   [7] compound

EXERCISE 8, SENTENCE TYPES   (1d)

Using subordinate and independent clauses, expand the following simple sentences into the sentence types indicated in parentheses.

Example   *Over 11 percent of all Americans are Black.*

(compound) *Over 11 percent of all Americans are Black, and most live in urban areas.*

(complex) *After the Civil War ended, many Blacks left the South.*

(compound-complex) *Now the migration has reversed, and they are returning to the South because job opportunities have increased there.*

1.   *Blacks are the largest single minority ethnic group in America.*

(compound) _____

(complex) _____

(compound-complex) _____

2.   *The second-largest minority in the United States is Spanish-speaking people.*

(compound) _____

(complex) _____

(compound-complex) _____

3.   *Nine and a half million Americans are Spanish-speaking.*

(compound) _____

(complex) _____

(compound-complex) _____

4.   *Over 5 million Spanish-speaking Americans are of Mexican origin.*

(compound) _____

(complex) _____

(compound-complex) _____

5. *The rest are Puerto Ricans, South Americans, or Filipinos.*

(compound) _____

(complex) _____

(compound-complex) _____

6. *Most of these people live in the five southwestern states.*

(compound) _____

(complex) _____

(compound-complex) _____

7. *Most of these states were actually part of Mexico at one time.*

(compound) _____

(complex) _____

(compound-complex) _____

8. *For 500 years, Spanish was the only language spoken in many parts of these states.*

(compound) _____

(complex) _____

(compound-complex) _____

9. *Migration from Mexico in search of jobs added to the population.*

(compound) _____

(complex) _____

(compound-complex) _____

10. *After World War II, Mexican-Americans began to think of themselves as a unified minority group.*

(compound) _____

(complex) _____

(compound-complex) _____

9
CASE (2)

The function of nouns and pronouns within clauses and sentences is indicated by their **case**. There are three cases in English: the **subjective case**, used for the subject of a verb or for a pronoun serving as a predicate complement; the **possessive case**, used to show ownership; and the **objective case**, used for the object of a verb, verbal, or preposition.

Nouns and pronouns change form to show their case. Nouns have a **common form**, such as *ancestor,* and a possessive form, such as *ancestor's*. Personal pronouns and relative or interrogative pronouns are **inflected**—that is, they have different forms for the subjective, possessive, and objective cases. The following table shows these various pronoun forms:

	PERSONAL PRONOUNS			**RELATIVE PRONOUNS**		
	Subjective	Possessive	Objective	Subjective	Possessive	Objective
		Singular			*Singular*	
First Person	I	my, mine	me	who	whose	whom
Second Person	you	your, yours	you			
Third Person	he, she, it	his, her, hers, its	him, her, it			
		Plural			*Plural*	
First Person	we	our, ours	us	who	whose	whom
Second Person	you	your, yours	you			
Third Person	they	their, theirs	them			

Using the correct case and form to indicate a particular function requires a little care.

SUBJECTIVE AND OBJECTIVE CASES

All parts of a compound subject should be in the subjective case. All parts of a compound object should be in the objective case.

SUBJECT	My *brother Sam* and *I* wanted to trace our ancestors.
OBJECT	Dad sent *him* and *me* to look in the family Bible.

After the conjunctions *as* and *than,* use the subjective case if a pronoun is the subject of an understood verb. Use the objective case if it is the object of an understood verb.

SUBJECT	The old Bible seemed to weigh more than *I* (weigh).
OBJECT	When it fell off the shelf, it hit my brother as well as (it hit) *me*.

An **appositive** is a word or phrase following a noun or pronoun that identifies or explains the noun or pronoun by renaming it. A pronoun in an appositive describing a subject or complement should be in the subjective case. A pronoun in an appositive describing an object should be in the objective case.

SUBJECT	*We* three—Sam, the Bible, and *I*—lay on the floor in a heap.
OBJECT	The big old book had claimed two *victims—me* and my brother.

Relative pronouns should be in the subjective case when they function as subjects: *who, whoever.* They should be in the objective case when they function as objects: *whom, whomever.* Remember that the case of the relative pronoun depends upon its function within the clause and not upon the function of the whole clause within the sentence.

SUBJECT	Sam, *who* got to his feet first, lifted the book to the desk. [*Who* is the subject of the subordinate clause modifying *Sam.*]
OBJECT	*Whom* we should look up first was the major question. [*Whom* is the object of the verb *look,* even though the whole clause *whom we should look up first* functions as the subject of the sentence.]

Pronouns following forms of the verb *be* (*is, are, was, were,* etc.) should be written in the subjective case because they function as complements renaming the subject.

It was *I* who decided that first we had to locate the family tree.

POSSESSIVE CASE

Be careful when forming the possessive case of personal pronouns. For most nouns, the *'s* possessive shows ownership. But personal pronouns show possession through inflection: *my, your, his, hers, its, theirs,* and so on. No apostrophe is used. Be particularly careful with the possessive form of *it.* The possessive is *its,* not *it's. It's* is the contraction for *it is.*

It's [It is] between the Old and New Testaments of the Bible, near *its* center.

The *'s* possessive is generally used for nouns naming living things. Conventionally, the *of* phrase is preferred for referring to inanimate objects.

ANIMATE	Sam's question, my children's birthdays
INANIMATE	the top of the desk, the pride of possession

There are many exceptions, including a number of familiar expressions: *a dollar's worth; for pity's sake; yesterday's news; heart's desire; last year's fashions.*
Nouns and pronouns preceding gerunds should be in the possessive case.

What was the reason for *my* falling on the floor?
My *brother's* tripping over the chair is a good one!

42

EXERCISE 9, CASE   (2)

In the following sentences, decide which of the pronouns in parentheses is correct.
Cross out the incorrect one.

Example   Nikhat invited me to accompany (her/~~she~~) to a Hindu festival.

1. She was happy to tell (we/us) about the Diwali festival.
2. (She/Her) and her family celebrate Diwali on the last day of the year.
3. The Hindu community celebrates Diwali on October 21, the end of (its/it's) year.
4. All (who/whom) are Hindu spend the day giving thanks.
5. Diwali is the most important of the New Year holidays, though Hindus celebrate (they/them) all.
6. The holiday celebrates Rama's return after slaying Ravana, (who/whom) was a demon.
7. Hindus use lights to show (them/their/they) joy at Rama's return.
8. The festival of Dussera, another of Rama's days, celebrates (his/he) actual victory over the demon.
9. Nikhat said (she/her) and (she/her) family celebrate Dussera ten days before Diwali.
10. (She and I/Me and her/She and me) helped prepare for Diwali by cleaning the house and buying new dishes.

In the following sentences, cross out any incorrect uses of case and write the
correction above the error. Write *correct* after correct sentences.

Example   Nikhat and ~~me~~ helped set out rows of lamps.

11. I lit the lamps and handed them to she.

12. Those whom can afford it light their houses with hundreds of lamps.

13. Hindus make resolutions to better theirselves each Diwali day.

14. Nikhat made more resolutions than me.

15. Lakshmi is a goddess whom is especially revered on Diwali day.

16. It is her who symbolizes wealth and prosperity for Hindus.

17. Doors are left ajar so Lakshmi can make her entrance.

18. Both children and adults dress in they finest clothes.

19. Nikhat says her and her family spend the day feasting and visiting.

20. After prayers, she and them eat a huge meal of traditional curry and sweet dishes.

21. Whomever studies Hindu culture soon realizes it has a 5,000 year history.

22. There is no fixed system that regulates whom prays, whom fasts, or whom meditates.

23. There is no single prophet or writer whom codified Hindu religious beliefs.

24. People who's backgrounds are in traditional Western culture find this hard to accept.

25. Each geographical region of India has it's own specific beliefs.

26. There are over 82,000 Hindus whom live and work in the United States.

27. Us knowing that Hinduism is taught in the home explained the family temple.

28. Hindu parents feel a great sense of responsibility for passing the culture on to they children.

29. Theirs is not a simple task.

30. Nikhat says her and her parents work hard to maintain Hindu customs.

10
ADJECTIVE AND ADVERB FORMS   (3)

In Section 3 we examined adjectives and adverbs as parts of speech with a particular function—modifying. **Adjectives** modify nouns, pronouns, or other noun substitutes. **Adverbs** modify verbs, adjectives, or other adverbs, and occasionally whole sentences. Both adjectives and adverbs limit or qualify the meaning of the words they modify.

Now that you are familiar with sentence patterns and types (Sections 5 and 8), as well as all the parts of speech, we can examine some other characteristics of adjectives and adverbs.

Some words, such as *fast, much, late,* and *well,* can function as **either adjectives or adverbs.**

ADJECTIVE   She is a *fast* runner. [*Fast* modifies the noun, *runner.*]

ADVERB   She ran *fast.* [*Fast* modifies the verb *ran,* telling how she ran.]

Linking verbs such as forms of the verb *be* (*is, are, was, were, become,* etc.) and verbs such as *seem, remain, prove,* and *stand,* as well as such verbs relating to the senses as *feel, look, smell, taste,* and *sound,* are followed by **predicate adjectives** that describe the subject of the sentence or clause.

You must be careful when you use such verbs since they may or may not be linking. *That meat tasted good* uses a linking verb and hence requires an adjective after the verb. However, in *I tasted the meat,* the verb *tasted* takes an object and hence is not a linking verb. In *She looked tired, looked* is a linking verb followed by the adjective *tired.* In *She looked away tiredly, looked* is not a linking verb. The modifiers *away* and *tiredly* do not describe the subject, *she,* but rather provide information about the verb and thus are adverbs.

Most adverbs are distinguished from their corresponding adjectives by the *-ly* ending: *grateful, gratefully; free, freely; pleasing, pleasingly.* However, an *-ly* ending does not automatically mean a word is an adverb. Some adjectives, such as *friendly, slovenly,* and *cowardly,* also end in *-ly.* Furthermore, some adverbs have two forms, one with *-ly* and one without: *quick, quickly; slow, slowly.* The key, as always, is to see what part of speech a word modifies or what role it plays in a sentence pattern when deciding whether it is an adverb or an adjective.

Adjectives and adverbs show degrees of quality or quantity by means of their **comparative and superlative forms.**

For the **comparative** form, which permits a comparison of two, *-er* is added to the adjective, or the adverb *more* is placed before it (*pretty, prettier; rapid, more rapid*). For the **superlative** form, which involves a comparison among three or more, *-est* is added to the adjective, or *most* is placed before it (*pretty, prettiest; rapid, most rapid*).

Most adjectives and a few adverbs of one syllable form the comparative and superlative with *-er* and *-est.* Adjectives of two syllables often offer a choice (*lovelier, loveliest* and *more lovely, most lovely*). Adjectives of three or more syllables and most adverbs usually use *more* and *most* in making their comparisons (*more industrious,* not *industriouser; more sadly,* not *sadlier*).

The comparative and superlative forms of the adjectives *good* and *bad* are irregular:

good   bad
better   worse
best   worst

Some adjectives and adverbs are absolute in their meaning and thus cannot logically be compared. Examples of such words include the following:

complete   final
dead   perfect
empty   unique

Practice: Identifying adjectives and adverbs   Underline once all the words that
function as adjectives in the following sentences. (Do not underline the articles.)
Underline twice all the words that function as adverbs. The answers are listed next.

[1] The oldest minority group in America are Indians. [2] In the early 1970's, there were over 800,000 Indians living in America. [3] The Indian population had almost doubled since 1950, the result of long-overdue improvements in health programs on reservations. [4] It is somewhat surprising to most Americans to learn that over half the Indians in America still live on federal reservations. [5] It is equally surprising to most people to learn that the Indians who live in cities are almost always at the very bottom of the poverty scale, or that the suicide rate among Indians was, at one time, 100 times that of whites. [6] This can be partially explained by observing that Indians are the only minority to be directly, daily, governed by government bureaucracy, and that no clear government policy has been established, either for assimilation or autonomy, for American Indians since the eighteenth century.

Answers to the Practice   *Adjectives:*   [1] oldest, minority   [2] early, over
[3] Indian, long-overdue, health   [4] surprising, most, over, federal   [5] surprising, most, very, poverty, suicide, one   [6] only, government, clear, government, American, eighteenth   *Adverbs:*   [3] almost   [4] somewhat, still   [5] equally, almost, always   [6] partially, directly, daily, no, either

46

EXERCISE 10-1, ADJECTIVE AND ADVERB FORMS   (3)

In the blanks, indicate with the appropriate abbreviation whether the adjectival (*adj*) or the adverbial (*adv*) form of the given word should be used.

Example   *strict*   Chinese painting is governed by _*adj*_ rules.

1. *unique*   Westerners tend to think of artists as _____ individuals.

2. *separate*   Each Western artist tries to adapt a _____ style or technique.

3. *thorough*   The Chinese artist, however, is _____ ruled by tradition.

4. *realistic*   Chinese painting must always be _____ .

5. *natural*   The size and proportion of objects must be _____ presented.

6. *identical*   The colors in the painting are _____ to the colors of the subject.

7. *free*   The details may be _____ selected.

8. *serious*   Treating detail abstractly, though, is a _____ violation of tradition.

9. *true*   A Chinese artist is _____ creative when he or she can copy the ancient masters.

10. *valuable*   The most _____ paintings are those whose subjects seem alive.

11. *actual*   Chinese folklore has many stories about painted subjects that _____ come alive.

12. *close*   For the Chinese, painting is _____ related to writing.

13. *virtual*   Writing and painting are done in _____ the same surroundings.

14. *interesting*   Most Western artists find an _____ scene and set up their easels.

15. *usual*   Western artists are _____ trained to draw from models.

16. *preferable*   A table or desk is _____ for Chinese painting.

17. *usual*   Drawing from memory is the _____ method in China.

18. *intense*   The Chinese artist must concentrate on his or her subject _____ .

19. *careful*   The planning of the composition must be done ———— .

20. *quick*   Above all, the act of painting must be ———— .

Write your own sentences, using the adjectival or adverbial form of the italicized word, as indicated.

Example   (*probable,* adjective) *The police had probable cause for the search.*

21. (*virtual,* adverb) ——————————————————————

22. (*total,* adjective) ——————————————————————

23. (*slow,* adverb) ——————————————————————

24. (*eventual,* adverb) ——————————————————————

25. (*usual,* adverb) ——————————————————————

26. (*sure,* adverb) ——————————————————————

27. (*real,* adverb) ——————————————————————

28. (*continual,* adjective) ——————————————————————

29. (*basic,* adjective) ——————————————————————

30. (*logical,* adverb) ——————————————————————

31. (*ordinary,* adverb) ——————————————————————

32. (*original,* adjective) ——————————————————————

33. (*typical,* adverb) ——————————————————————

34. (*frequent,* adjective) ——————————————————————

35. (*excellent,* adverb) ——————————————————————

36. (*late,* adverb) ——————————————————————

37. (*relative,* adverb) ——————————————————————

38. (*primary,* adverb) ——————————————————————

39. (*heavy,* adverb) ——————————————————————

40. (*fair,* adverb) ——————————————————————

EXERCISE 10–2, COMPARATIVE AND SUPERLATIVE FORMS   (3)

In each blank, write the appropriate comparative or superlative form of the modifier given in italics to complete the sentence correctly.

Example   *fast*   Chinese painting is done *faster*_____ than is Western painting.

1. *careful*   A Chinese painter must be _____ than a Western artist.

2. *bad*   Erasing and painting over mistakes are the _____ violations of tradition for Chinese artists.

3. *bad*   Taking too long to finish a painting is _____ than throwing a painting away.

4. *similar*   The materials used are _____ to a letterer's than to a Western artist's materials.

5. *frequent*   The painter draws on silk _____ than any other artist.

6. *good*   Only the _____ grades of silk are used.

7. *good*   A Chinese artist may not choose the _____ of two grades of paper.

8. *painstaking*   Of all the materials used, brushes are the _____ chosen.

9. *precise*   Chinese brushes are _____ than Western brushes.

10. *large*   The _____ brush has a diameter of about 2 inches.

11. *small*   The _____ has a diameter of one-third of an inch.

12. *large*   Even this is still _____ than most Western artists use.

13. *regulated*   The sizes of the brushes are _____ than are their materials.

14. *familiar*   Chinese artists, like all other artists, become _____ with one set of brushes they keep for daily use.

15. *prized*   Often, the brushes are their _____ possessions.

16. *beautiful*   They may also be their _____ possessions.

17. *intricate* The handles are _____ carved than the handles of Western brushes.

18. *simple* The _____ sets may have bamboo or wooden handles.

19. *expensive* _____ sets may have gold, quartz, or horn handles.

20. *famous* The _____ artists use very individualistic materials.

Write sentences using the proper form—comparative or superlative—of the listed modifiers.

21. (*low,* superlative)

_____

22. (*less,* superlative)

_____

23. (*bad,* comparative)

_____

24. (*bad,* superlative)

_____

25. (*well,* superlative)

_____

26. (*badly,* superlative)

_____

27. (*good,* superlative)

_____

28. (*good,* comparative)

_____

29. (*obnoxious,* comparative)

_____

30. (*speedy,* comparative)

_____

11
VERB FORMS   (4–5)

Section 2 sketches the general role verbs play, but it only begins to suggest the amount of information a verb actually conveys. The single word comprising a verb (or the few words of a verb phrase) tells us not only the exact nature of an action or condition but also

1. the time when it occurs and whether the action is completed or continuing (**tense**);

2. whether or not the verb passes its action to an object (is **transitive**, **intransitive**, or **linking**);

3. whether the subject is performing or receiving the action (**voice**);

4. the attitude of the speaker or writer (**mood**).

TENSES

Verbs show present, past, and future time by means of their three tenses. Each of these tenses is further subdivided into categories, according to whether the action or condition is continuing (in progress) or completed at the time indicated. The following table lists, explains, and gives examples of the categories of tense. Notice which helping verbs are used to form each of the tenses.

TENSE	TIME	EXAMPLE
Present	Present or habitual action	I *call* my parents.
Present perfect	Action completed at an indefinite time in the past or extending up to the present time	I *have called* my parents every Sunday.
Present progressive	Present action continuing or in progress	I *am calling* my parents now.
Present perfect progressive	Continuing action occurring up to but not including the present	I *have been calling* my parents.
Past	Past action	I *called* my parents.
Past perfect	Past action completed before another past action	I *had called* my parents before lunch.
Past progressive	Continuing action that occurred in the past	I *was calling* my parents.
Past perfect progressive	Continuing past action that occurred before another past action	I *had been calling* my parents when you arrived.
Future	Future action	I *shall/will call* them later.
Future perfect	Future action that will be completed before another future action	I *will have called* them before I see you again.

TENSE	TIME	EXAMPLE
Future progressive	Continuing action that will occur in the future	I *will be calling* them again next Sunday.
Future perfect progressive	Continuing action that leads up to a point in the future	If I arrive late, the reason is I *will have been calling* my parents.

REGULAR AND IRREGULAR VERBS

The verb previously used to illustrate tenses, *call,* is a **regular verb.** Most verbs are regular—that is, the past tense and past participle (the combining form used with many helping verbs) are formed by adding *-ed* to the present tense form: for example, *help + ed* and *show + ed* yield *helped* and *showed.* If the present tense form of a regular verb ends in *e,* the past tense and past participle are formed by simply adding *d: hoped, filed.*

Irregular verbs, as the term suggests, follow another pattern. Of the more than 200 irregular English verbs, about twenty have the same form for the present tense, past tense, and past participle: *cut, cut, cut.* Many change an internal vowel for the past tense and past participle: *keep, kept, kept.* Some irregular verbs have three distinct forms, a different one for each of the tenses, present, past tense, and past participle: *forgive, forgave, forgiven; do, did, done.* The following list shows the three forms for the most commonly used irregular verbs:

PRESENT INFINITIVE	PAST	PAST PARTICIPLE
awake	awoke, awaked	awaked
arise	arose	arisen
bear (carry)	bore	borne
bear (give birth to)	bore	borne, born
beat	beaten	beaten
become	became	become
begin	began	begun
bet	bet	bet
bid	bade, bid	bidden, bid
bite	bit	bitten
blow	blew	blown
break	broke	broken
bring	brought	brought
burst	burst	burst
buy	bought	bought
catch	caught	caught
choose	chose	chosen
come	came	come
cut	cut	cut
dig	dug	dug
dive	dived, dove	dived
do	did	done
draw	drew	drawn
drink	drank	drunk
drive	drove	driven
eat	ate	eaten
fall	fell	fallen

PRESENT INFINITIVE	PAST	PAST PARTICIPLE
feel	felt	felt
find	found	found
fly	flew	flown
forget	forgot	forgotten, forgot
forgive	forgave	forgiven
freeze	froze	frozen
get	got	got, gotten
give	gave	given
go	went	gone
grow	grew	grown
hang (suspend)	hung	hung
hang	hanged	hung
hid	hid	hidden
hit	hit	hit
hurt	hurt	hurt
keep	kept	kept
know	knew	known
lay (place)	laid	laid
lead	led	led
leave	left	left
let	let	let
lie (recline)	lay	lain
lose	lost	lost
make	made	made
mean	meant	meant
pay	paid	paid
read	read	read
ride	rode	ridden
ring	rang	rung
rise	rose	risen
run	ran	run
see	saw	seen
set	set	set
shake	shook	shaken
shine	shone	shone
shrink	shrank, shrunk	shrunk
sink	sank, sunk	sunk
speak	spoke	spoken
spin	spun	spun
spring	sprang, sprung	sprung
stand	stood	stood
steal	stole	stolen
stink	stank	stunk
strike	struck	struck
swear	swore	sworn
swim	swam	swum
swing	swung	swung
take	took	taken

PRESENT INFINITIVE	PAST	PAST PARTICIPLE
teach	taught	taught
tear	tore	torn
tell	told	told
think	thought	thought
throw	threw	thrown
wake	woke, waked	woken, waked
wear	wore	worn
weave	wove, weaved	woven, weaved
weep	wept	wept
win	won	won
wind	wound	wound
wring	wrung	wrung
write	wrote	written

The verb *be* is also an irregular verb. It appears often in many forms, and it is used frequently with the combining forms of other verbs. Study it carefully.

SINGULAR	PLURAL	SINGULAR	PLURAL
Present Tense		*Present Perfect Tense*	
I am	we are	I have been	we have been
you are	you are	you have been	you have been
he, she, it is	they are	he, she, it has been	they have been
Past Tense		*Past Perfect Tense*	
I was	we were	I had been	we had been
you were	you were	you had been	you had been
he, she, it was	they were	he, she, it had been	they had been
Future Tense		*Future Perfect Tense*	
I will be	we will be	I will have been	we will have been
you will be	you will be	you will have been	you will have been
he, she, it will be	they will be	he, she, it will have been	they will have been

Practice: Identifying verb tenses   *Name the tenses of the verbs in the following sentences. The answers are listed at the end of this section.*

[1] The term "Chicano" comes from one of two possible origins. [2] "Chicano" may have come from the Aztecs' name for themselves, "Mexicano"; the *x* may have been pronounced as a *sh* sound. [3] Through the influence of other languages, the first consonant and vowel disappeared. [4] Eventually the *sh* sound became a *ch* sound, resulting in "Chicano." [5] Other people claim that "Chicano" is a combination of "chico," the Spanish word for "small," and "Mexicano." [6] Whatever its origins are, the word is not used in Mexico, and though the Aztecs may have used it first, it now stands for something new: people of Mexican ancestry who live in North America. [7] Many Chicanos resent the label "Mexican-American," which they feel Anglo-Saxon society has been imposing on them. [8] Conservative members of the Mexican-American community, however, have been refusing, in some cases, to accept "Chicano." [9] They feel that "Chicano" is a word that has been created by militants who demand political

rights, and they have refused to associate with the militants. [10] "Hispanic-American" or "Latino" also has proponents in the Mexican-American community. [11] Creating a name with which an entire ethnic minority will identify themselves is a virtual impossibility.

SPECIAL PROBLEMS WITH VERB TENSES

Problems writers face in using verbs correctly sometimes arise from difficulties with tense forms. Several of the most common problems are discussed next.

Writers sometimes omit necessary verb endings, especially if they do not audibly pronounce these endings when speaking. The two most frequently omitted endings are *-s* and *-ed*. The *-s* form is required for present tense verbs used with singular nouns, third person singular pronouns (*he, she, it*), and indefinite pronouns such as *each, someone,* and *everybody*.

> He *likes* the sweaters that his Scottish aunt *knits.*

For the present tense verbs ending in *o,* the form is *-es: goes.* For the verbs *be* and *have,* the *-s* forms are *is* and *has.*

> He *is* very fond of the last sweater she sent him, because it *goes* with the tweed jacket he *has.*

The *-ed* form is required for the past tense and past participle of all regular verbs. When the next word following the verb in a sentence begins with a similar sound, the *-ed* can be hard to hear and may be difficult to remember when you write. Be particularly careful to include it when you write the past tense for constructions such as *used to* and *supposed to.*

> He was *supposed* to write her a thank-you note. [Not *He was **suppose** to write.*]

Writers sometimes use nonstandard forms of irregular verbs. Remember that although most English verbs are regular, a great many are irregular. *See* is an irregular verb, so you should not write *I seed him yesterday.* instead of *I saw him yesterday.*

Also, the principal parts of an irregular verb are not interchangeable—that is, you need to select the correct tense for the time you wish to indicate. *I done my homework.* is incorrect because *done* is the past participle form (*do, did, done*); it requires a helping verb and cannot be used for the past tense. *I did my homework.* is correct.

Writers sometimes have trouble choosing the appropriate tense sequence for verbs in main and subordinate clauses in complex sentences. When the verb in the main clause is in any tense except the past or past perfect tense, the verb in the subordinate clause should be in whatever tense the meaning requires.

> Because our old refrigerator *broke,* we *need* a new one. [The need is in the present but is the result of a past event.]
> The sales clerk *promises* they *will deliver* the new refrigerator on Tuesday. [The promise occurs in the present but refers to a future event.]

When the verb in the main clause is in the past or past perfect tense, the verb in the subordinate clause should usually be in the past or past perfect tense, too—unless the subordinate clause states a general truth.

The clerk *said* that he *had checked* the delivery schedule. [He checked before he made the statement.]

BUT

We *learned* later that clerks *promise* quickly, but stores *deliver* slowly. [Here the subordinate clause is offered as a general truth and so is in the present tense.]

Answers to the Practice   [1] present   [2] present perfect, present perfect   [3] past   [4] past   [5] present, present   [6] present, present, present perfect, present, present   [7] present, present, present perfect progressive   [8] present perfect progressive   [9] present, present, present perfect, present, present perfect   [10] present   [11] future, present

EXERCISE 11-1, VERB TENSES   (4–5)

Change the present tense verbs in each of the following sentences to past tense by rewriting the sentences with past tense verbs in the blanks provided. Be sure to choose the correct forms for irregular verbs.

Example   The art of Chinese painting thrives in Chinese-American communities.

The art of Chinese painting thrived in Chinese-American communities.

1. Surprisingly, Chinese paintings done in America resemble those done in China.

    _____

2. The ancient rules and traditions that rule Chinese art keep it consistent.

    _____

3. The artist spreads silk or paper on a floor or table.

    _____

4. The artist's left arm pins the silk or paper in place.

    _____

5. The artist holds the brush in his or her right hand.

    _____

6. Ancient Chinese paintings have been drawn on cloth other than silk.

    _____

7. Eventually silk has come to be favored.

    _____

8. In fact, some painters cut their art into stones or walls.

    _____

9. An artist uses a large brush to make wide, bold strokes.

    _____

10. The large brushes contain bristles made of sheep, goat, or pig hair.

    _____

11. The small brushes are reserved for delicate lines.

___

12. These often require rabbit, weasel, fox, or deer hair.

___

13. Some famous artists buy very odd materials for their brushes.

___

14. One artist reportedly prefers wolf hair for broad strokes.

___

15. For him, the fine work demands brushes made from mouse whiskers.

___

16. Another claims to own a set with fine brushes made from the discarded hair of human babies.

___

17. Traditionally, Chinese painting takes only one color.

___

18. Therefore, the artists' ink-mixing tools receive as much attention as their brushes.

___

19. The ink mixes lampblack, pine soot, and glue, pressed into a cake.

___

20. Each artist grinds the ink on a stone slab.

___

21. He or she then pours a few drops of water into the ground ink.

___

22. Careful control of the water gives a thick, thin, light, or dark quality to the ink.

___

23. Artists value ink-mixing secrets very highly.

___

24. Subtle shadings of ink produce an artist's entire range of colors.

___

25. Though some artists use watercolors, ink is still more highly regarded.

___

Name _____ Date _____ Score _____

EXERCISE 11-2, SPECIAL PROBLEMS WITH VERB TENSES (4–5)

In the blank in each sentence, write the correct form of the listed verb in the tense indicated.

Example (*come,* present perfect) Often the most American-seeming sports

*have come* from other countries.

1. (*be,* present perfect) Ice skating _____ popular in northern Europe for centuries.

2. (*know,* present) No one _____ who attached wheels to ice skates first.

3. (*be,* past) There _____ several attempts to popularize roller skating.

4. (*skate,* past perfect) A showman and musician, Joseph Merlin, once

_____ into a concert hall playing a violin.

5. (*take,* past) When he crashed through a huge mirror, the sport

_____ a giant leap backward.

6. (*play,* past perfect progressive) The violin he _____ was broken, too.

7. (*begin,* past) Inventors _____ trying to perfect roller skates.

8. (*build,* past) A French citizen _____ a pair with a single row of wheels.

9. (*gain,* past perfect) By 1823, the sport _____ sudden popularity.

10. (*wear,* past progressive) Professionals _____ them in skating exhibitions.

11. (*work,* past perfect progressive) John Tyner _____ to perfect the first practical skate.

12. (*use*, past)   Waitresses in beer gardens in Germany

_____ to wear the skates to make their work less tiring.

13. (*lead*, past)   The popularity of skating _____ London businessmen to open the first public rink.

14. (*ask*, past)   A Paris opera company _____ for an opera to be performed on skates.

15. (*go*, present)   It _____ without saying that one had to be both daring and muscular to try the early skates.

For each of the following sentences, select the appropriate verb for the tense sequence from the choices in parentheses. Cross out the incorrect choice.

16. Roller skating caught on in America after an inventor named Plimpton (design/designed) the first modern skate.

17. The wheels on the Plimpton skate (turn/turned) when the skater's foot is tipped to one side.

18. At last there was a steerable roller skate that (does/did not) require superhuman balance and strength.

19. Because he (had understood/understood) social status, Plimpton was wildly successful with skating rinks in America.

20. He (built/had built) very large, lavishly decorated rinks in New York and Newport, where the wealthiest families lived.

21. The socially prominent families adopted the sport of skating immediately, once they (saw/were seeing/had seen) the beautiful rinks.

22. Once manufacturers (began/begin) to mass produce skates, the sport became inexpensive.

23. Formerly it had been the sport of the wealthy, but now the middle and lower classes (had taken/took/take) up skating.

24. Skating rinks popped up all over America, and for the price of renting skates—then a quarter—anyone (can/could) join in.

25. Thus a sport invented in the winters of northern Europe (is/was) transplanted to America.

12
TRANSITIVE, INTRANSITIVE, AND LINKING VERBS   (4)

A **transitive verb** transmits or passes action from a subject to an object.

> She *bought* a ticket.

An **intransitive verb** does not transmit action and has no object or complement.

> The train *arrived* on time.

Some verbs can be either transitive or intransitive. For example, in the sentence *She watched the train.*, the verb *watched* is transitive; it is followed by the direct object *train*. However, if the sentence is changed to *She watched carefully.*, the verb becomes intransitive; it has no object.

Two pairs of verbs that are often confusing and used incorrectly as a consequence are *lie, lay* and *sit, set*. If you remember that *lie* and *sit* are intransitive but *lay* and *set* are transitive, it will be easier to use them correctly. To help you distinguish their uses, the principal parts of the four verbs are illustrated here:

	PRESENT	PAST	PAST PARTICIPLE
INTRANSITIVE	I *lie* down.	I *lay* down.	I *have lain* down.
TRANSITIVE	I *lay* the book down.	I *laid* the book down.	I *have laid* the book down.
INTRANSITIVE	I *sit* down.	I *sat* down.	I *have sat* down.
TRANSITIVE	I *set* my watch.	I *set* my watch.	I *have set* my watch.

Practice A: *Identifying transitive and intransitive verbs*   *In each of the following sentences, underline transitive verbs once and intransitive verbs twice. The answers are listed at the end of this section.*

[1] Alex Haley started, or at least speeded up, Americans' current interest in looking for their families' cultural and historical roots. [2] Haley's *Roots* appeared first as a bestselling book, and then was developed into a television miniseries. [3] On television, *Roots* drew one of the largest audiences in history, night after night. [4] In addition, the book was serialized in several national magazines. [5] Haley also wrote and published articles that described the intricate detective work which led him to the story of his African ancestors. [6] Haley, who was born in Ithaca, New York, was six generations away from these ancestors, who eventually were taken to Henning, Tennessee. [7] His discovery of his heritage not only rekindled interest in genealogy, but also resulted in a story that dramatically recounts Black America's emergence from slavery.

A **linking verb** joins the subject of a sentence to its complement, the predicate adjective that describes the subject or the predicate noun that renames the subject. A linking verb expresses a condition and frequently acts as an equal sign. For example, *the apples are ripe* means the same as *apples = ripe*. Because a linking verb does not convey action from a subject to an object, it can never have an object.

The most common linking verbs are forms of *be, become, seem, appear, feel, look, smell, taste,* and *sound.* Verbs pertaining to the five senses can be either linking or transitive, depending on how they are used. Remember that a linking verb states a condition, but a transitive verb passes action to an object.

TRANSITIVE VERB	LINKING VERB
The cat *smells* a mouse.	The cat *smells* terrible since its fight with a skunk.
She *looked* her opponent straight in the eye.	Her opponent *looked* nervous.
He *sounds* the alarm.	His voice *sounds* hoarse.
Mother *felt* my forehead.	I *felt* faint and dizzy.
Taste the stew.	Does the stew *taste* too salty?

Practice B: Identifying linking verbs *In each of the following sentences, underline the transitive verbs once and the linking verbs twice. The answers are listed at the end of this section.*

[1] Haley had only a vague memory of three African words. [2] These words were all that remained of the story of his original ancestors. [3] Haley wasn't even sure of their origin; the words simply sounded African. [4] Haley began quickly interviewing his older relatives, but their stories had become tangled by repeated retellings. [5] A linguist helped Haley to locate the origin of his bloodline and established the origin of the three words in Gambia. [6] The task that once seemed impossible had begun in earnest. [7] Haley began gathering details of his ancestors' lives. [8] He searched census records, wills, plantation records, cargo invoices, tax records. [9] This wealth of facts allowed Haley to reconstruct the daily lives of his ancestors.

Answers to Practice A   *Transitive:* [1] started, speeded   [3] drew   [5] wrote, published, described, led   [7] rekindled, recounts   *Intransitive:* [2] appeared, was developed   [4] was serialized   [6] was born, was, were taken   [7] resulted

Answers to Practice B   *Transitive:* [1] had   [4] began interviewing   [5] helped, established   [6] had begun   [7] began gathering   [8] searched   [9] allowed *Linking:* [2] were   [3] was[n't], sounded   [4] had become   [6] seemed

EXERCISE 12-1, TRANSITIVE AND INTRANSITIVE VERBS   (4)

For each of the listed verbs, first write a sentence using it as a transitive verb, and then another sentence using it as an intransitive verb. You may use the verb in any tense you wish.

Example   *drink*

(transitive) _*I drank all of it.*_____

(intransitive) _*I drank with gusto.*_____

1. *wind*

   (transitive) _____

   (intransitive) _____

2. *begin*

   (transitive) _____

   (intransitive) _____

3. *flip*

   (transitive) _____

   (intransitive) _____

4. *draw*

   (transitive) _____

   (intransitive) _____

5. *do*

   (transitive) _____

   (intransitive) _____

6. *burst*

   (transitive) _____

   (intransitive) _____

7. *blow*

   (transitive) _____

   (intransitive) _____

8. *freeze*

   (transitive) _____

   (intransitive) _____

9. *grow*

   (transitive) _____

   (intransitive) _____

10. *know*

    (transitive) _____

    (intransitive) _____

11. *lay*

    (transitive) _____

    (intransitive) _____

12. *lead*

    (transitive) _____

    (intransitive) _____

13. *return*

    (transitive) _____

    (intransitive) _____

14. *run*

    (transitive) _____

    (intransitive) _____

15. *swim*

    (transitive) _____

    (intransitive) _____

EXERCISE 12-2, TRANSITIVE, INTRANSITIVE, AND LINKING VERBS   **(4)**

In each of the following sentences, select the correct verb from the choices in parentheses. Cross out the incorrect choice.

Example   I believe I'll (~~sit~~/set) to work tracing my family history.

1. Have you (set/sat) as a goal the discovery of your family genealogy?
2. Many organizations have (set/sit) themselves to work maintaining old records.
3. It is amazing where many of these old records (lie/lay).
4. You first should (sit/set) down with all your relatives who know bits of family history.
5. (Sit/Set) yourself the objective of learning all they know.
6. It does no good to (lie/lay) around and wonder.
7. (Sit/Set) a schedule so you can interview each one.
8. I found that many of our family records (lie/lay/laid) in little villages in Alsace-Lorraine.
9. If you (sit/set) enough value on discovering your genealogy, you may have to travel to another country.
10. In the field of genealogy, you don't just (sit/set) and study old records.

For each of the listed verbs, first write a sentence using it as a linking verb, and then write a sentence using it as a transitive verb. You may use the verb in any tense you wish.

Example   *feel*

(linking) _I feel a song coming on._

(transitive) _I feel pretty good._

11. *become*

(linking) ——————————————————————————

(transitive) ——————————————————————————

12. *grow*

(linking) ——————————————————————————

(transitive) ——————————————————————————

13. *act*

   (linking) _____

   (transitive) _____

14. *taste*

   (linking) _____

   (transitive) _____

15. *smell*

   (linking) _____

   (transitive) _____

16. *prove*

   (linking) _____

   (transitive) _____

17. *watch*

   (linking) _____

   (transitive) _____

18. *turn*

   (linking) _____

   (transitive) _____

19. *look*

   (linking) _____

   (transitive) _____

20. *sound*

   (linking) _____

   (transitive) _____

13
ACTIVE AND PASSIVE VOICE VERBS   (5)

Transitive verbs can either be active voice or passive voice verbs. An **active voice verb** indicates that the subject performs the action and transmits it to an object: *Carla called her cousin in Mexico City.* A **passive voice verb** indicates that the subject receives the action performed by someone or something else: *Carla was called by her cousin from Mexico City.*

Passive voice verbs enable us to emphasize the receiver of the action rather than the performer, or agent, of the action. For example, in the sentence *Carla packed her suitcase.*, the subject is *Carla*. The emphasis is on what she is doing. In the sentence *The suitcase was packed by Carla.*, however, the subject is *suitcase*. The emphasis is not on Carla, the agent, but on what happened to the suitcase. Sometimes the agent in a passive voice sentence is not even identified: *The suitcase was packed.*

The passive voice is formed by using the past participle of the main verb with the appropriate form of the verb *be* to indicate tenses. Like active voice verbs, passive voice verbs also have perfect and progressive forms. The following table lists, explains, and illustrates the various passive voice verb forms:

TENSE	TIME	EXAMPLE
Present	Present or habitual action	I *am called* to the telephone.
Present perfect	Completed action in the immediate past	I *have been called* to the telephone.
Present progressive	Present action continuing or in progress	I *am being called* to the telephone now.
Present perfect progressive	Continuing action occurring up to but not including the present	I *have been being called* to the telephone all morning.
Past	Completed past action	I *was called* to the telephone.
Past perfect	Past action completed before another past action	I *had been called* to the telephone, so I ran down the stairs.
Past progressive	Continuing action that occurred in the past	I *was being called* to the telephone when I tripped.
Past perfect progressive	Continuing past action that occurred before another past action	I *had been being* urgently *called* to the telephone, until I shouted that I had fallen down.
Future	Future action	I *shall/will be called* to the telephone no more.
Future perfect	Future action completed before another future time	I *shall/will have been called* at home by my boss tomorrow, however.
Future progressive	Action in progress at a future time	In fact, I *shall/will be being called* daily for progress reports.

TENSE	TIME	EXAMPLE
Future perfect progressive	Continuing future action that leads up to another future time	I *shall/will have been being called* for weeks by the time my broken leg heals.

Obviously, we do not often need to write sentences using passive voice perfect progressive verb forms. Nevertheless, the other passive voice forms are widely used in writing, particularly for technical and scientific subjects in which the receiver of an action is more important than the agent: *The results of the survey were tabulated, and the findings were reported to the review board.*

Keep in mind, however, that a passive voice sentence is longer and less forceful than an active voice sentence. Passive voice requires the addition of at least one helping verb, and a prepositional phrase if you identify the agent of the action. Active voice sentences are more direct, more economical, and more forceful, as the following comparison shows:

PASSIVE VOICE   The meeting was called to order by the president.

ACTIVE VOICE   The president called the meeting to order.

When you write, be aware of verb voice so that you select verbs in the voice that best achieves the emphasis you want.

Practice: Identifying passive voice verbs   Underline all the passive voice verb phrases in the following sentences. The answers are listed next.

[1] One may find, like Haley did, that family records have not been kept in a very orderly fashion. [2] Stories may have been forgotten, birth certificates may be lost or misplaced, and, if your research takes you back far enough, you may find that records simply were not kept in certain areas in pioneer or colonial times. [3] In America, particularly, a foreign language may be needed in order to pursue records back very far at all. [4] It is these difficulties, after all, that make genealogy fascinating. [5] It wouldn't be much fun at all simply to go to a library and look in a big record book to discover the origins of your ancestors.

Answers to the Practice   [1] have been kept   [2] may have been forgotten, may be lost, [may be] misplaced, were kept   [3] may be needed

EXERCISE 13, ACTIVE AND PASSIVE VOICE VERBS (5)

Rewrite the following sentences, changing the passive voice verbs to active voice verbs. Try to retain the verb tense of the original sentence. If an agent is not supplied in the original sentence, provide an appropriate one in your revision.

Example   One of the African words was discovered by Alex Haley to be a name.

Alex Haley discovered one of the African words was a name.

1. His "roots" were traced to 1750 in The Gambia, West Africa.

2. Haley's bloodline was discovered to begin in the village of Juffure.

3. Kunta Kinte was found to be the name of Haley's African ancestor.

4. He was referred to as "The African" by Haley's oldest relatives.

5. The village was a Mandinka village which had been peaceful and agrarian.

6. The Moslem religion was practiced by the Mandinkas.

7. The Arabic language and the Koran were known by all Mandinkas.

8. Their livelihood had been derived, for generations, from harvesting rice and cotton.

9. In smaller, outlying villages, goats were herded.

10. Kunta's basic education in Arabic, history, and mathematics had been completed by the time he was ten.

11. At 17, Kunta was kidnapped by slave traders and sent to America.

_____

12. During the three-month ocean voyage, one-third of the captured Africans were killed by disease and the inhuman conditions.

_____

13. After having been auctioned off, Kunta was renamed "Toby."

_____

14. Kunta had been so enraged by these humiliations that escape was attempted by him four times.

_____

15. He was permanently crippled by his captors as punishment.

_____

16. Finally, Kunta realized that Africa would not be seen by him again.

_____

17. The facts of Kunta Kinte and his descendants were fashioned into gripping fiction by Haley.

_____

18. Talent, inner strength, and resilience were demonstrated by each generation born in America.

_____

19. After they had been emancipated by the Civil War, Kunta's descendants moved to Tennessee.

_____

20. Haley's maternal grandmother was born in Tennessee, and the three African words had been remembered by her.

_____

14
MOOD (5d–f)

English has three moods. The **indicative mood** expresses a statement: *I will go*. The **imperative mood** expresses a direct command or request: *Go do what I told you*. In sentences in the imperative mood, the understood subject is always *you*. The **subjunctive mood** is now mainly used to express wishes and conditions contrary to fact: *I wish that I were at home. If I were you, I would leave now*. The subjunctive should also be used in *that* clauses that express formal demands, resolutions, recommendations, requests, or motions: *He moved that the motion be tabled*.

The subjunctive mood uses special forms in several tenses, persons, and numbers of the verb *be* and in the third person singular, present, and present perfect tenses of all verbs. The following tables pinpoint these variations:

Subjunctive Mood: *To Be*

	SINGULAR	PLURAL
PRESENT TENSE	I *be* [not *am*] you *be* [not *are*] he, she, it *be* [not *is*]	we *be* [not *are*] you *be* [not *are*] they *be* [not *are*]
PAST TENSE	I *were* [not *was*] you were he, she, it *were* [not *was*]	we were you were they were
PRESENT PERFECT TENSE	I have been you have been he, she, it *have* been [not *has*]	we have been you have been they have been
PAST PERFECT TENSE	had been (all persons and numbers)	

Subjunctive Mood: *To Speak*

	SINGULAR	PLURAL
PRESENT TENSE	I speak you speak he, she, it *speak* [not *speaks*]	we speak you speak they speak
PAST TENSE	I spoke you spoke he, she, it spoke	we spoke you spoke they spoke
PRESENT PERFECT TENSE	I have spoken you have spoken he, she, it *have* spoken [not *has* spoken]	we have spoken you have spoken they have spoken
PAST PERFECT TENSE	had spoken (all persons and numbers)	

The following sentences illustrate the correct use of the subjunctive:

I demand that this defendant *be found* guilty.

My lawyer has insisted that the judge *have delivered* her opinion by tomorrow morning.

If this woman *be* a citizen, as she claims, why have we found no public record of her existence?

They would not have asked that we *be* consulted if they *were* not interested in our opinions.

If Fargo *were* a Republican, he could not have been elected.

The subjunctive mood also survives in a few idiomatic expressions:

Far be it from me . . .   Long live the king!
Suffice it to say . . .   Come what may . . .
Heaven help us!   Be that as it may . . .
The devil take the hindmost.   Glory be to God!

EXERCISE 14, MOOD   (5)

Select the correct verb from the choices in parentheses. Cross out each incorrect choice.

Example   I wish I (~~was~~/were) in that class.

1. If a person (is/be) teaching a class on ethnic history, should that person be a member of an ethnic minority?
2. If such a person (was/were) well trained, why complain?
3. A knowledge of the subject (is/be) really all that is required.
4. Such a person (read/reads) and (perform/performs) research in ethnic history.
5. (Be it/It is) resolved that the student union (requires/require) that all ethnic-studies courses be taught by minorities.
6. Such a demand (was/were) frequent not too long ago.
7. We think it impossible that all such courses (be/are) taught by minorities.
8. Ethnic-studies instructors (are/be) in great demand.
9. The requirement that such instructors (are/be) the only instructors involved in these programs is misguided, in many people's opinions.
10. Is it essential that Elizabethan history (is/be) taught by an Elizabethan?
11. The two examples (are/be) not similar.
12. I prefer that such a course (is/be) taught by someone who can speak about the psychological dimensions of life in a minority group.
13. Students prefer that such a perspective (is/be) given by a student.
14. Most important is the necessity that all information included in the course (is/be) accurate.
15. I wish that this issue (was/were) resolved.

Write sentences using the mood indicated for each of the following verbs listed.

Example   (*be,* formal demand, subjunctive) *Be it resolved that the motion pass.*

(*be,* condition, subjunctive) *If the case be such, heaven help us.*

(*give,* imperative) *Give me the money.*

(*be,* wishes, subjunctive) *I wish I weren't here.*

16. (*jump,* imperative) _____

17. (*love,* indicative) _____

18. (*succeed,* subjunctive) _____

19. (*meet,* formal demand, subjunctive) _____

20. (*watch,* imperative) _____

21. (*discover,* condition, subjunctive) _____

22. (*complete,* formal demand, subjunctive) _____

23. (*finish,* imperative) _____

24. (*see,* condition, subjunctive) _____

25. (*choose,* wishes, subjunctive) _____

The following sentences are in the indicative mood. Rewrite them, using the subjunctive mood appropriately.

Example   What if the student government wants no ethnic studies at all?

What if the student government were to want no ethnic studies at all?

26. We asked the director to explain the ethnic-studies program.

_____

27. The school expects her to be responsible for the entire program.

_____

28. She ensures that all courses taught in the program are taught professionally.

_____

29. She requires that every instructor has the appropriate degrees and training.

_____

30. She prefers that each of her instructors has taught the class previously.

_____

74

15 BASIC GRAMMAR REVIEW (1–5)

For each of the following sentences, write in the blank the correct form of the word listed at the left. Note that verbs may require a change in tense, voice, or mood, or the addition of auxiliaries, to be correct.

Example   *be*   Everyone assumes that the Pilgrims _were_ _____
a singular group of people with a single purpose.

1. *who/whom*   These people, _____ were the first
immigrants to America, were themselves a pluralistic
society.

2. *They/Their*   _____ immigrating to America
demonstrated their radical view of society.

3. *quiet/quietly*   They were not a people to remain _____
wherever they were.

4. *separate*   Years before, they _____ from the
Church of England.

5. *live*   Many of them _____ in Holland before
immigrating to America.

6. *actual*   But only about one-third of the 102 people on board the

    Mayflower _____ were Pilgrims.

7. *be*   The rest of the passengers _____
volunteers or recruits.

8. *themselves/theirselves*   The Pilgrims called _____ ''Saints.''

9. *They/Their*   _____ calling the others ''Strangers'' was
no accident.

10. *different/differently*   These people must have seemed _____ to the religious Pilgrims.

11. *It's/Its*   _____ true that many "Stranger" families were mainly drunkards or criminals.

12. *be*   Puritan law required that both men and women

    _____ placed in the stocks for public drunkenness.

13. *cause*   Stranger children _____ at least two early problems.

14. *blow*   On the voyage one child almost _____ up the *Mayflower* while he played near the powder supply.

15. *he/him*   This same child's brother, as mischievous as

    _____ , got lost; the entire colony

searched for _____ for days.

16. *charge*   Their mother _____ with being "a common gossip."

17. *hang*   Ten years after the landing, their father

    _____ for murder.

18. *bad*   Thus, whole families of rather unwholesome people formed

the _____ element in society.

19. *recruit*   The Strangers _____ by the merchants who backed the colony.

20. *sit/set*   Strangers and Pilgrims alike had _____ their sights on a new life in the New World.

21. *lie/lay*   Imagine the shock that _____ ahead for them.

22. *who/whom* All the settlers had agreed to send goods back to the

merchants, _____ would sell the goods
at a profit.

23. *plentiful* Opportunity must have been _____
in America than in England, in order to tempt the Pilgrims
to attempt the crossing.

24. *take* The crossing _____ nine weeks.

25. *kill* One sailor _____ during the crossing.

26. *quick* Since he had not been sympathetic to the Pilgrims, they

_____ decided his death was a good
omen.

27. *grow* Strangers and Saints immediately _____
accustomed to hard work.

28. *near* During the first year, _____ half the
settlers died.

29. *drink; who/whom* Since they were afraid to drink the water, the settlers

_____ more beer per person than any

other group for _____ we have figures.

30. *real* Even the first Thanksgiving was _____
not a religious festival, as we sometimes think.

31. *involve* The "harvest festival" _____ games,
dancing, singing, feasting, and drinking.

32. *complete* The usual image of the Pilgrims may be

_____ false.

33. *more/most* They were less religious and _____
radical than most people believe.

34. *go*   It _____ without saying that "ancestors who came over on the *Mayflower*" were immigrants, too.

35. *have*   And even the 102 Pilgrims _____ minority groups among them.

16
SENTENCE FRAGMENTS   (6)

A **sentence fragment** lacks either a subject or a predicate or both and is not a complete statement. Usually, a fragment occurs because the writer has mistaken a phrase or subordinate clause (see Sections 6 and 7) for a complete sentence. Consequently, fragments can often be corrected by attaching them to an adjacent sentence.

COMPLETE STATEMENT: INDEPENDENT CLAUSE
American music offers something for everybody.

FRAGMENT: SUBORDINATE CLAUSE
Because it has borrowed something from everybody.

COMPLETE STATEMENT: COMPLEX SENTENCE
American music offers something for everybody because it has borrowed something from everybody.

Sometimes a comma is required to attach the fragment to an adjacent sentence.

Our music owes a lot to ethnic groups. *Particularly Black song writers and musicians.*
Our music owes a lot to ethnic groups, *particularly Black song writers and musicians.*
Denied the opportunity to learn to read and write. Enslaved Blacks recorded their history in song.
Denied the opportunity to learn to read and write, enslaved Blacks recorded their history in song.

By reading a sentence aloud, you can usually tell if a comma is needed or not.

Another way to correct a sentence fragment is to rewrite the fragment as a complete sentence containing both a subject and a verb.

The blues originated in the Black community. *Eventually becoming popular throughout the country.*
The blues originated in the Black community. *It eventually became popular throughout the country.*

Remember, to be a sentence a group of words must have a subject and a predicate and must not be introduced by a subordinating conjunction. Prepositional phrases, verbal phrases, appositives renaming or explaining nouns or noun substitutes, and other word groups lacking a subject or a verb are not sentences. The following examples show these types of fragments and suitable revisions:

PREPOSITIONAL PHRASE	Bessie Smith was a great blues singer. *With a powerful style.*
REVISION	Bessie Smith was a great blues singer *with a powerful style.*
VERBAL PHRASE	Her style became a legend. *To inspire generations of singers.*
REVISION	Her style became a legend *to inspire generations of singers.*

SUBORDINATE CLAUSE	Bessie's music lived on in Billie Holiday and others. *Even after she died in 1937.*
REVISION	*Even after she died in 1937,* Bessie's music lived on in Billie Holiday and others.
APPOSITIVE	Bessie Smith's blues style influenced Janis Joplin. *A young pop singer of the 1970's.*
REVISION	Bessie Smith's blues style influenced Janis Joplin, *a young pop singer of the 1970's.*
COMPOUND PREDICATE	People who heard Bessie sing called her "the Empress of the Blues." *And never forgot her.*
REVISION	People who heard Bessie sing called her "the Empress of the Blues" *and never forgot her.*

Practice: Identifying sentence fragments   Underline all the sentence fragments in the following paragraph. The answers are listed next.

[1] The National Newspaper Publishers Association. [2] Formed in 1940. [3] This group represents 125 Black-owned newspapers in the United States. [4] Functioning not only as a trade association. [5] The NNPA helps Black newspapers with all sorts of business problems. [6] Even problems which they share with white-owned newspapers. [7] Such as circulation, revenues, and delivery schedules. [8] Despite these problems. [9] With the help of the NNPA, the Black press is now thriving in America. [10] Reaching well over 25 million readers each week.

Answers to the Practice   The following items are fragments: 1, 2, 4, 6, 7, 8, 10.

EXERCISE 16, SENTENCE FRAGMENTS   (6)

Revise the following word groups, eliminating fragments in two ways: (a) by joining the groups to form one complete sentence; and (b) by rewording them as necessary to form two separate sentences.

Example   Published in New York in 1827. *Freedom Journal* was the nation's first newspaper published by Blacks.

a. *Published in New York in 1827, Freedom Journal was the nation's first newspaper published by Blacks.*

b. *Freedom Journal was published in New York in 1827. It was the nation's first newspaper published by Blacks.*

1. The editors of *Freedom Journal* were Samuel Cornish and J. B. Russwum. One of the first American Blacks to earn a college degree.

   a. _____

   b. _____

2. Cornish was a freeborn Black. Who also started the first Presbyterian Church in America.

   a. _____

   b. _____

3. All the other New York papers were owned by whites. And very critical of freed slaves.

   a. _____

   b. _____

4. White papers were particularly critical of allowing ex-slaves to vote. To which *Freedom Journal* was a response.

   a. _____

   b. _____

5. Forced to close within two years. *Freedom Journal* was hampered by disagreements over editorial policy.

   a. _____

   b. _____

6. The editors of the paper urged Blacks to educate themselves. But could not agree and dissolved the partnership.

   a. _____

   b. _____

7. They were undecided on the question of whether Blacks should stay in America. Or return to help colonize Africa by settling in Liberia.

   a. _____

   b. _____

8. There were many other Black papers printed before the Civil War. But had equally short lives.

   a. _____

   b. _____

9. Forty Black-owned newspapers printed between 1829 and 1860. None really lasted very long at all.

   a. _____

   b. _____

10. That these newspapers were founded at all and survived for a while. This shows that a Black audience for newspapers existed at the time.

   a. _____

   b. _____

Revise the following paragraph, eliminating sentence fragments. You may join groups of words to form complete sentences, or you may reword fragments, adding missing subjects and predicates to form complete sentences. Write out your revision on your own paper.

Starting your own business may be one of the oldest forms of the American Dream. Dating from the early days in the Colonies. When immigrants from the Old World came to America to make their fortunes. America has a long tradition of entrepreneurship. Which may help explain the country's rapid growth from a colonial outpost. To a major economic leader. For example, the invention of the modern textile factory in 1813 by Francis Cabot Lowell. This made New England a manufacturing center. George Westinghouse was 22 years old. When he invented the airbrake. He used the profits from the airbrake to develop the first industrial-scale generators and transformers. And produced alternating current. To allow wide use of electricity. Edwin Land developed a new kind of camera. Which other people thought was just a novelty. So he sold it with the backing of his own lens-making company. Which he had named Polaroid Corporation.

17
COMMA SPLICES AND FUSED SENTENCES   (7)

A **comma splice** occurs when two main clauses are joined by a comma without a coordinating conjunction. A **fused sentence** (also called a **run-on sentence**) occurs when two main clauses are run together without any punctuation.

COMMA SPLICE	Immigrants change the nation, they are also changed by it.
FUSED SENTENCE	Immigrants change the nation they are also changed by it.

Comma splices and fused sentences are similar types of errors, and they have similar solutions. In both cases, the independent clauses require clear signals to tell the readers where one complete thought stops and another begins.

The conventions of written English provide only two such signals: the period and the semicolon. Two other alternatives are also acceptable. The thoughts may be coordinated, joined by a comma and a coordinating conjunction (*and, but, or, nor, for, so, yet*), or one thought may be subordinated to the other and joined by a subordinating conjunction. The following sentences illustrate these four solutions for the comma splice and fused sentence:

PERIOD	Immigrants change the nation. They are also changed by it.
SEMICOLON	Immigrants change the nation; they are also changed by it.
COORDINATION	Immigrants change the nation, but they are also changed by it. Immigrants change and are changed by the nation.
SUBORDINATION	Even though immigrants change the nation, they are also changed by it.

Notice that when the subordinate clause precedes the main clause, a comma joins the two. You may be wondering why a comma is acceptable in the middle of *Even though immigrants change the nation, they are also changed by it.* but not in *Immigrants change the nation, they are also changed by it.* Remember, the issue is not where the comma appears as much as it is *why* it appears. In the first instance, one idea is subordinate and functions as a modifier of the main clause. The comma helps to signal the subordinate relationship and marks the beginning of the main clause. In the second instance, the ideas are not subordinate, and, consequently, they are expressed in independent clauses. A comma used between them would be a false signal, indicating a connection that does not grammatically exist.

Why is the comma in *Immigrants change the nation, but they are also changed by it.* acceptable? The coordinating conjunction *but* grammatically establishes the connection between the two complete thoughts. The comma signals that relationship.

Practice: Identifying comma splices and fused sentences   *Decide which of the following sentences are correct, which contain comma splices, and which are fused. The answers are listed at the end of this section.*

[1] A major choice which faces many members of ethnic or minority groups in America is the choice between assimilation and autonomy. [2] People find themselves deciding whether they should preserve their ethnic culture or consciously try to become "as

American as apple pie," this is one of the few countries where people even have that choice. [3] Most countries throughout history have attempted, even using law or military power, to preserve only one culture the majority culture was frequently the culture of the political, ethnic, or social group which happened to be in power at the time. [4] Even today, many countries that consider themselves "emerging" nations wish to define their national culture as the only one, dominant culture of their nation and expect minorities to conform to the dominant culture.

REVISING SENTENCES WITH MULTIPLE ERRORS

When a sentence contains more than two fused independent clauses, more than one comma splice, or both comma splices and fused independent clauses, a combination of remedies is usually needed. Rewriting a sentence using only periods, only semicolons, or only coordinating conjunctions is likely to result in a choppy, awkward, and illogical or unfocused revision.

FAULTY SENTENCE	Our town holds its ethnic festival everybody turns out, the food and entertainment are wonderful.
POOR REVISION	Our town holds its ethnic festival; everybody turns out; the food and entertainment are wonderful.
BETTER REVISION	When our town holds its ethnic festival, everybody turns out because the food and entertainment are wonderful.

Unless fused or spliced sentence elements are parallel—that is, of equal rank and therefore expressed in parallel grammatical form—repeating the same punctuation or conjunction does not create an effective revision. Notice that the preceding final revision focuses the ideas and clarifies the time sequence and the cause-effect logic by means of the subordinating conjunctions *when* and *because.*

Similarly, in the revision of the following example, a relative pronoun is used to subordinate less important information. To avoid awkward length and to handle two relatively independent ideas, the clauses have been divided into two separate sentences.

FAULTY SENTENCE	The ethnic festival has been held every July for the past twenty years it attracts huge crowds, they get bigger every year.
EFFECTIVE REVISION	The ethnic festival, which attracts huge crowds, has been held every July for the past twenty years. The crowds get bigger every year.

Answers to the Practice   [1] correct   [2] comma splice   [3] fused   [4] correct

EXERCISE 17-1, COMMA SPLICES AND FUSED SENTENCES   (7)

Revise each of the following faulty sentences in four ways to correct the spliced or fused independent clauses: (a) use a period to form two separate sentences; (b) use a semicolon between independent clauses; (c) use a coordinating conjunction and a comma to form a compound sentence; and (d) use a subordinating conjunction or relative pronoun (with any necessary commas) to form a complex sentence.

Example   Dozens of Black newspapers have started up many famous Black Americans have worked with these papers.

a. _started up. Many famous_

b. _started up; many famous_

c. _started up, and many famous_

d. _Since dozens . . . , many famous_

1. The *Freedom Journal* was first to demand equal rights, many of these papers have shared that message.

    a. _____

    b. _____

    c. _____

    d. _____

2. Frederick Douglass was a famous early Black writer, he published the *North Star* in New York.

    a. _____

    b. _____

    c. _____

    d. _____

3. W.E.B. DuBois became editor of *The Crisis* he also helped found the NAACP.

    a. _____

    b. _____

c. _____

d. _____

4. Marcus Garvey was an editor of *Negro World* there he advocated emigration back to Africa.

   a. _____

   b. _____

   c. _____

   d. _____

5. These publishers helped change minds in America, they sometimes suffered for their beliefs.

   a. _____

   b. _____

   c. _____

   d. _____

6. A paper like *The Living Way* might have its office burned, the messages of Black papers were heard.

   a. _____

   b. _____

   c. _____

   d. _____

7. The *Chicago Defender* told Blacks of the jobs in northern industry, thousands moved north.

   a. _____

   b. _____

   c. _____

   d. _____

8. Black publishers asked President Truman to integrate the armed services, he ordered their complete integration immediately after World War II.

   a. _____

   b. _____

   c. _____

   d. _____

EXERCISE 17-2, COMMA SPLICES AND FUSED SENTENCES   (7)

The following sentences contain comma splices, fused independent clauses, or both. Revise them, correcting the errors and clarifying the logic. You may add, omit, or rearrange some words to achieve an effective revision.

Example   Few sports are truly American, some are.

_____ *Although few sports are truly American, some are.* _____

1. White-water boating is a major new sport in America, it involves using canoes or kayaks.

_____

2. Both canoes and kayaks have uniquely American histories both were invented by native Americans.

_____

3. Canoes are long, sleek boats, they were developed by Indians of the Northeast and Great Lakes region.

_____

4. The hull is a deep, V-shape it was originally made of wood.

_____

5. Later, a frame of thin wooden ribs was made first, then a covering of thin, scraped bark was laid over the frame.

_____

6. Modern canoes are made of aluminum or fiberglass the design has never really changed, however.

_____

7. The canoe's hull will carry mountains of equipment, the boat itself is light enough to be carried by one or two people.

_____

8. Sailboats require near-perfect skill and balance, canoes don't.

_____

9. Canoes are versatile, they're fun on lakes or in mountain rapids.

___

10. The kayak is even more lightweight, it was developed by the Eskimos of northern Canada and Greenland.

___

11. Kayaks have a wood or bone frame, seal skin is stretched over it.

___

12. Like the canoes, the modern kayak may be made of plastic, aluminum, or fiberglass, it is designed to hold only one person, or two at the most.

___

13. The passengers sit flat on the bottom of the kayak a watertight flap seals them into the craft.

___

14. The kayak is watertight, it's almost impossible to sink.

___

15. It turns upside down, the pilot can turn it back upright with a twist of the hips.

___

16. The name of this maneuver honors its inventors it is called "the Eskimo roll."

___

17. Kayak enthusiasts are only interested in rapids the kayak is perfectly suited for rapids.

___

18. Kayak pilots carry a single oar, it has two blades.

___

19. They can use this oar to paddle rapidly, they also use it as a lever to fend off rocks and obstacles.

___

20. Both the Indians and Eskimos needed lightweight, maneuverable boats, these are the same qualities that make canoeing and kayaking popular today.

___

18
SUBJECT AND VERB AGREEMENT   (8a)

When subjects and verbs do not agree, readers are likely to misunderstand a writer's message. Suppose you have written *The first two quarters of the game was exciting.* in a letter to a friend. Reading the sentence, your friend understands that the game was exciting but doesn't quite know what the first two quarters have to do with it. Your reader has perceived the subject of the sentence to be *game.* Because *game* is a singular noun and *was* is a singular verb, the two fit together. If you had written *The first two quarters of the game were exciting.,* your friend would quickly see that *quarters* is the subject because it fits the plural verb *were.* Your reader would understand the message correctly: You found half the game exciting, but not necessarily all of it.

Subjects and verbs should agree in **person** and **number. Agreement in person** is achieved if the verb form corresponds to the first, second, or third person pronoun form of the subject. For example, *She buy new sneakers.* is a faulty sentence because the third person pronoun *she* does not agree with the verb *buy.* In the present tense, the *-s* form of the verb is required for third person singular pronouns and all singular nouns: *She buys.* Agreement in person causes relatively few problems for writers because the *-s* form is the only exceptional verb form requiring special attention. (See *Special Problems with Verb Tenses,* Section 11.)

Agreement in number between subjects and verbs, however, can be more troublesome. Most writers are well aware that a singular subject requires a singular verb and a plural subject requires a plural verb. Agreement errors most often arise when the writer is uncertain about whether a subject is singular or plural or when intervening words obscure the real subject. The following guidelines can help you avoid subject-verb agreement errors:

1. If words or phrases come between the subject and the verb, be sure the verb agrees with the subject, not with an intervening noun or pronoun.

FAULTY	The final miles of the race was grueling.
CORRECT	The final *miles* of the race *were* grueling.

Singular subjects followed by expressions such as *with, along with, together with,* and *as well as* take singular verbs, even though they suggest a plural meaning. These expressions are not considered part of the subject.

FAULTY	Joan, together with her sisters, play in the semifinals tonight.
CORRECT	*Joan,* together with her sisters, *plays* in the semifinals tonight.

2. If the subject is an indefinite pronoun such as *everyone, somebody, another, each, either,* and *neither,* use a singular verb.

FAULTY	Everybody are here, but neither of the judges have arrived yet.
CORRECT	*Everybody is* here, but *neither* of the judges *has* arrived yet.

The indefinite pronouns *all, any, most, more, none,* and *some* take either a singular or a plural verb, depending on whether the noun to which the pronoun refers is singular or plural.

SINGULAR	*All* of the *soap is* gone.
PLURAL	*All* of my *socks are* dirty.

3. If two or more subjects are joined by *and,* use a plural verb.

FAULTY | Football and rugby is only for the hearty.
CORRECT | *Football and rugby are* only for the hearty.

However, if the parts of a compound subject refer to the same person or thing, use a singular verb. Also use a singular verb if a compound subject is understood to be a unit.

SINGLE REFERENT | The play's *star and inspiration has stormed* off the stage.
SINGLE UNIT | *Macaroni and cheese was* his favorite lunch.

4. If two or more subjects are joined by *or* or *nor,* the verb should agree with the nearest subject.

FAULTY | My assistants or my secretary have the keys to the lockers.
CORRECT | My assistants or my *secretary has* the keys to the lockers.
FAULTY | My secretary or my assistants has the keys to the lockers.
CORRECT | My secretary or my *assistants have* the keys to the lockers.

5. If an expletive (such as *there* or *it*) precedes the verb, locate the true subject and make sure the verb agrees with it, not with the expletive.

FAULTY | There is many reasons for his success.
CORRECT | There *are* many *reasons* for his success.

6. If the subject is a singular collective noun (such as *assembly, audience, jury, flock*), use a singular verb when the group is acting as a unit. Use a plural verb when the members of the group are acting separately.

AS A UNIT | The *subcommittee addresses* the issue tomorrow.
AS INDIVIDUALS | The *staff take* turns answering the director's questions.

7. If the sentence contains a predicate noun, the verb should agree with the subject, not with the predicate noun.

FAULTY | Material things is a prime necessity with you.
CORRECT | Material *things are* a prime necessity with you.

8. If a relative pronoun (*who, which, that*) is used as the subject, the verb should agree with the pronoun's antecedent.

SINGULAR ANTECEDENT | They will release *one* of the men *who has* been injured. [Antecedent of *who* is *one.* The information *has been injured* is intended to describe only the one man.]
PLURAL ANTECEDENT | Here is one of the *shoes that were* missing. [Antecedent of *that* is *shoes.* The information *were missing* is intended to describe all the shoes.]

9. If a subject is plural in form but singular in meaning (such as *news, physics, linguistics*), use a singular verb. Similarly, titles of novels, plays, songs, and the like take singular verbs, even if their form is plural. Subjects indicating sums or quantities also usually take singular verbs.

College *athletics is* big business these days.
Wales and Nightingales was a popular record album.
Ten years is a long career in professional sports.

EXERCISE 18-1, SUBJECT AND VERB AGREEMENT   (8)

Select the correct verb from the choices in parentheses. Cross out the incorrect form.

Example   Gypsies still (comprise/~~comprises~~) the most mysterious ethnic group.

1. University sociologists and anthropologists (knows/know) relatively little about them.

2. A great deal of popular lore about Gypsies (is/are) false.

3. But many of the stereotypes (turn/turns) out to be true to some degree.

4. The origin of the Gypsy people (is/are) hidden in mystery.

5. The word "Gypsy" (derive/derives) from the word "Egyptian."

6. At one time, the Gypsies (was/were) thought to have come from Egypt.

7. Some Gypsies still (believe/believes) they are of Egyptian origin.

8. It is now believed that their original homeland (was/were) India.

9. Romany, the Gypsy language, (has/have) similarities to Sanskrit.

10. Nobody (know/knows) why the Gypsies migrated from India.

11. Some (was/were) as far west as Persia by the fifth century.

12. News of Gypsies (was/were) recorded in southeastern Europe by the 1300's.

13. There (is/are) evidence that Gypsies arrived in Virginia, Georgia, Louisiana, and New Jersey during the 1600's.

14. The fate of these first arrivals (remain/remains) unknown.

15. Those early arrivals (was/were) deportees from various countries.

16. A significant number of Gypsies (was/were) living in the U.S. by the 1880's.

17. Until the 1930's, Gypsy travel (was/were) by way of horse-drawn caravan.

18. Now, Gypsies (own/owns) as many cars and trucks as anyone else.

19. Gypsies (call/calls) themselves *Rom.*

20. There (is/are) many difficulties in studying the Rom.

21. The Rom (live/lives), as they always (have/has), in an alien culture.

22. They (maintain/maintains) sharp boundaries between themselves and others.

23. Investigating the Rom (is/are) like trying to find out about a secret society.

24. The Rom do not mingle with the *gadje,* which (is/are) their name for all non-Gypsies.

25. Most Americans never (come/comes) into contact with a Gypsy.

26. There (is/are) Gypsies in all the states of the U.S.

27. The largest concentrations of the Rom (is/are) to be found in New York, Virginia, Illinois, Texas, and Massachusetts.

28. Estimates of the total Gypsy population in the U.S. (range/ranges) from 500,000 to a million.

29. There are four major tribes of the Rom who (live/lives) in this country.

30. The culture of the Rom (varies/vary) according to the tribe and the country to which a particular family (belong/belongs).

31. The customs or cultural tradition of one group (do/does) not necessarily apply to another.

32. One of the most striking features of Gypsy life (is/are) the "extended family."

33. A Gypsy family, along with other families, often (form/forms) an economic unit called a *Kumpania.*

34. These *Kumpaniyi* (is/are) rather fluid associations for organizing labor.

35. The *Kumpania* (parcel/parcels) out jobs.

36. *Wortacha* (is/are) much smaller units, such as partnerships.

37. Some groups who (is/are) often called Gypsies are not, in fact, Gypsies at all.

38. The Irish Tinkers, for example, are Celtic and (speak/speaks) a Celtic dialect.

39. There (has/have) always been large numbers of Gypsies who did not travel.

40. Perhaps because they (are/is) so mysterious, the Rom are fascinating.

EXERCISE 18-2, SUBJECT AND VERB AGREEMENT   (8)

Write sentences that contain appropriate forms of the given verbs and that use the words given as subjects and modifiers.

Example   (*Cable television,* present tense of *have*)

Cable television has become very popular.

1. (*Foremost causes of failure,* a form of *be*)

_____

2. (*These, disasters,* a form of *be*)

_____

3. (*One, people, that,* a form of *be*)

_____

4. (*Committee* [with its individuals acting separately], present tense of *arrive*)

_____

5. (*Motivation and persistence,* present tense of *result*)

_____

6. (*These,* a form of *be, decisions*)

_____

7. (*Either you or one of the others,* present tense of *be*)

_____

8. (*Algebra, trigonometry,* form of *be*)

_____

9. (*Fifty dollars,* form of *be, high price*)

_____

10. (*Network television,* present tense of *be*)

_____

11. (*Most of the news,* present tense of *seem*)

_____

12. (*None of the group,* form of *be*)

_____

13. (*Spaghetti and meatballs,* present tense of *taste*)

_____

14. (*Professors and students,* present tense of *cooperate*)

_____

15. (*Airplanes and trains,* present tense of *provide*)

_____

16. (*These,* form of *be, kinds*)

_____

17. (*Assembly* [acting as a unit], form of *be*)

_____

18. (*Neither the captain nor the sailors,* present tense of *believe*)

_____

19. (*Girl, with blue eyes,* present tense of *appear*)

_____

20. (*Justifications,* present tense of *involve, an essential matter*)

_____

21. (*Everybody,* present tense of *know*)

_____

22. (*Here, options,* form of *be*)

_____

23. (*Motivation,* present tense of *comprise, essential* [adjective])

_____

24. (*Nobody,* present tense of *see*)

_____

25. (*Hope* [noun], *desires* [noun], *neither, nor,* form of *be*)

_____

19
PRONOUN AND ANTECEDENT AGREEMENT   (8b–c)

Pronouns should agree with their antecedents in number. If the **antecedent,** the word or words for which the pronoun stands, is singular, the pronoun should be singular; if the antecedent is plural, the pronoun should be plural.

SINGULAR ANTECEDENT	The dog wanted its nightly run.
PLURAL ANTECEDENT	The dogs wanted their nightly run.

Antecedents such as *anyone, anybody, someone, somebody, each, every, everyone,* and *everybody* are singular and require singular pronouns. Collective nouns, such as *band, assembly, organization, mob, army, family, team, class,* and *brigade,* require singular pronouns when the group is being considered as a unit and plural pronouns when the individual members of the group are being considered separately.

GROUP AS A UNIT	The crew has finished its work.
MEMBERS OF GROUP CONSIDERED SEPARATELY	The crew have decided to quit their work.

A plural pronoun is used to refer to two or more antecedents joined by *and.* A singular pronoun is used to refer to a singular antecedent joined by *or* or *nor.* If one of the antecedents is singular and the other is plural, the pronoun should agree in number with the antecedent that is nearer.

ANTECEDENTS JOINED BY *AND*	Artists and artisans know their stuff.
SINGULAR ANTECEDENTS JOINED BY *OR* OR *NOR*	Either Jack or Joe must have missed his connecting flight.
COMBINATION OF SINGULAR AND PLURAL ANTECEDENTS	Neither the coach nor the players flagged in their desire.

The demonstrative adjectives *this, that, these,* and *those* agree in number with the nouns they modify. In constructions with *kind of* and *sort of,* the demonstrative adjective modifies *kind* and *sort,* and the following noun should be singular, not plural.

INCORRECT	These kind of situation are bad.
CORRECT	This kind of situation is bad.
	These kinds of situations are bad.

Historically, masculine pronoun forms (*he, him, his*) have been used to refer to antecedents such as *one, none, everybody,* and other indefinite pronouns, as well as to antecedent nouns of indeterminate gender. In recent years, this "common gender" use of masculine pronouns has been recognized as imprecise at best and discriminatory at worst.

Unless all the members of a group are known to be male, it is inappropriate to use a masculine pronoun when referring to them. For example, to write *Every employee should fill out his time card correctly.* is inaccurate if some of the employees are women. By the same token, not all secretaries, librarians, and nurses are female. Be equally careful about the blanket use of feminine pronouns if the antecedent refers to men as well.

If you wish to avoid common gender when referring to antecedents that include both males and females, you can use one of the following methods:

INSTEAD OF	*Each job applicant must submit his resume.*
USE BOTH MASCULINE AND FEMININE PRONOUNS	*Each job applicant* must submit *his or her* resume.
USE THE PLURAL FOR BOTH ANTECEDENT AND PRONOUN	*All job applicants* must submit *their* resumes.
RECAST THE SENTENCE TO REMOVE THE PRONOUN	Each job applicant must submit a resume.

Practice: Avoiding inappropriate common-gender pronouns   *In which of the following sentences is the use of common-gender pronouns inappropriate? The answers are listed next. Your instructor may ask you to revise those sentences that use pronouns inappropriately.*

[1] Although Gypsy children are supposed to show respect for their elders, they are really quite pampered. [2] Corporal punishment is rare for the Romany child, and he is always the center of attention. [3] A Gypsy child is treated as if he were a small adult. [4] His or her wishes are as respected as are those of adults. [5] Timidity is not very highly thought of among the Rom, so children are encouraged to speak up. [6] A Gypsy child also spends more time with her parents than do other children. [7] From the age of eight or nine, boys accompany their fathers on work assignments, while the girls begin to work around the home and to accompany their mothers.

Answers to the Practice   Sentences 2, 3, and 6 should be revised to avoid common-gender pronouns because the persons they refer to may be either female or male.

EXERCISE 19-1, PRONOUN AND ANTECEDENT AGREEMENT (8)

In each of the following sentences, select the correct form of the pronoun from the choices in parentheses. Cross out the incorrect choice.

Example   A Gypsy will not force (his or her/~~his~~/~~their~~) children to attend school.

1. Since Gypsies work only when necessary, (he or she/they) are free to travel almost at will.
2. In fact, "Traveler" is another common name for (this/these) kinds of people.
3. Neither the Gypsy father nor son feels that formal education is relevant to (his/their) way of life.
4. Among the Gypsies, nobody can read or write (his or her/their) native language, Romany, since it is a spoken tongue only.
5. Many Gypsies pay no taxes because (he or she/they) own no taxable property.
6. Since (his or her/their) work is irregular and at low-paying jobs, Gypsies' income taxes are low, at the very least.
7. The Rom (themselves/itself) love to talk about the days of horse-drawn caravans.
8. With (their/its) unusual lifestyle, this ethnic group has always fascinated the non-Gypsy.
9. Novels, songs, plays, and operas have romanticized the Gypsy and (his/their) wanderings.
10. Yet at the same time, persecution of the Gypsies has followed (him/them) everywhere.
11. (These/This) nomads were often hounded from one locale to another.
12. Even the *Sinte,* nonnomadic Gypsies, found hostility and discrimination directed at (it/them).
13. Signs that "No Gypsies Are Allowed" were posted in exactly (that/those) kinds of places where the Rom might camp.
14. Local authorities felt the Rom were using local services without paying (their/his/its) share of taxes.
15. They said that the Rom were dirty, that (he or she/they/it) stole things or cheated people.
16. Sometimes the charges were true, but often (its/their) truth was unfounded or exaggerated.
17. Fortunately, the Rom have friends and supporters and (these/this) people have helped them.

18. Some countries aid the Rom by setting up special camping and housing facilities for (it/them).

19. In the 1970's, a number of international organizations were formed to provide aid; (it/they) carefully included Gypsies in the planning.

20. Anyone who follows the Gypsy way of life will have (his/his or her/their) problems.

21. People who study the Rom say (their/his) carefree, romantic life is a myth.

22. The Gypsy's life is one of constant insecurity, since (he or she/they) will do little planning for the future.

23. A young Gypsy man or woman cannot choose (their/his or her) mate but must usually marry the person (his or her/their) parents choose.

24. Kinship relations are the cornerstone of Gypsy society, so (they/it) do not trust matrimony to chance or luck.

25. The groom's parents arrange the marriage, but he won't be forced into (them/it) if he objects.

26. The groom's family often pays several thousand dollars to the bride's family; they accept (it/them) as a gesture of good will.

27. The money is not a profit; (they/it) will be used to pay for the wedding and to buy household items for the new couple.

28. Although arranged marriages and the "bride price" are integral parts of Gypsy culture, (its/their) enforcement is not as rigid as it was in earlier times.

29. Like parents in the rest of the world, the Rom are seeing increased freedom demanded by (their/his or her) children.

30. Parents still arrange the marriages, but now the bride and groom may be in love; (they/he or she) used to marry without ever meeting beforehand.

EXERCISE 19-2, PRONOUN-ANTECEDENT AND SUBJECT-VERB AGREEMENT

Revise the following sentences, correcting errors of pronoun-antecedent and subject-verb agreement. Revise to avoid common-gender pronouns where their use is inappropriate.

Example   In Gypsy culture, people of either sex achieve higher status as he or she grows older.

In gypsy culture, people of either sex achieve higher status as they grow older.

1.   When they are a young girl, Gypsy females assist with the housework.

2.   After they marry, Gypsy girls are then under the control of their mother-in-law instead of their mother.

3.   But either age or children of her own helps the Gypsy woman achieve independence.

4.   An increasing number of children increase her status accordingly.

5.   Many times, it is Gypsy women who deals with outsiders such as school officials.

6.   If somebody is successful at this task, their status rises again.

7.   Gypsy men and women look forward to having children, and he or she especially look forward to having grandchildren.

8.   Grandchildren mean true independence, for a grandparent has their children and their children's children to look after them in old age.

9.   The Gypsy community do not, of course, maintain group homes for their elderly.

10. The elderly are cared for by their own family in his or her own home.

11. A young Gypsy man, as well as young women, gain status as children are born and grow up.

---

12. The economics are simple; the more children, the more status.

---

13. When a father is ready to marry his children off, his position in the various tribal or family organizations are secure.

---

14. These sort of positions lead to roles of leadership and authority.

---

15. One of the things he will be expected to handle are family problems.

---

16. Older males spend more time on the affairs of the Gypsy band rather than the affairs of his own family.

---

17. Should their judgment prove sound, someone who is well respected may become a *Rom Baro,* a "Big Man."

---

18. A Big Man provides help for his followers and serve as a liaison with non-Gypsies if necessary.

---

19. A Big Man is the leader not only of his family, but also the band brings their individual problems to him as well.

---

20. Several economic units or, in other words, a group of families rely on the leadership of a *Rom Baro.*

---

21. He officiates at weddings and funerals; negotiating with the police or paying bail are included among his duties.

---

22. A *Rom Baro* must be skilled at persuasion and discussion to handle this kind of difficulties.

---

23. Neither the Big Man nor his followers expects coercive power to be used.

---

24. All that a *Rom Baro* is allowed in managing Gypsy affairs is his powers of persuasion; if they fail, he may be replaced.

---

25. While there are more than one *Rom Baro,* there really is no single "King of the Gypsies."

20
REFERENCE OF PRONOUNS (9)

Pronouns conveniently spare us the awkwardness of having to repeat nouns monotonously in our writing. However, pronouns are more general and less precise than their antecedents, the names of people, places, and things. Consequently, writers must be careful to make pronoun references very clear. If the reader is unsure to what antecedent a pronoun refers, the pronoun becomes a source of confusion.

Pronoun reference problems usually result from vague usage. The following discussion addresses the most common usage problems.

1. A pronoun should clearly refer to only one antecedent, and that antecedent should be located as near to the pronoun as possible. Don't make the reader search for and choose among remote antecedents.

    VAGUE   When Ray told his father about the accident, *he* was calm.

Who was calm, Ray or his father? Readers are used to associating a pronoun with the noun that most closely precedes it, in this case *father.* However, *Ray* and *he* are both subjects of their clauses, so the parallel positions of the two words suggest that Ray was calm. The reader cannot be sure which noun is really the intended antecedent.

    CLEAR   Ray was calm when he told his father about the accident.

    CLEAR   His father was calm when Ray told him about the accident.

    CLEAR   When Ray told his father about the accident, his father was calm.

    VAGUE   The neighbors decided to celebrate the Fourth of July with a block party. The morning was sunny, but by late afternoon rain began to fall. Clearing out a garage, *they* moved the picnic tables under its roof.

Neighbors is the only sensible antecedent for *they,* but because the pronoun is several sentences away from its antecedent, the reader must back-track to find the correct reference.

    CLEAR   . . . Clearing out a garage, the neighbors moved the picnic tables under its roof.

    CLEAR   When rain interrupted their Fourth of July block party, the neighbors cleared out a garage and moved the picnic tables under its roof.

2. The pronouns *this, that,* and *which* should not be used to refer to the general idea of a preceding clause or sentence. Always supply a specific antecedent.

    VAGUE USE OF   The dog slipped his leash but did not run away, *which*
    WHICH AND *THIS*   showed his training. *This* resulted from his going to obedience school.

What showed the dog's training, that he slipped his leash or that he did not run away? Was slipping the leash, not running away, or showing training the result of obedience school?

    CLEAR   The dog slipped his leash, but the fact that he did not run away showed his training. This training resulted from his going to obedience school.

3. Although we commonly use *it* and *they* for general, indefinite references in informal speech, nouns should be used in writing for exactness and clarity. *You,* used in speech to mean people in general, should be replaced by nouns such as *people, person,* or the pronoun *one. You* is correct, however, when used as the subject in writing directions or when the context is clearly *you, the reader* (as in *You should sand the surface before painting it.*).

VAGUE USE OF *IT,*   *It* says in the newspaper that *you* can still get tickets
THEY, AND *YOU*   because *they* have added two more performances.

CLEAR   The newspaper says people can still get tickets because
the theater has added two more performances.

4. A sentence containing two or more different uses of the pronoun *it* can be confusing. Especially when *it* is used as an idiom in one place in a sentence (as in *it is cold*) and as a definite pronoun referring to a specific noun in another place, the reader may have trouble keeping the uses straight.

CONFUSING   My wife and I were hiking along the mountain trail
when *it* began to snow, but we decided *it* was time
to turn back in case *it* drifted shut.

CLEAR   When the snow began to fall, my wife and I were hiking
along the mountain trail, but we decided to turn back
in case it drifted shut.

5. A pronoun should refer to a noun that is actually expressed, not to one that is merely implied. For example, a pronoun should not refer to a noun that functions as an adjective or to a word whose form does not correspond to that of the pronoun.

VAGUE   Joan's form was excellent when *she* played on the college golf
team, but now she has no time for *it.*

The possessive *Joan's* implies but does not express *Joan,* the correct antecedent for *she.* Neither the adjective *golf,* nor the verb *played,* nor the nouns *form* or *team* provide an appropriate antecedent for *it.*

CLEAR   When Joan played on the college golf team, her form was excellent,
but now she has no time for golf.

EXERCISE 20-1, REFERENCE OF PRONOUNS   (9)

Revise the following sentences, correcting vague, remote, and implied pronoun references.

Example   It says in this book that most Amish are farmers.

The author of this book says that most Amish are farmers.

1.   They say the Amish and the Gypsies are more similar than you think.

_____

2.   They have an oral rather than a written culture.

_____

3.   They use a language other than English.

_____

4.   When an Amish father and son speak, he speaks in German.

_____

5.   The Amish respect their elderly and care for them at home. This is why they do not accept Social Security benefits.

_____

6.   The Amish are a branch of the Mennonites, and they are direct descendants of the Swiss Anabaptists.

_____

7.   The Anabaptists believed in separation of church and state, in adult baptism, and in the refusal to bear arms or take oaths of any sort, which resulted in persecution and harassment.

_____

8.   The first "Amish ships" came to America in the early 1700's. Each ship carried enough families to make an Amish congregation possible. They were soon followed by more.

_____

9.   You can't determine, however, when the first few Amish families came to America with other groups of immigrants.

_____

10. The supply of cheap land they found in Pennsylvania was an Amish paradise, but it soon grew in such numbers that the Amish traveled westward for more land.

---

11. The Old Order Amish is the largest and most conservative group of Amish in modern America, which are found in twenty states and other North and South American countries, as well.

---

12. There are no Amish to be found in Europe, which is ironic, since it was their homeland.

---

13. It will be slight variations in religious practice, dress, and lifestyle that make it possible to distinguish among the Amish from different regions.

---

14. The Amish reject almost all the advances of modern civilization, including autos, television, radio, higher education, politics, movies, jewelry, watches, and even life insurance, which creates their distinctive way of living.

---

15. Even the clothes they wear haven't changed, in any way you could see, for 250 years.

---

16. The men wear black hats and the women wear black bonnets outdoors. It was ordered by the Bible, according to the Amish.

---

17. The Amish can almost be described by the things they shun. Belts, collars, lapels, pockets, sweaters, neckties, gloves, or jewelry are all considered ornamental, and they avoid them.

---

18. Young men are clean-shaven, whereas married men must let their beards grow; they avoid mustaches.

---

19. You can't use makeup or ornamentation of any kind, even including sun glasses or wedding rings, since they do not wish to appear "worldly."

---

20. The reasons for this include thrift, the desire to avoid worldliness, and conservatism; this is a religious principle with the Amish.

EXERCISE 20-2, PRONOUN REVIEW   (2, 8-9)

Revise the following sentences, correcting errors in pronoun case, pronoun-antecedent
agreement, and vague pronoun reference.

Example   What you notice most about the Amish is that they forbid the use
of automobiles.

_*What one notices most about the Amish is that they
forbid the use of automobiles.*_

1. The Amish also forbid motorcycles, bicycles, and tractors; it is a threat to their
culture.

2. Any sick Amish farmer will find their fields tended by their concerned neighbors.

3. If their barn burns down, all the neighbors will unite and build another in a day.

4. At one time, the Amish rejected doctors and hospitals, but now it is approved by
most of them.

5. Amish women used to have their babies at home, but now most are in hospitals.

6. Amish funerals are simple. A wooden coffin is made by an Amish carpenter, and the
service is held at home. There are no flowers or elaborate monuments, not even a
caretaker. He is as conservative about death as he is about life.

7. Amish farms are, according to experts, among the best in the world, which
demonstrates the Amish farmers' skill and training pays off.

8. You may find three to five generations of Amish living on a single farmstead.

9. Some of them are so prosperous and so populated that they look like small villages.

10. Using horses gives the Amish farmers advantages and disadvantages; they are cheap, but slow.

_____

11. You can also fertilize the fields with a horse.

_____

12. The principles that govern Amish life allow them to use gasoline engines, however, and other machinery such as sprayers, cultivators, balers, and haymaking equipment.

_____

13. It says in this article that a stationary tractor is often used to power them.

_____

14. The Amish farmer whom uses any rolling equipment uses a horse to pull them, however.

_____

15. Problems are rare; the Amish farmer is a master of his trade, and this is what his children learn as they help him.

_____

16. Amish farm products are choice, and the family members or the farmer himself sell it for top prices, sometimes at farmers' markets.

_____

17. In addition, most of what him and his family eat is grown at home.

_____

18. Thus, large families are no burden; on the contrary, it is a necessity.

_____

19. The use of horses rather than tractors makes them work longer, harder hours.

_____

20. A large family is often a supply of cheap labor, they say.

_____

21
SHIFTS IN POINT OF VIEW   (10)

Point of view in a sentence is the vantage point or focus the writer provides for the reader. Unless grammar or meaning necessitates changing that focus, a sentence's subjects, verb tenses, mood, and voice, and pronoun person and number should work together to maintain a consistent point of view.

Most needless shifts occur in compound and complex sentences. The writer may begin with one focus but carelessly change to another in midsentence. The shift in point of view can distract and confuse the reader, as the following example shows:

> Terry liked to cook Chinese food, but the right ingredients were hard to find.
> [Subject changes from *Terry* to *ingredients*; voice changes from active to passive.]

The sentence focuses on Terry at the beginning, suggesting that he, his activities, or his interests are going to be emphasized. But when the sentence's subject shifts to *ingredients* in the second clause, the reader's initial assumptions are disturbed. What happened to Terry? The reader is left wondering just what the real focus of the sentence is. The following sentence illustrates a consistent point of view:

> *Terry* liked to cook Chinese food, but *he* had a hard time finding the
> right ingredients.

Sometimes the meaning of a sentence requires a shift in point of view. A change from one subject to another or a change in time, number, or person may be needed to keep the reader's attention in the right place and to convey the intended meaning clearly. For example, the sentence *I will wash the dishes while the cupcakes are baking.* contains shifts in subject, tense, voice, and number (first person, singular pronoun subject *I* to third person, plural noun subject *cupcakes*; active future tense verb *will wash* to passive present progressive tense verb *are baking*). These shifts are natural and necessary to convey the ideas in the sentence. *Needless* shifts in point of view, like those that follow, can make writing confusing and unfocused.

NEEDLESS SHIFT OF SUBJECT	She hated to study and, as a result, the grades she received were bad. [Subject changes from *she* to *grades*.]
REVISION	She hated to study and, as a result, she received bad grades.
NEEDLESS SHIFT OF VOICE	After a great deal of time had been spent in preparation, they started on their journey. [Voice changes from passive to active.]
REVISION	After they had spent a great deal of time in preparation, they started on their journey.
NEEDLESS SHIFT OF PERSON	When a person becomes ill, you should see a doctor. [Person changes from third, *a person*, to second, *you*.]
REVISION	When a person becomes ill, he or she should see a doctor.
NEEDLESS SHIFT OF NUMBER	If one tries hard, they will succeed. [Number changes from singular to plural.]
REVISION	If one tries hard, he or she will succeed.

NEEDLESS SHIFT OF TENSE	The mechanic first adjusts the carburetor and then set the points. [Tense changes from present to past.]
REVISION	The mechanic first adjusted the carburetor and then set the points.
NEEDLESS SHIFT OF MOOD	You must be careful; take no chances. [Mood changes from indicative to imperative.]
REVISION	Be careful; take no chances.

Another type of shift, from indirect to direct quotation (called a **shift of discourse**), is also particularly annoying to readers. Shifts from indirect to direct quotation usually involve a shift of verb tense and the omission of quotation marks.

NEEDLESS SHIFT OF DISCOURSE	The waiter asked Martha whether she wanted chopsticks or does she prefer a fork.
REVISIONS	The waiter asked Martha whether she wanted chopsticks or preferred a fork.
	The waiter asked Martha, "Do you want chopsticks, or do you prefer a fork?"

EXERCISE 21-1, SHIFTS IN POINT OF VIEW   (10)

The following sentences contain shifts in point of view. For each, indicate the type
of shift by writing the appropriate abbreviation—*s* (subject), *v* (voice), *t* (tense),
m (mood), *p* (person), *n* (number), or *d* (discourse)—at the end of the sentence.
Then revise the sentences to eliminate the shifts.

Example   For people wanting to learn more about the Amish, you may have
a hard time learning much about them. *P*

*People waiting to learn more about the Amish may have
a hard time learning much about them.*

1. Don't expect much information from an Amish farmer, but you should be prepared
for a shrug of the shoulders.

2. "It has always been so" is likely to be a farmer's answer any time they are asked about
Amish customs.

3. If an Amish farmer has been prosperous, they may retire at the age of fifty.

4. Then he stayed on at the farmstead, after turning the farm over to his sons.

5. Amish farm houses must be large since so many generations lived there.

6. The Old Order Amish have no church buildings, so services and ceremonies are held
in the farm houses, on a rotating schedule.

7. The Amish must make their homes not only large but also versatile; for this reason,
moveable partitions often are used instead of inner walls on the ground floor.

8. The Amish hold church services every other Sunday, so the pews are hauled by them
from one home to the next.

9. It is not clear to outsiders whether the Amish religion forbids the use of colors or is it forbidden to mix colors.

---

10. Inside an Amish home, one will find all the colors you see anywhere else.

---

11. The Amish love bright colors, so purple dishes or red walls or yellow furniture are often favored by them.

---

12. However, the Amish use only one color for each object, so fancy prints, plaids, or stripes were absent.

---

13. Much of the furniture in an Amish home is handmade, or they buy it secondhand at auctions and flea markets.

---

14. Rugs or carpets are not allowed by the Amish, although they often use linoleum.

---

15. There are no curtains, mirrors, photographs, or paintings in an Amish home; in fact, cameras were not permitted.

---

16. It was a sign of one's vanity and pride to have your picture made.

---

17. Wallpaper is forbidden, as was electric appliances.

---

18. Telephones are prohibited by the Amish, and they use oil lamps for light.

---

19. People have wondered why are electricity, indoor toilets, running water, even doorbells prohibited, even though the Amish in some districts are allowed to use gasoline-powered washing machines.

---

20. While the pattern of forbidden items and customs seems strange to an outsider, the Amish accept the prohibitions as just the way things have always been.

EXERCISE 21-2, SHIFTS IN POINT OF VIEW (10)

The following paragraphs illustrate just how confusing and distracting shifts in point of view can be to a reader trying to follow a writer's train of thought. After reading the paragraphs, use your own paper to write revisions that eliminate the shifts.

A typical day on an Amish farm begins well before dawn. Prayers are the first necessity, and then about two hours of chores are done by the family members. Cows, chickens, and hogs are fed, and then the farmer prepared the horses for the day's work. Breakfast is served around 6 A.M. and is preceded by prayer, and a prayer follows the meal. An hour later, everyone was in the fields. If one is there during a particularly busy season, you will see men and women together in the fields. Otherwise, Amish women work at household duties; without modern appliances, food preparation and storage took most of the day. At 11 A.M. the bell is rung for the noon meal, and the Amish eat a large noon meal. Less than two hours later, the men and women were back at work, and the work is done usually until four in the afternoon. The farmer and his family feed their livestock again; then equipment was cleaned and put away. A large supper is served, and afterward the family has about an hour and a half together, and then it is bedtime.

Because their religious beliefs rather limit their choices, the Amish do not take advantage of many recreational activities. If you believe that the "English" world is too worldly, then what does that leave one to do for fun? First of all the Amish had little time left over after all their work. Except for business trips that are absolutely necessary, you stay away from cities. Take this attitude, and what cultural activities are left open for you. The Amish do not attend operas, ballets, or concerts; movies, art shows, bars, restaurants, and sporting events are not frequented, either. At home, television, telephones, radios, popular magazines, and books are all forbidden, and the Amish do not dance or play cards. The Amish do not celebrate political holidays like the Fourth of July or Washington's Birthday; Christmas and Easter are celebrated, emphasizing their religious aspects.

Another factor that restricted the Amish is the ban on automobiles. You can ride in someone else's car, but you can't own one. You have to wonder why do the Amish insist more strongly on this ban than on any other? Ask an Amish person and they say that horses are mentioned in the Bible, and cars are not. Automobiles are expensive and unreliable, according to the Amish, while it is believed that horses are neither. If you consider the situation carefully, one can see that the automobile would give the Amish, particularly the young, far too easy access to the worldly city. It would be easy to leave the farm. Driving into town in search of leisure activities would take time away from work. To be Amish means to be a hard worker, and the automobile was simply too easy an escape from the farm and its rigorous demands on your time and energy. The Amish have experienced enormous pressure to allow automobile ownership. One group broke off from the Old Order Amish and now allows its members to own autos; occasionally the Old Order Amish lose a member to this group, the Beachy Amish. In addition, traveling by buggy has become dangerous on modern highways; lights have had to be installed by the Amish on their buggies for night travel on public roads.

Of course, like all cultures, the Amish culture provides recreation for its creators. Besides asking questions about the things they do, you might ask what do they do for recreational activities. Much of the Amish social life revolves around religion, as does almost all of the rest of their lives. A great deal of socializing took place before and after church services. Religious holidays and weddings are also celebrated, and the Amish young people hold "singings" on Sunday nights. Friends and relatives are visited on Sundays when no services are held. If you're Amish, one is fond of picnics and family outings of all sorts, particularly if they involve cooking and eating special foods. The Amish are fond of reading; religious books, the Bible, farm journals, and local papers are read by both children and adults. There is, in fact, an Amish newspaper. Its name, fittingly enough, is *The Budget*. Chess and checkers are played, and young children play at their own athletic games. Many adult males chew tobacco, and smoking is even practiced by the Amish in some districts. Drinking is forbidden, but certainly not strictly forbidden. You can easily find Amish who "take a nip" now and then. One sees that despite their forbidding lists of bans, the Amish are fairly tolerant of a bit of light drinking.

22
MISPLACED PARTS: MODIFIERS (11)

As a general rule, modifiers should be positioned as close as possible to the words they modify. Word order is crucial to meaning in English; readers depend on word order to follow a writer's train of thought. The following sentence illustrates what happens when a modifier is misplaced, violating the principle of word order:

She gave the fish hook to her brother baited with a worm.

After a moment's thought, the reader can untangle the sentence, being reasonably certain it is not the brother but the hook that is baited with a worm.

However, the following sentence cannot be untangled so easily:

The bartender handed a glass to the customer that was half full.

In this case, either the customer or the glass may be half full. Only the writer knows for sure.

Modifiers should be positioned so that the writer's intended meaning is unambiguous. The following discussion identifies some of the more common problems caused by misplaced sentence parts:

1. Adverbial modifiers such as *almost, even, hardly, just, merely, only, nearly*, and *scarcely* should be placed immediately before the words they modify.

AMBIGUOUS MODIFIER	He had only a face a mother could love. [Is his face all of him a mother could love?]
REVISION	He had a face only a mother could love. [*Only* placed thus conveys the idea the writer intends, that no one but a mother could love that face.]

2. Modifying phrases and clauses should refer clearly to the words they modify. The **squinting modifier** is an ambiguous construction so located that it can modify what precedes it and what follows it.

UNCLEAR MODIFYING PHRASE	It is the car that won the race which has yellow wheels.
REVISION	It is the car which has yellow wheels that won the race.
UNCLEAR MODIFYING PHRASE	She had a meal in a restaurant that was low in price.
REVISION	She had a meal that was low in price in a restaurant.
SQUINTING MODIFIER	The cow he was milking irritatedly switched her tail.
REVISIONS	The cow he was irritatedly milking switched her tail.
	The cow he was milking switched her tail irritatedly.

3. As a general rule, infinitives should not be split. An infinitive is split when an adverbial modifier is positioned between the *to* and the verb: *to not go*. It is not always incorrect to split an infinitive; sometimes a sentence sounds more awkward when the writer attempts to avoid a split. But because a split infinitive usually registers in the reader's mind as unharmonious, you should avoid splitting infinitives if possible.

AWKWARD   I want to, if I can, leave the office early.

REVISION   I want to leave the office early, if I can.

4. Generally speaking, sentence parts such as subject and verb, verb and object, and parts of verb phrases should not be separated unless the result of the separation adds greatly to the effectiveness of the sentence.

AWKWARD SEPARATION	He realized, after many hours, that his course of action was wrong.
REVISION TO REMOVE AWKWARDNESS	After many hours, he realized that his course of action was wrong.
EFFECTIVE SEPARATION	The squad leader, sensing that the enemy was near, ordered the platoon to take up defensive positions.

Practice: Identifying misplaced parts   *In the following sentences, underline the misplaced words or phrases that make the sentences unclear or awkward. The answers are listed next.*

[1] The Statue of Liberty was neglected virtually for 97 years, which became a symbol of hope for immigrants. [2] People finally realized that the statue's deterioration was serious in 1984. [3] A century almost of salty air, high winds, and industrial pollution had made the statue unsafe for tourists. [4] Ellis Island has been deserted for decades, where many immigrants first touched American soil. [5] Many of the buildings have been vandalized in the Ellis Island complex. [6] In 1984, private citizens groups and businesspeople began for the preservation of these landmarks gathering funds. [7] By the Statue's 100-year anniversary, these preservationists hope once again that the Statue of Liberty will be welcoming visitors.

Answers to the Practice   [1] virtually, which became a symbol of hope for immigrants
[2] in 1984   [3] almost   [4] where many immigrants first touched American soil
[5] in the Ellis Island complex   [6] for the preservation of these landmarks
[7] once again

EXERCISE 22-1, MISPLACED WORDS, PHRASES, AND CLAUSES   (11)

Revise the following sentences, placing the adverbs so that the relationships to the words they modify are clear and the meanings are unambiguous.

Example   Once carefully school children were taught the history of the Statue of Liberty.

Once school children were carefully taught the history of the Statue of Liberty.

1. Edward de Laboulaye proposed a gift to America first from the people of France.

_____

2. He proposed that the gift commemorate American independence at a dinner party in 1865.

_____

3. Laboulaye was admired by the French highly for his scholarship and his statesmanship.

_____

4. One of the guests was F. A. Bartholdi at Laboulaye's dinner party.

_____

5. The young sculptor was noted for his heroic style already.

_____

6. Bartholdi was 31 years old only.

_____

7. No one was surprised when he received the commission really.

_____

8. He was commissioned to create simply a fitting gift.

_____

9. Entirely the idea for a statue of the Goddess of Liberty was his.

_____

10. To New York Bartholdi took the steamer *Pereire* in June of 1871.

_____

11. He caught his first glimpse after 13 days at sea of New York Harbor.

_____

12. Bartholdi admired the huge monuments of the past of the classic civilizations.

_____

13. Most he admired the Colossus of Rhodes.

_____

14. For centuries the Colossus was a lighthouse that marked the entrance to a harbor.

_____

15. Of his career, Bartholdi was to dedicate 15 years to creating his "modern Colossus."

_____

16. He had of all his plans a clear conception when he returned to France that fall.

_____

17. Broken chains would symbolize freedom at her feet.

_____

18. A torch would offer enlightenment to people in darker lands in her hand.

_____

19. Bartholdi knew in scale that his statue must be gigantic.

_____

20. The symbol of freedom must match obviously the importance of the idea.

_____

Revise the following sentences, relocating words, phrases, and clauses so their relationships to the words they modify are clear and the meanings are unambiguous.

Example   In 1875 Bartholdi finished of the statue a 48-inch model.

In 1875 Bartholdi finished a 48-inch model of the statue.

21. The sculptor wanted the finished statue to be in height 151 feet.

_____

22. Ten feet wide would be the face.

_____

23. The Goddess of Liberty would around the waist be 35 feet.

_____

116

24. It would be difficult to build the statue just strong enough to bear its own weight.

_____

25. The statue also had the winds and tide to face of New York Harbor.

_____

26. The design also had to allow to the torch maintenance workers.

_____

27. A framework was designed by A. G. Eiffel which would support the massive statue.

_____

28. Of iron, Eiffel proposed a central framework of beams and pylons.

_____

29. The exterior of the statue was formed of less than one-fourth of an inch thick copper sheets.

_____

30. One-fourth the size of the final statue from a model Bartholdi plotted the lines of the final copper sections.

_____

31. The final sections of copper were over latticed molds hammered into place.

_____

32. Into place workers hammered the copper sheets using huge mallets.

_____

33. Finally four large sections were assembled which would the final statue complete.

_____

34. Half a million rivets almost were used to assemble the four sections and the framework.

_____

35. The statue was first in Paris assembled, where the final adjustments could be made.

_____

36. It was disassembled after the final fit was assured then.

_____

37. In huge wooden boxes, the copper skin of the statue was packed.

_____

38. Fifty boxes were nearly required for the exterior alone.

_____

39. Another thirty-six boxes were needed for the ironwork packaging.

_____

40. The trip was by truck and special train to the port.

_____

41. The dismantled statue by the French warship *Isère* was brought to New York.

_____

42. The ship entered New York with the statue in 1885 in its holds.

_____

43. New Yorkers for nearly a year and a half watched the reassembly of Liberty.

_____

44. On October 28, 1886, finally the statue was dedicated and the torch lit.

_____

45. Bartholdi was ironically disappointed in the glow of the statue's torch.

_____

**EXERCISE 22–2, SPLIT INFINITIVES
AND SEPARATED SENTENCE PARTS**   **(11)**

Revise the following sentences correcting awkwardly split infinitives.

Example   Bartholdi did not know how brightly Liberty's torch was to eventually glow.

Bartholdi did not know how brightly Liberty's torch was to glow eventually.

1. Laboulaye expected French city governments to enthusiastically underwrite the cost of the Statue of Liberty.

2. A few cities, a few businesses, and a few wealthy people volunteered to quickly make large contributions.

3. After eight years, Laboulaye had less than half the money needed to completely pay for the statue.

4. In 1879 he decided to enormously step up his efforts to raise money.

5. A nation-wide lottery was held to swiftly bring in the necessary money.

6. This scheme helped Laboulaye to finally meet his goal.

7. In America, however, the cash was proving more difficult to easily raise.

8. The statue was ready to at last be shipped, but the pedestal was not completed.

9. A sum of $100,000 was needed to fully finance the construction of the pedestal.

10. When the *Isère* arrived with the statue, the French flag had to be disappointingly flown over an unfinished pedestal.

_____

11. New York's average citizens were able to in only a few weeks raise the rest of the money for the pedestal.

_____

12. Joseph Pulitzer was the publisher whom the public had to happily thank for this feat.

_____

13. Pulitzer, born in Hungary himself, decided it would be disgraceful to sheepishly accept France's gift without a finished pedestal.

_____

14. He used his paper, the *World,* to immediately launch a fund-raising campaign.

_____

15. Pulitzer used the cause of Liberty to of course boost his paper's circulation.

_____

16. Announcements of special fund-raising events, editorials, and news stories all helped to constantly keep the statue in the public eye.

_____

17. The paper even went so far as to daily print lists of contributors.

_____

18. The *World* printed letters to sentimentally portray school children giving their nickels and pennies.

_____

19. Most of the contributions were to only amount to a dollar or less.

_____

20. Pulitzer's campaign was able to by rousing public spirit complete the pedestal-building fund.

_____

Revise the following sentences, eliminating awkward separation of sentence parts. If a sentence is satisfactory without revision, write *satisfactory* in the blank below it.

Example   President Grover Cleveland on October 28, 1886, unveiled the statue.

On October 28, 1886, President Grover Cleveland un-veiled the statue.

120

21. John Greenleaf Whittier on the theme of national government delivered a speech.

_____

22. The French anthem and the United States anthem were both played by military bands.

_____

23. The flag of France on the statue's face was used as a drape.

_____

24. All the guns, as the flag fell to reveal the statue, in and around the harbor fired a deafening salute.

_____

25. The French consider as a symbol of government by the people the Statue of Liberty.

_____

26. Students of democracy in European countries considered the United States the first working democracy.

_____

27. In 1801 America had peaceably transferred, as a result of popular elections, power to another administration.

_____

28. The United States was in its successful application of democracy alone.

_____

29. The statue became for immigrants a symbol of freedom and opportunity.

_____

30. The statue has come to symbolize the United States.

_____

31. Of course it was for millions of immigrants who poured into New York harbor the first sight of America.

_____

32. A U.S. Immigration Station was on nearby Ellis Island established.

_____

33. It opened on January 1, 1892, its doors for the first time.

_____

34. Over 2,500 people passed on that first day through the facilities at Ellis Island.

_____

35. The ground floor was the baggage room of the main building.

_____

36. Upstairs they received in the Great Hall medical and legal examinations.

_____

37. As many as 5,000 people a day could be examined.

_____

38. More than a million during 1907 arrived.

_____

39. There were between 1910 and 1914 over five million immigrants.

_____

40. Most of these immigrants only four or five hours stayed on Ellis Island.

_____

41. One-fifth of the immigrants were for medical or legal reasons detained longer.

_____

42. Two percent of the immigrants were only barred from entering the United States.

_____

43. More than half of all Americans are today descended from immigrants who went through Ellis Island.

_____

44. Ellis Island was in 1954 closed and abandoned by the government.

_____

45. Its ownership was transferred, becoming part of the Statue of Liberty National Monument, to the National Park Service.

_____

23
DANGLING MODIFIERS   (12)

A **dangling modifier** does not logically modify anything in a sentence. Sometimes it seems to modify a certain word but cannot because such a relationship does not make sense. In other instances, there is nothing it could possibly modify.

One type of dangling modifier is the **dangling participle**. Because it functions as an adjective, a participle or participial phrase must have a substantive (noun or noun substitute) to relate to. If the substantive is not present, the participle has nothing to modify. One remedy for a dangling participle is to supply a word it can logically modify. Another solution is to expand the dangling modifier into a full subordinate clause.

DANGLING PARTICIPLE	*Tied to the mast,* the storm lashed at him.
REVISION	Tied to the mast, he was lashed by the storm. [Making *he* the expressed subject supplies the appropriate word for the participial phrase to modify.]
DANGLING PARTICIPLE	*Running in a race,* the finish is hardest.
REVISION INTO SUBORDINATE CLAUSE	When you are running in a race, the finish is hardest.

Dangling gerund phrases, like dangling participles, lack a word they can logically modify. These dangling constructions are usually prepositional phrases with the gerund serving as the object of the preposition. To correct a dangling gerund phrase, you must supply a word that the phrase can modify. Another solution is to recast the sentence so that the gerund is no longer part of a modifying phrase but is instead the subject or object of the verb.

DANGLING GERUND	*After mowing the lawn,* the lemonade tasted very good.
REVISION BY SUPPLYING SUBJECT	After mowing the lawn, I found the lemonade tasted very good.
REVISION BY RECASTING SENTENCE	Mowing the lawn made the lemonade taste very good to me.

A **dangling infinitive** must also have a word to modify logically. Like a gerund, an infinitive can substitute for a noun, so an alternative method for correcting a dangling infinitive is to recast the infinitive as a noun substitute rather than a modifer.

DANGLING INFINITIVE	*To win at tennis,* practice is required.
REVISIONS	To win at tennis, one must practice.
	To win at tennis requires practice.

As with other types of modifiers, participles, gerunds, and infinitives can also be misplaced. They can be situated near nouns with which they have no connection instead of near nouns they logically modify.

MISPLACED PARTICIPLE	*Fleeing down the alley,* the police caught the thief.
REVISION	The police caught the thief fleeing down the alley.

MISPLACED GERUND	*Playing with the symphony*, she loved her job.
REVISION	She loved her job playing with the symphony.
MISPLACED INFINITIVE	*To stick to a diet*, her doctor told her she needed will power.
REVISION	Her doctor told her she needed will power to stick to a diet.

An **elliptical clause** is one that has an implied or understood, rather than a stated, subject or verb—for example, *While tying his shoes, he broke a lace.* In the preceding sentence, the subject and auxiliary verb (*he was*) of the subordinate clause are implied. An elliptical clause dangles if its implied subject is not the same as the subject of the main clause. To correct a dangling elliptical clause, be sure the objects of both clauses agree, or supply the omitted subject or verb.

DANGLING ELLIPTICAL CLAUSE	*While eating our supper*, the rain began to fall.
REVISIONS	While eating our supper, we noticed that the rain had begun to fall.
	While we were eating our supper, the rain began to fall.

Practice: Identifying dangling and elliptical modifiers   *In the following sentences, underline the dangling or elliptical modifiers. The answers are listed next.*

[1] Having survived for hundreds of years, ethnologists call the Aleut culture the oldest civilization in North America. [2] While once being almost extinct, adaptation to their environment has served the Aleuts well. [3] Being never numerous, the lower forty-eight states have lured many Aleuts away from Alaska. [4] However, over 3,000 Aleuts still make their homes on the Aleutian and Pribilof Islands. [5] While coming to terms with the modern world, great changes in the Aleut way of life are not very likely.

Answers to the Practice   [1] Having survived for hundreds of years   [2] While once being almost extinct   [3] Being never numerous   [5] While coming to terms with the modern world

EXERCISE 23-1, DANGLING PARTICIPLES AND GERUNDS   **(12)**

Revise the following sentences to eliminate all dangling or misplaced participles and gerunds. Write the word *satisfactory* in the blank if the sentence requires no revision.

Example   Uninformed about Alaskan people, the Aleuts are sometimes mistakenly called Eskimos.

The Aleuts are sometimes mistakenly called Eskimos by those who are uninformed about Alaskan people.

1. Living in the Aleutians for over 9,000 years, ethnologists say the Aleuts are neither Eskimo nor Indian.

2. Rivaling in their history the ancient cultures of Europe, experts think the Aleuts are a distinct ethnic group with their own language and culture.

3. Hunting in northern Asia, mastodon and caribou herds led nomadic tribes farther and farther north.

4. Locked up in ice 10,000 years ago, a land bridge from Siberia to Alaska was exposed by the ocean's lower level.

5. Pursuing their food sources, this land bridge permitted the crossing of the Bering Strait.

6. Keeping to the woods as they traveled eastward and southward, Indian tribes descended from one group of these nomads.

7. Staying close to the northern shores, the descendants of the sea-faring nomads are called Eskimos or *Inuit*.

8. Traveling south to the Aleutian Islands, *Unangan* was the original name for the Aleuts for themselves.

9. Seldom frozen, the Aleuts found the waters around the southern islands more hospitable.

    _____

10. Being rich in cod, halibut, and shellfish, the Aleuts benefited from a ready food supply.

    _____

11. Migrating annually to the southern waters, the islands forced seals and whales into narrow, easily hunted straits.

    _____

12. Using the _baidarka_ or skin boat, the violent currents and stormy weather of these straits were tamed.

    _____

13. Hunting in the open sea was possible, equipped with the _baidarka._

    _____

14. Marveling at their skill, open sea hunting, according to anthropologists, is the most demanding kind of hunting undertaken by human beings.

    _____

15. Practiced from early childhood and passed from father to son, Aleuts developed their mastery of hunting at sea to its highest level among any people.

    _____

16. A father would begin to teach crouching and balancing exercises, starting at the age of one year.

    _____

17. Adding to the food gained by hunting, the islands offered summer berries, edible native plants, and the eggs of nesting birds.

    _____

18. Prospering on such diets, their average life span was extended.

    _____

19. Resulting from the Aleuts' intelligence and preservation of tribal lore, a fairly comfortable life on the cold islands could be made for themselves.

    _____

20. Prospering and settling down, a distinct culture was preserved.

    _____

EXERCISE 23-2, DANGLING INFINITIVES AND ELLIPTICAL CLAUSES (12)

Revise the following sentences to eliminate dangling or misplaced infinitives and elliptical clauses. Write the word *satisfactory* in the blank if the sentence requires no revision.

Example   To survive in a bleak environment, skill and knowledge are required.

_____ *To survive in a bleak environment requires skill and knowledge.*

1. To illustrate the advanced nature of the ancient Aleut culture, they used numbers in advanced ways.

_____

2. To enumerate dates and keep track of possessions, very high numbers could be used by the Aleuts.

_____

3. While using these great numbers with ease, most other primitive people's arithmetic was limited to much smaller numbers.

_____

4. When studying anatomy, the corpses of their own dead were analyzed.

_____

5. While merely speculating about anatomy in other cultures, Aleuts were able to name every bone and muscle with great precision.

_____

6. To aid the sick, acupuncture and even brain surgery were used.

_____

7. To help repair major wounds, much like modern physicians, Aleuts used bone needles and sinew threads to close cuts.

_____

8. When disposing of their dead, embalming and storing in cool caves were advanced practices.

_____

9. To protect themselves from the constant rain, the waterproof intestinal lining of sea lions made waterproof clothing.

---

10. To make waterproof baskets, the Aleuts wove grass strands.

---

11. To decorate their baskets and clothing, roots and herbs and octopus ink were mixed.

---

12. To add stability in violent winds, Aleut houses were built partially underground.

---

13. When designing roofs to withstand Aleutian winds, sod roofs placed over rafters of whale rib proved sturdy.

---

14. To make efficient use of these structures, a home might cover an area of 1,500 square feet and house five families.

---

15. While eventually populating the entire chain of islands, Anangula, the central island, probably was the site of the first settlement.

---

16. While growing in number, the islands to the east and west were also settled.

---

17. Although prospering as a culture, never did the population exceed 16,000.

---

18. To study the culture of the Aleuts, the islands were the sites of several major anthropological studies in 1948.

---

19. To thrive in such surroundings, Aleuts have lived in harmony with their environment.

---

20. To demonstrate a longer continuous existence as a culture in one place than any other people, one example of a successful society is the Aleut.

24
OMISSIONS (13)

Omissions in sentences may occur because of the writer's haste, carelessness, or lack of proofreading. A few types of omissions occur, however, because the writer is not fully aware that certain omissions common in speech can be very confusing in writing. Omissions of this sort typically fall into three categories: omitted prepositions and verbs, omissions in compound constructions, and incomplete comparisons.

1. Be sure to proofread carefully. Proofreading is difficult for almost everyone. When we have written a sentence or paragraph, we have trouble seeing our own omissions because we tend to "fill in" anything that is missing. We listen to our thoughts rather than see what is actually written on the page. Keep a list of errors you have difficulty seeing when you are proofreading. You may notice an emerging pattern that will help you to spot mistakes more easily in the future. When you proofread, do it slowly and do it some time after you have finished the final draft—when the words will be less familiar to you. Read a line at a time, using a ruler or sheet of blank paper under each line as you read it. This technique will help to isolate the line on which you are concentrating and eliminate distractions from other sentences on the page.

Careless omissions usually involve the little words our minds fill in but our pens fail to record: articles and prepositions.

CARELESS OMISSION	The car was little, green one.
REVISION	The car was *a* little, green one.
CARELESS OMISSION	I saw it parked next the gas pump.
REVISION	I saw it parked next *to* the gas pump.

2. Be sure to write out relationships that are merely implied in speech. In casual speech we may say *This type motorcycle is very powerful.* or *We were roommates last semester.*, but in writing we need to supply the prepositions.

OMISSION	Gasoline consumption the last few years has decreased.
REVISION	Gasoline consumption *during* the last few years has decreased.

3. Be sure compound constructions are complete. Check the verbs and prepositions in particular. When we connect two items of the same kind with a conjunction, we frequently omit words that unnecessarily duplicate each other; however, these omitted words must in fact be the same as words that do appear in the sentence: *She can [climb] and will climb the mountain.* Too often, omitted words are not duplicates of stated ones, and the result is an illogical sentence.

OMISSION	She is interested and experienced at mountain climbing.
REVISION	She is interested *in* and experienced at mountain climbing.
OMISSION	On the other hand, I never have and never will go mountain climbing.
REVISION	On the other hand, I never have *gone* and never will go mountain climbing.

Sometimes duplicate words should be repeated in a compound construction. Otherwise the expressed meaning may be illogical.

OMISSION — They lost the game because of a lack of speed and good blocking. [It is doubtful that the game was lost because of good blocking, but the reader might understand that to be the case.]

REVISION — They lost the game because of a lack of speed and *a lack of* good blocking.

4. Be sure all comparisons are clear, complete, and logical. Avoid illogical use of *than any of* or *any of*. Do not compare items that are logically not comparable. Make sure not only that comparisons are complete but also that both terms of the comparison are given and that the basis of the comparison is stated. The following sentences illustrate omissions that create illogical comparisons:

ILLOGICAL USE OF *THAN ANY OF* — She is the best player than any of them.

REVISION — She is the best player *on the team.*

ILLOGICAL COMPARISON — The vegetables here are as high in price as any other region.

REVISION — The vegetables here are as high in price as *those in* any other region.

GRAMMATICALLY INCOMPLETE COMPARISON — This horse is as fast, if not faster than, the other.

REVISION — This horse is as fast *as,* if not faster than, the other horse.

TERMS OF COMPARISON INCOMPLETE — I like biology more than Jan.

REVISION — I like biology more than Jan *does.*

BASIS OF COMPARISON NOT STATED — This brand costs less.

REVISION — This brand costs less *than other popular brands.*

EXERCISE 24, OMISSIONS   (13)

Revise the following sentences, correcting omissions and comparisons that are illogical or incomplete. Write the word *satisfactory* if the sentence requires no revision.

Example   Peter the Great dispatched Vitus Bering to Alaska to see the land bridge still existed.

Peter the Great dispatched Vitus Bering to Alaska to see if the land bridge still existed.

1. Bering sailed in two ships, the *St. Peter* and *St. Paul,* to the Aleutian Islands.

2. Bering died on his second expedition to the Aleutians 1741.

3. Survivors of the expedition took the pelts of sea otters back Russia.

4. Sea-otter fur was the most prized than any of the furs available in Europe.

5. The next twenty-five years, over 10,000 Aleuts died.

6. The Aleuts could not supply enough furs by trading the Russians.

7. Eventually, the Aleuts were enslaved and forced hunt otters.

8. Finally, the Russian fur trade moved on to exploit fur seals of Pribilof Islands.

9. Seal fur proved as valuable, if not more valuable than, otter fur.

10. In 1867, when United States purchased Alaska, only 6,000 Aleuts remained.

11. Paradoxically, the Russian elements are as striking, if not more striking than, older influences on modern Aleut culture.

12. The Aleuts themselves are more proud of their Russian heritage.

_____

13. A Russian Orthodox church is centerpiece in many Aleut village.

_____

14. Most Aleuts have Russian names, result of Russian ancestry.

_____

15. Others received Russian names baptism, since Aleuts originally did not use surnames.

_____

16. Most Aleuts are short compact, but Cossack ancestry has produced some tall, slender Aleuts.

_____

17. Some Aleuts still play the *balalaika,* a type string instrument native to Russia.

_____

18. Some favorite Aleutian foods are Russian origin.

_____

19. The Aleutians have been dominated by outsiders more than most other American ethnic groups.

_____

20. After 1867, the Aleuts' affairs were administered the Bureau of Indian Affairs.

_____

21. Government services provided the Aleuts were often low quality.

_____

22. In 1971, the Alaska Native Claims Settlement Act deeded 44 million acres of land to Eskimo, Indian, Aleut populations.

_____

23. The Aleuts chose land around their villages and previous settlements for their share of the acreage being returned.

_____

24. Fortunately that acreage includes most the land around Dutch Harbor, the principal deep-water port in the Aleutians.

_____

25. It is in the waters around Dutch Harbor the gas and oil drilling has started which may the Bering Strait and its people well known.

_____

25
AWKWARD AND CONFUSED SENTENCES (14)

Sometimes sentences are clumsy, meaningless, or, in some instances, absurd. Often it is difficult to determine exactly which violation of grammar is involved. The reason may be a combination of violations or simply a heavy-handed or vague and illogical manner of saying something. However, awkwardness may be the result of faulty predication or mixed construction—sentence faults that occur when a sentence begins with one kind of construction but ends with another, incompatible one.

Faulty predication results if the verb or complement is not appropriate to the subject of a sentence.

INAPPROPRIATE VERB	The data make several errors.
REVISION	The data contain several errors.
INAPPROPRIATE COMPLEMENT	His daughter is the reason he stayed at home today.
REVISION	His daughter's illness is the reason he stayed at home today.

In the first faulty sentence, action is illogically attributed to the subject, *data*. In the second faulty sentence, the linking verb *is* joins a subject and complement that are not equal. Because the verb *to be* in its various forms equates what precedes and follows it, the two sides of such an "equation" must be logically compatible. *His daughter is the reason* makes no sense.

Another common cause of faulty predication is the construction of definitions and explanations that use *is when, is where, is what,* or *is because.* Remember that the linking verb *is* functions as an equal sign between the subject and the words that rename or define it; equivalent terms must be used on both sides.

ILLOGICAL USE OF *WHEN*	A hurricane is when the winds in a tropical storm exceed 75 miles per hour.
CORRECTED SENTENCE	A hurricane occurs when the winds in a tropical storm exceed 75 miles per hour.
ILLOGICAL USE OF *WHERE*	Skydiving is where people jump from airplanes into free-fall.
CORRECTED SENTENCE	Skydiving is jumping from an airplane into free-fall.
ILLOGICAL USE OF *WHAT*	The direct object is what receives the action of the verb.
CORRECTED SENTENCE	The direct object receives the action of the verb.
ILLOGICAL USE OF *BECAUSE*	The reason she laughed is because the joke was funny.
CORRECTED SENTENCE	The reason she laughed is the joke was funny.

To avoid a **mixed construction,** attempt to maintain throughout a sentence the type of construction you establish in the first part of the sentence. Frequently, mixed constructions are caused by unnecessary shifts between active and passive voice verbs within a sentence, as the following example illustrates:

| MIXED CONSTRUCTION | Although he had the best intentions, many errors were made. |
| SMOOTH CONSTRUCTION | Although he had the best intentions, he made many errors. |

Sometimes mixed constructions occur when the writer forgets the true subject of a sentence and constructs a predicate that fits a word in a modifying phrase or clause.

MIXED CONSTRUCTION	By packing my suitcase tonight will give me more time for breakfast tomorrow.
REVISIONS	Packing my suitcase tonight will give me more time for breakfast tomorrow.
	By packing my suitcase tonight, I will have more time for breakfast tomorrow.

The best way to avoid writing awkward, confused, or mixed sentences is to evaluate each statement critically. Is it clear? Is it precise? Is it logical? Is it sensible? Is it to the point?

EXERCISE 25, AWKWARD SENTENCES AND MIXED CONSTRUCTIONS   (14)

Revise the following sentences, correcting awkward, confused, and mixed constructions. Write the word *satisfactory* if the sentence requires no revision.

Example   By becoming extremely popular is when an ethnic food hides its origins.

Extremely popular ethnic foods may have origins that are difficult to discover.

1.   The submarine sandwich makes several different names for itself.

_____

2.   In Ohio, a "Poor Boy" is what they call a submarine sandwich.

_____

3.   The mid-Atlantic states are where they call submarines "Hoagies."

_____

4.   A submarine calls itself a "Hero" sandwich in New York City.

_____

5.   The reason for the names is because as people moved from the source of the original sandwich, the name changed.

_____

_____

6.   The original of the sandwich was Benny Capalbo's, a grocery store on Long Island.

_____

7.   Benny migrated from Salerno, Italy, in 1913, where his sandwich had already been invented by him.

_____

_____

8.   He claimed to have invented the sandwich, what he called a "grinder."

_____

9. The reason for the name was because of the bread Benny bought from the bakery around the corner.

_____

_____

10. By leaving it unglazed and baking it for less than 20 minutes makes you really have to grind away to eat it.

_____

_____

11. Although he had made his sandwich for his family for years, it wasn't until 1926 that one was sold by Benny.

_____

_____

12. The grinders were what made his little grocery store so successful.

_____

13. The bread is the crucial ingredient, since a day or two is when it will stay fresh.

_____

14. All the other ingredients consist of any well-stocked Italian grocery.

_____

15. The traditional grinder is where you slice the bread lengthwise.

_____

16. Salami, provolone cheese, sliced tomatoes, and shredded lettuce are what go between the slices.

_____

_____

17. The reason for the difference in taste between one grinder and another is because of the dressing.

_____

_____

18. This mixture of olive oil, salt, and black pepper is what makes infinite variations in taste possible.

_____

_____

19. New London was where Benny's grocery store was on Long Island.

_____

20. New London was also what the Navy chose as a location for a submarine base.

_____

_____

21. Twelve thousand hungry young sailors and thousands more Coast Guardsmen contained the success of Benny's business.

_____

_____

22. Benny sold 400 to 500 sandwiches to the base commissary each day.

_____

23. Where the ships stopped at other ports, the sailors tried to describe their favorite sandwich.

_____

_____

24. The reason for the varied ingredients is because the sandwich makers tried to duplicate the grinder with locally available meats, cheeses, and dressings.

_____

_____

25. The farther the sailors traveled from New London, the names and ingredients of the sandwiches change more.

_____

_____

26. Benny's success eventually lowered as competitors in New London began supplying grinders.

_____

_____

27. After the end of the war, Benny's Navy customers were discharged from the service.

_____

_____

28. By returning to their homes across the country spread the fame of Benny's grinders even farther.

_____

_____

29. Since he never patented his sandwich made it safe and profitable to copy it.

_____

30. The reason there is a "sub shop" in almost every town in the United States is because of Benny Capalbo and his grinders.

_____

_____

26 SENTENCE FAULTS REVIEW   (6–14)

Revise the following sentences, correcting fragments, fused sentences, comma splices, faulty agreement, faulty reference of pronouns, unnecessary shifts, misplaced and dangling modifiers, and awkward constructions.

Example   The first American flag was planted at the North Pole by Matthew A. Hensen.

The first American flag at the North Pole was planted by Matthew A. Hensen.

1. Hensen, a Black scientist who was with Peary's expedition, reaches the pole 45 minutes before the rest of the party.

2. Born in poverty, in his teen years school was not attractive to Hensen.

3. He, as an aide to Perry, taught himself surveying and navigation, not in school.

4. He even learned anthropology and becomes an expert on the customs of Eskimos.

5. Forwarding his manuscripts to the Academy of Science, Thomas Jefferson discovered a Black farmer, Benjamin Banneker, who was a self-taught mathematical genius.

6. Writing a treatise on entomology and recording the tides.

7. Banneker's interests were wide ranging, he wrote on astronomy and even predicted a solar eclipse.

8. Banneker was able to learn so fast that errors in his borrowed textbook were soon being corrected by him.

9. Banneker eventually became an assistant to the Geographer of the United States in this office he helped create the plan for Washington, D.C.

---

10. Blacks, before the Civil War, could not register patents in their own names he was a slave.

---

11. Although some free Blacks did register patents. This was rather uncommon.

---

12. You can easily discover this if one simply checks records at the Patent Office.

---

13. The first patent taken out by a Black inventor were granted in 1821 to Thomas L. Jennings, a tailor.

---

14. Since then, 1,000 patents has been registered in the names of more than 400 Black inventors.

---

15. Never patenting them, some Black inventors didn't bother with registration at the Patent Office.

---

16. Lewis Temple never patented, which doubled the whaling catch in New England, his harpoon.

---

17. Every Black almost who registered a patent before the 1870's was self-taught.

---

18. Andrew Beard invented the Jenny Coupler, one of the devices that hold railroad cars together.

---

19. Mechanisms that oil machinery automatically was invented by Elijah McCoy.

---

20. His name became so synonymous with successful inventions that people begin to refer to good inventions as "the real McCoy."

---

21. Granville T. Woods invented the third rail for electric railways, and it was patented by him in 1901.

---

22. Woods patented more than fifty inventions, who never finished elementary school.

_____

23. The automatic traffic light in 1923 was invented by Garrett Morgan.

_____

24. Used on the safety helmets of firefighters, Morgan also developed a breathing device.

_____

25. He proved the worth of his device in a rescue in the Lake Erie tunnel by using it himself.

_____

Ten incomplete statements follow. Replace the dots with your own words, creating complete sentences from the fragments.

Example   Jodie likes . . . better . . .

Jodie likes pizza better than she likes tacos.

26. Neither training nor education . . . necessary . . .

_____

27. Stuck in the mud . . .

_____

28. If a brand . . . costs about the same . . .

_____

29. . . . used more . . .

_____

30. Someone will plead your case if you give . . . your version of the facts.

_____

31. The jury . . . cast . . . votes by secret ballot.

_____

32. . . . flying through the air . . .

_____

33. Overtime . . . when work continues because the orders aren't filled.

_____

34. I served . . . covered with whipped cream.

_____

35. . . . nearly . . .

___

Revise the following sentences to make plural subjects and verbs singular and singular subjects and verbs plural. Be sure that the subjects and verbs agree in number in each of your revisions. Also, be sure that you have changed pronouns and the articles *a, an,* and *the* where necessary, so that they agree with the nouns to which they refer.

Example   The automatic refrigeration system for trucks changes the way we eat.

Automatic refrigeration systems for trucks change the way I eat.

36. The refrigerator for the truck eliminates the problems of food spoilage.

___

37. The system was invented by a Black man, Frederick M. Jones.

___

38. Lewis Latimer's skill drew the attention of the white inventor of the day.

___

39. He worked closely with Alexander Graham Bell.

___

40. As one of the "Edison Pioneers," he worked even more closely with Edison.

___

41. As education became more available to Blacks, their successes became more conventional.

___

42. The Black chemist, physician, or educator made an appearance.

___

43. Black triumph began to occur in the laboratory or classroom.

___

44. The early law regarding slaves has held back a generation of Black inventors.

___

45. That any patent at all was registered by the early Black inventor is a tribute to Black ingenuity, practicality, and curiosity.

___

142

27
NUMBERS, ABBREVIATIONS, AND SYLLABICATION   (16–18)

NUMBERS

In writing for general readers, **numbers** are usually spelled out if they can be expressed in one or two words and are less than 100: *four, ninety-nine, fifteen.* Scientific, business, and technical writing, however, tend to favor using figures over spelled-out numbers, especially if numbers are used extensively, because figures are clearer and less time consuming to read. Often, business, scientific, and technical writers use the "rule of ten": isolated numbers of ten or less are spelled out, whereas numbers greater than ten are written as figures. For example, *The machine took two years to design and 12 years to be accepted by the industry.*

A good rule of thumb for writing numbers is to follow the conventions of the field to which your readers belong. (You can find these conventions in the style manual for that field.) The most important thing is to be consistent in your use of numbers. The following guidelines explain the prevalent conventions for general, nontechnical writing:

1. Spell out numbers or amounts less than 100; use figures for larger numbers or amounts.

My son is *twelve.*
We saw *thirty-five* horses.
The mountain is *15,000* feet high.

2. Use figures for dates and addresses.

July 4, 1776	1426 Homer Avenue
1914–1918	Route 2
908 B.C.	P.O. Box 606

3. The suffixes *-st, -nd, -rd,* and *-th* should not be used after dates if the year is given.

May 1, 1985	May 1st of last year

4. Figures are ordinarily used in the following situations:

DECIMALS	2.67
	3.14159
PERCENTAGES	45% *or* 45 percent
MIXED NUMBERS AND FRACTIONS	10½
SCORES AND STATISTICS	The vote was 67–24 against the plan.
IDENTIFICATION NUMBERS	Flight 457
	Channel 6
VOLUME AND CHAPTER NUMBERS	Volume 2
	Chapter 3
	page 17

ACT, SCENE, AND LINE NUMBERS	Act IV, Scene 1, lines 10–11
NUMBERS FOLLOWED BY SYMBOLS	8″ × 10″
	55 mph
	89°
EXACT AMOUNTS OF MONEY	$35.79
TIMES	9:30 P.M.
	2:45 A.M.
	11:00 A.M.
BUT	quarter to three, eleven o'clock

5. Except in legal or commercial writing, a number that has been spelled out should not be repeated as a figure in parentheses.

LEGAL	The easement is twenty (20) feet wide.
STANDARD	The ladder is twenty feet long.

6. Numbers that begin sentences should always be spelled out. If such a number is long or falls into a category of numbers usually expressed in figures (e.g., 40,000; 33 1/3), recast the sentence to eliminate its beginning with a number.

One thousand five hundred refugees stepped off the boat.
Off the boat stepped 1,500 refugees.

ABBREVIATIONS

Abbreviations should generally be avoided in writing, with a few standard exceptions. These exceptions and other conventions governing the use of abbreviations include the following:

1. The abbreviations *Mr., Mrs., Ms.,* and *Dr.* are appropriate only before surnames, as in *Mr. Brown, Mrs. Sanchez, Ms. Trent, Dr. Jacobson.*

2. Abbreviations such as *Hon., Rev., Prof., Sen.,* and *Gen.* are appropriate only when both the surnames and given names or initials are given, as the *Rev. Oscar Smith.*

3. The abbreviations *Jr., Sr., Esq., M.D., D.D., J.D., LL.D.,* and *Ph.D.* are used when a name is given, as in *John Roberts, Jr. is the new district manager.* However, academic degrees are also used alone in abbreviated form, as in *Gloria Jones received her M.A. last year and is now working toward her Ph.D. in economics.*, in all but the most formal writing situations.

4. The abbreviations *B.C.* (before Christ), *A.D.* (*anno Domini,* after Christ), *A.M.* or *a.m.* (*ante meridiem,* before noon), *P.M.* or *p.m.* (*post meridiem,* after noon), *Vol.* or *vol.* (volume), *No.* or *no.* (number), and *$* are used only when specific dates, times, and figures are given, as in *12 B.C., No. 4, $50.00.* The twentieth century's two world wars are abbreviated—*World War I* and *World War II; WW I* and *WW II* should not be used.

5. Latin abbreviations such as *i.e.* (that is), *e.g.* (for example), and *etc.* (and so forth) are appropriate in most contexts. However, avoid using *etc.* in formal writing and do not use it as a catch-all in any type of writing. Instead of saying, for example, *I like seafood such as shrimp, clams, etc.,* say *I like such seafood as shrimp and clams.*

144

6. Personal names and names of countries, states, months, days of the week, and courses of instruction should be spelled out. For example, *On September 17 we studied Germany and France in our history class.* instead of *On Sept. 17 we studied Ger. and Fr. in our hist. class.* Three exceptions are the District of Columbia, abbreviated *D.C.* when it follows the city name, Washington; the United States, abbreviated *U.S.A.* (or *USA* or *U.S.*); and the Soviet Union, abbreviated *U.S.S.R.* (or *USSR*). The names of states may, of course, be abbreviated when they are parts of addresses.

7. Names of agencies, organizations, corporations, and persons commonly referred to by initials do not need to be spelled out unless you believe your reader will not be familiar with them. In that case, spell out the name the first time you use it and place the abbreviation in parentheses. Thereafter you may use the abbreviation by itself: *The president of the United Auto Workers (UAW) refused to comment on the UAW's negotiations with Ford.*

Use abbreviations such as *Inc., Co., Bros.,* or *&* (for *and*) only if they are part of a firm's official title, as in *MacLaren Power & Paper Co.*

8. The words *street, avenue,* and *boulevard* should be spelled out. References to a subject, volume, chapter, or page should also be spelled out. The only exceptions are special contexts such as addresses and footnotes.

SYLLABICATION

Syllabication, or word division, at the end of a line properly occurs only between syllables. If you are in doubt about where a word's syllable breaks occur, consult your dictionary. When you must divide a word between one line and the next, place the hyphen, which indicates the break, after the first part of the divided word, not before the remainder of the word at the beginning of the next line: *inter- esting,* not *inter -esting.*

Dictionaries indicate syllabication by means of dots: in·ter·est·ing. However, not every syllable division is an appropriate place to break a word at the end of a line. Three general rules govern word division at ends of lines:

1. Do not divide one-syllable words or words pronounced as one syllable (*thrust, blanched, stream*).

2. Do not divide a word so that a single letter stands alone on a line. If necessary, leave the line short and carry the whole word over to the next line.

INCORRECT	The neighbors moved a- way.
CORRECT	The neighbors moved away.

3. Divide hyphenated compound words at the hyphen only, to avoid awkwardness.

AWKWARD	The committee re-ex- amined the issue.
IMPROVED	The committee re- examined the issue.

EXERCISE 27-1, NUMBERS AND ABBREVIATIONS   (16-17)

Assume an audience of general readers. Cross out incorrectly expressed numbers in the following sentences. Then write the correct forms in the blanks at the right.

Example   I became a citizen on June 20th, 1981, at the age of 22.   *20, twenty-two*

1.   25 candidates reported for the ceremony.   ————————————————

2.   She will arrive in thirty (30) days.   ————————————————
3.   On January Twenty-third, we observe Martin Luther King's birthday.   ————————————————
4.   I am 6 feet tall and weigh two hundred pounds.   ————————————————
5.   Their address is forty-three One Hundred Twenty-third Street.   ————————————————
6.   They saved $2,500 and spent one hundred fifty-nine dollars and seventy cents of it on airfare.   ————————————————

7.   Reduce your weight by fifteen percent.   ————————————————
8.   I ran the one-hundred-yard dash in nine and two-fifths seconds   ————————————————
9.   The assignment is on page two hundred forty-nine of Chapter 11.   ————————————————
10.   We arrived at eleven twenty A.M. and left at ten P.M.   ————————————————
11.   Buy 10 jalapenos, 1 pound of masa, and 2 pimientos.   ————————————————
12.   The radius was twenty six-hundredths of an inch.   ————————————————
13.   Phone me at five seven two 3 one nine one at 7 o'clock.   ————————————————

14.   25 times 25 equals 625.   ————————————————
15.   His grade point average for the term was two point nine.   ————————————————
16.   Physics three hundred thirty-two is the last of the twelve physics courses offered.   ————————————————
17.   They will arrive at three fifteen A.M. on track seven.   ————————————————
18.   I was driving fifty mph when the hose burst.   ————————————————

19. We drive 2 miles Monday through Friday
    and 5 miles on Saturday.
    _____

20. At half-time the score was tied at fourteen
    to fourteen.
    _____

Cross out inappropriate abbreviations in the following sentences. Then write the corrections in the blanks at the right.

Example   W̶m̶., a s̶o̶c̶ major, has a high
               average.   *William, sociology*

21. The fruits, lemons, oranges, etc. are grown
    in FL.
    _____

22. Her office is on Westview St.
    _____

23. She was the Sr. member of the firm.
    _____

24. She made the firm many $, I believe.
    _____

25. He has previously lived in Ger. and Eng.
    _____

26. John Werdt, Sr., and John Werdt, Junior
    are certainly highly dissimilar persons.
    _____

27. Walter Cronkite retired from the CBS eve.
    news in 1981.
    _____

28. I don't know whether the Dr. will
    approve.
    _____

29. The Lamson Co. manufactures hardware
    specialties.
    _____

30. I like the month of Aug. better than I do
    the month of Feb.
    _____

31. Rev. McIntosh preached an inspiring
    sermon on tolerance.
    _____

32. The No. is either four dollars or five $.
    _____

33. He drove his new Cad. to the Co.
    meeting.
    _____

34. They settled in the Blue Ridge Mtns.
    of Va.
    _____

35. Span. is an easier language than Fren.
    or Ger. for English speakers to learn.
    _____

36. Ms. Jare could not find the answer in
    vol. 9 of the encyclopedia.
    _____

37. Hon. George Dorain will address the
    meeting of the Hibernian Society at
    121 Birch Ave.
    _____

38. The Jr. looked a great deal like his
    father, Matt Brown, Sr.
    _____

39. The boss told Sandy to bring his wife
    with him to the office New Yrs. Eve
    party.
    _____

40. Way back in B.C., Gen. Julius Caesar won
    some important Roman victories.
    _____

EXERCISE 27-2, SYLLABICATION   (18)

Some of the following word groups contain errors in word division or hyphenation. In the blanks to the right, show by means of slashes where the words should be divided. If a word cannot be divided, write *ND* (no division) and then write out the whole word. If a word division is acceptable, copy the word as it is given. For each word in question, indicate each of its syllable points with a dot. Indicate any hyphens with a dash.

Example

twe-
lve *ND twelve*

leth-
al *le / thal*

re-en-
list *re- / en · list*

yearn-
ed *ND yearned*

1. flatt-
er _____

2. gho-
ul _____

3. gi-
ant _____

4. ghos-
tly _____

5. gyro-
stabilizer _____

6. merchan-
dise _____

7. aff-
inity _____

8. raz-
zle-dazzle _____

9. utopia-
nism _____

10. must-
ache _____

11. a-
cute _____

12. e-
rupt _____

13. trimm-
ing _____

14. longwind-
ed _____

15. hind-
rance _____

16. non-
support _____

17. in-
flation _____

18. high-
strung _____

19. malig-
nant _____

20. barb-
aric _____

21. pre-
medical   _____

22. pre-
judice   _____

23. court-
martial   _____

24. ver-
y   _____

25. post-
office   _____

26. re-en-
actment   _____

27. coll-
ective   _____

28. e-
qual   _____

29. pre-his-
tory   _____

30. inacc-
essible   _____

31. exh-
ibition   _____

32. learn-
ed [adjective]   _____

33. defi-
nite   _____

34. re-
al   _____

35. pre-
sent [adjective] _____

36. int-
elligent   _____

37. guil-
ty   _____

38. undou-
btedly   _____

39. pre-
sented [verb]   _____

40. o-
pen   _____

28 MANUSCRIPT MECHANICS REVIEW (16-18)

The following sentences contain errors involving numbers, abbreviations, and word division. Assume a general audience and rewrite the sentences, correcting the errors.

Example   Akiba Horowitz landed in New York in eighteen-ninety.

*Akiba Horowitz landed in New York in 1890.*

1. Horowitz, a Russ. immigrant, quickly Americanized his name to Conrad Hubert.

2. Horowitz opened a small restaurant, whe-re he met Joshua Lionel Cowen.

3. Cowen was the owner of the Lionel Train Co.

4. Hubert closed his restaurant and became a salesm-an for Cowen's toys.

5. Cowen had invented an artificial plant w/ flowers that lit up.

6. He called this invention the Dec. flowerpot.

7. Cowen had no real int. in the future of the elec. flowerpot.

8. He was glad to sell his rights and lice-nses in the invention to his salesman, Hubert.

9. The 1st thing Hubert did was throw away the plant and the pot.

10. He designed better batteries & bulbs.

_____

11. Then he sealed the 2 inside a long cylindrical tube.

_____

12. He obtained patent number seven hundred thousand four hundred ninety seven.

_____

13. He later received patent # seven hundred thousand six hundred fifty.

_____

14. He called his patented invention "a port. elec. light."

_____

15. We commonly refer to his device today as a fla-shlight.

_____

16. Hubert called his company the Ever Ready Co.

_____

17. He sold his business in nineteen fourteen.

_____

18. Within only 12 years, Hubert had made his fortune.

_____

19. At his death, his estate was worth eight million dollars.

_____

20. Almost all his $ was made w/ his modification of the electric flowerpot.

_____

29
END PUNCTUATION (19)

Three punctuation marks signal the end of a sentence: the period, the question mark, and the exclamation point. The **period** signals the end of an assertion or a mild command. It is also used at the end of an indirect question.

ASSERTION	She mailed the letter.
MILD COMMAND	Please mail the letter.
INDIRECT QUESTION	He asked if she had mailed the letter.

A period is also used for abbreviations—for example, *Jr., Ms., Mr., Mrs., Ph.D., C.P.A.* Omit the period in abbreviations that serve as names of organizations or government agencies: *NAACP, UNESCO, NCTE, NSF, AMA, USAF, IBM.*

The **question mark** signals the end of a direct question. It is also used to indicate doubt or uncertainty about the correctness of a statement. When used to express uncertainty, the question mark is placed in parentheses. A good substitute for (?) is simply to say *about.*

DIRECT QUESTION	Have you paid the bills?
EXPRESSIONS OF UNCERTAINTY	This house is 150 (?) years old.
	This house is about 150 years old.

A polite request phrased as a direct question is usually followed by a period rather than a question mark. Phrasing a request as a question rather than as a command is considered to be courteous and tactful, but the underlying intention of such a statement is not interrogative.

POLITE REQUEST	Will you please mail your payment as soon as possible.

A period rather than a question mark is used for an indirect question because such a statement implies a question but does not actually ask one. Although the idea expressed is interrogative, the actual phrasing is not.

DIRECT QUESTION	Had he turned off the water?
INDIRECT QUESTION	He wondered whether he had turned off the water.

The **exclamation point** signals the end of an emphatic or exclamatory statement. It is also used for emphatic commands and for interjections. Interjections are exclamatory words and phrases capable of standing alone: *Oh!, Ouch!, My goodness!*, and so forth.

EXCLAMATORY STATEMENT	Help! I'm drowning!
INTERJECTION WITH EMPHATIC COMMAND	Ouch! Stop pinching me!

Be careful not to overuse exclamation points in your writing. Inexperienced writers tend to use exclamation points for indicating everything from mild excitement to full-scale disaster. Whereas exclamation points used sparingly can provide genuine emphasis, too many of them will make the tone of your writing seem hysterical. Furthermore, your reader may begin to distrust you; like the boy in the fable who falsely cried "Wolf!" too often, you will not be able to attract your reader's attention with an exclamation point if you have previously misused it.

Practice: Using end punctuation   Supply the missing end punctuation in the following paragraph. The answers are listed next.

[1] Which is the most successful minority group in America [2] The answer, of course, depends on the definition of success being used [3] What are the easiest aspects of success to measure [4] Many sociologists claim that education and job status, if not representative of success in themselves, are easily measured components of success [5] In 1972, a survey of eight ethnic groups revealed that, in proportion to population size, Russian-Americans comprise the most successful ethnic group [6] Isn't it true that they represent only 1.2 percent of the population, yet hold 2.7 percent of all professional jobs [7] That's almost two and a half times the ratio of Anglo-Saxons in professional jobs [8] In addition, Russian-Americans surveyed in 1972 had completed an average of 16.0 years of schooling [9] That means the average Russian-American has graduated from college [10] The next closest group, Americans of English, Scot, or Welsh origin, have an average of 12.9 years of schooling, which merely means that the average person in this group has graduated from high school and that some have gone on to college [11] Russian-Americans have been very, very successful in America, indeed

Answers to the Practice   [1] America?   [2] used.   [3] measure?   [4] success.
[5] group.   [6] jobs?   [7] jobs! *or* jobs.   [8] schooling.   [9] college.
[10] college.   [11] indeed! *or* indeed.

154

EXERCISE 29, END PUNCTUATION   (19)

Circle any errors involving the use of periods, question marks, or exclamation points in the following sentences; then write the correct forms in the blanks at the right. If the punctuation is correct, write *correct* in the blank.

Example   She asked if I knew when the most
                      Russians immigrated?   *immigrated.*

1. Didn't the Russians populate much of Alaska before it was purchased by the U.S. in 1867.   _____

2. I don't know whether those Russians remained or not?   _____

3. There were Russian settlements in California by 1912!   _____

4. Russians began emigrating to the U.S. in record numbers in 1880.   _____

5. I wonder if world-wide economic conditions were responsible?   _____

6. Many of these people were only technically "Russian," however.   _____

7. No one knows how many were Jewish, Polish, Ukranian, or Byelorussian?   _____

8. Did many Russians come to America after the 1918 Bolshevik revolution?   _____

9. In fact, this second wave was very unlike the first wave of Russian immigrants?   _____

10. These were Russians from the upper and middle classes!   _____

Punctuate each of the following sentences as indicated, changing the wording if necessary so the sentence will be appropriate to the end punctuation requested.

Example   Time, according to the old adage, waits for no one.

(question) *Doesn't the old adage say that time waits for no one?*
(exclamation) *Time waits for no one!*

11. I wonder, like many others, if Russian-Americans are surprised by this turn of events.

    (question) _____

    (exclamation) _____

12. Vladimir asked if we had seen the newspaper.

    (question) _____

    (exclamation) _____

13. What a great idea!

(period) _____

(question) _____

14. Doesn't it take a long time to learn Russian?

(exclamation) _____

(period) _____

15. I question whether this is really necessary or not.

(question) _____

(exclamation) _____

Write sentences with end punctuation appropriate to the instructions indicated.

Example (expression of uncertainty) _*Bake the casserole*_

*for fifty minutes?*

16. (indirect question) _____

_____

17. (polite request phrased as a question) _____

_____

18. (mild command) _____

_____

19. (direct question) _____

_____

20. (assertion) _____

_____

21. (interjection with assertion) _____

_____

22. (expression of uncertainty) _____

_____

23. (emphatic command) _____

_____

24. (indirect question) _____

_____

25. (polite request phrased as a question) _____

_____

30
COMMAS, MAIN CLAUSES,
AND SUBORDINATE CLAUSES   (20a–b)

The **comma** is the most frequently used (and misused) punctuation mark. It is an internal punctuation mark that indicates relationships between sentence elements. One of its principal functions is to signal relationships between clauses. (See also Sections 7 and 17.)

1. A comma separates main clauses (independent clauses) joined by the coordinating conjunctions *and, but, or, nor, for, so,* and *yet.* The comma always precedes the coordinating conjunction.

She was a good student, and she was also a good athlete.

When you use a comma with a coordinating conjunction, be sure that the conjunction introduces an independent clause and not just a compound sentence part. For example, no comma is necessary before the conjunction linking compound predicate nouns (see Section 5).

INCORRECT   She was a good student, and also a good athlete.

CORRECT   She was a good student and also a good athlete.

If two main clauses are not joined by a coordinating conjunction, use a semicolon between them (see also Section 33).

She was a good student; she was also a good athlete.

A semicolon may also be used before the coordinating conjunction when one or both of the main clauses are very long or are internally punctuated with commas.

She was a good student, getting nearly all *A*'s in even the most difficult courses;
and she was also a good athlete with many conference records to her credit.

2. A comma separates introductory words, phrases, or subordinate clauses from the main clause. Such introductory elements function as modifiers—either adverbial modifiers qualifying the verb or the whole main clause or adjectival modifiers qualifying the subject of the main clause. A comma following a modifying word, phrase, or clause signals the reader that the main clause is about to begin.

INTRODUCTORY PARTICIPLE   Depressed, George thought about all his
                               unpaid bills.

INTRODUCTORY   Without enough money for his tuition, he
PREPOSITIONAL PHRASE   looked for a part-time job.

INTRODUCTORY   Because he could type well, he found work
SUBORDINATE CLAUSE   as a temporary secretary.

Be sure not to confuse modifying verbal phrases with verbals used as subjects. An introductory verbal modifier needs a comma; a verbal used as a subject does not.

INTRODUCTORY VERBAL MODIFIER	Having learned to type in high school, he now put his skill to use.
VERBAL AS SUBJECT	Having learned to type in high school was a blessing now that he needed to earn money for tuition.

3. The comma may be omitted after a very short introductory clause or phrase if there is no chance the reader will misunderstand your meaning. Remember that your use of a comma may be your reader's only clue to the exact meaning you intend. Note, for example, the following sentence: *Watching my sister Barbara was no fun.* The sentence might mean that Barbara is my sister. On the other hand, it might mean that Barbara was watching my sister.

CLEAR	Watching my sister, Barbara was no fun.
CONFUSING	After rolling the ball fell into the hole.
CLEAR	After rolling, the ball fell into the hole.
CONFUSING	In case of fire escape down the stairs instead of using the elevator.
CLEAR	In case of fire, escape down the stairs instead of using the elevator.
CLEAR	Before breakfast we went for a walk.
CLEAR	Next Tuesday my vacation begins.

The decision to use a comma after short introductory elements is sometimes a matter of emphasis. If, when you say a sentence aloud, you find yourself pausing for emphasis, a comma is probably desirable to ensure that the reader will distinguish the same emphasis.

CLEAR	Unfortunately my car needs new tires.
COMMA USED FOR EMPHASIS	Unfortunately, my car needs new tires.

EXERCISE 30-1, PUNCTUATION BETWEEN CLAUSES   (20a–b)

Insert a caret (ᴧ) to show where punctuation should be placed between main clauses
or between an introductory element and the main clause in each of the following
sentences. Then indicate whether the sentence requires a comma (,) or a semicolon (;)
by writing the correct punctuation mark in the blank at the right. If the sentence
requires no additional punctuation, write *NP* in the blank.

Example   Cities with names like Odessa and Moscow indicate
regions where Russian immigrants settled.   *NP*

Between 1880 and 1910 almost two million Russians
found their way to America.   ᐳ

1. Many of the Russians in this first wave were Polish, Jewish,
   or Byelorussian. ————

2. Because they were traveling with Russian passports American
   immigration officials listed them as Russians. ————

3. During the early years of immigration officials used the country
   of birth to classify immigrants for statistical purposes. ————

4. For the sake of convenience and speed in processing the flood of
   immigrants individual ethnic heritage may have been overlooked. ————

5. The second great wave of Russian immigrants was in 1918 but those
   who came were upper and middle class Russians fleeing the
   Bolshevik revolution. ————

6. They were professionals who either brought fortunes with them
   or expected to remake fortunes in America. ————

7. The second wave of Russians included people like Prince Matchabelli
   and other perfumers and jewelers. ————

8. Vladimir Zworykin entered with this group and later invented television. ————

9. Vladimir Nabokov also fled the Bolsheviks he later created a revolution
   in literature with his experimental novels. ————

10. Thus we can thank Russia for television, perfume, and art novels. ————

11. Russian-Americans and their descendants also gave us roller coasters
    and helicopters. ————

12. A Russian-American, Allen Funt, created *Candid Camera* not
    only did he create a television show but he also added its slogan
    to the English language. ————

13. Leonard Nimoy is of Russian-American heritage and is most famous as *Star Trek's* Mr. Spock. _____

14. Nimoy is a talented actor and he also writes poetry and scripts, as well as directs. _____

15. Norman Lear is also of Russian-American descent he is best known for his innovative situation comedies on television, especially *All in the Family.* _____

16. It is somehow fitting that so many of his programs feature ethnic characters. _____

17. As you may also know many of his programs present minorities in positive ways. _____

18. Responsible for publicizing the ecology movement Barry Commoner also claims Russian descent. _____

19. In some quarters Commoner is called the "Paul Revere of Ecology." _____

20. Russians continue to come to America in the 1970's over 110,000 Russian Jews left Russia. _____

21. The official policy of the U.S.S.R. is that Jews may emigrate from Russia if they wish. _____

22. Between 1971 and 1976 almost 8,000 Russian Jews settled in New York City alone. _____

23. Today the best estimate of the Russian population in America places it at 2.5 million. _____

24. In Alaska's first settlement of Russians 191 men and one woman started a fur-trading outpost on Kodiak Island. _____

25. That first settlement was named Three Saints Bay and was founded in 1784. _____

26. Even smaller the second settlement was inhabited by only ninety-five Russians. _____

27. Established as an agricultural settlement for the Kodiak Island post the second settlement was at Fort Ross California. _____

28. In 1841 the Russian interest at Fort Ross was sold to John Sutter. _____

29. Since Sutter built a mill on the property it became known as Sutter's Mill. _____

30. Unfortunately for Sutter gold was discovered there in 1848 and his mill and property were destroyed in the gold rush of 1849. _____

EXERCISE 30-2, PUNCTUATION BETWEEN CLAUSES (20a-b)

Expand each of the core sentences in the following ways: first, by adding another main clause; second, by adding an introductory subordinate clause; third, by adding an introductory phrase. Use appropriate internal punctuation.

Example His only possession was his passport.

(main clause) *His only possession was his passport, but he liked traveling light.*

(subordinate clause) *Because he liked traveling light, his only possession was his passport.*

(phrase) *When traveling, his only possession was his passport.*

1. The women shook hands.

   (main clause) _____

   (subordinate clause) _____

   (phrase) _____

2. The boat finally docked.

   (main clause) _____

   (subordinate clause) _____

   (phrase) _____

3. People are funny animals.

   (main clause) _____

   (subordinate clause) _____

   (phrase) _____

4. She offered to share her food.

   (main clause) _____

   (subordinate clause) _____

   (phrase) _____

5. You have ruined your suit.

(main clause) _____

(subordinate clause) _____

(phrase) _____

6. Waiting in line requires patience.

(main clause) _____

(subordinate clause) _____

(phrase) _____

7. He hated to wait in line.

(main clause) _____

(subordinate clause) _____

(phrase) _____

8. I visit my dentist twice a year.

(main clause) _____

(subordinate clause) _____

(phrase) _____

9. He learned to type in high school.

(main clause) _____

(subordinate clause) _____

(phrase) _____

10. Inez bought her book last week.

(main clause) _____

(subordinate clause) _____

(phrase) _____

31

COMMAS: NONRESTRICTIVE AND RESTRICTIVE SENTENCE ELEMENTS (20c–f)

Nonrestrictive elements are nonessential modifying words, phrases, or clauses that add useful but incidental information to a sentence. **Restrictive elements** are essential modifying words, phrases, or clauses that affect a sentence's basic meaning. Nonrestrictive sentence elements are set off with commas; restrictive elements are not.

We noted previously, in Section 30, that commas can be crucial to the reader's understanding of the writer's meaning. In the case of nonrestrictive and restrictive elements, the presence or absence of commas is particularly important because the meaning can be quite different, depending upon their use. A simple example illustrates the difference:

NONRESTRICTIVE	Children, *who hate vegetables,* should take vitamins.
RESTRICTIVE	Children *who hate vegetables* should take vitamins.

In the first sentence, the subordinate clause *who hate vegetables* can be removed without changing the sentence's basic message: *All* children ought to take vitamins. The subordinate clause adds the incidental information that all children also dislike vegetables.

The second sentence says something very different. Its meaning is that the *only* children who ought to take vitamins are those who hate vegetables. In this sentence, the subordinate clause *restricts* the category, children, to those hating vegetables.

This is the crucial point: Readers have no way of knowing whether the writer intends the category to be all-inclusive (nonrestrictive) or limited (restrictive) unless the commas are used (or omitted) correctly. The words are identical in both sentences.

A reader can occasionally distinguish whether a sentence element is restrictive or nonrestrictive even though the writer has misused commas.

RESTRICTIVE BUT INCORRECTLY PUNCTUATED	A waiter, *who gives good service,* gets generous tips.
NONRESTRICTIVE BUT INCORRECTLY PUNCTUATED	Max *who gives good service* gets generous tips.

If the reader follows the signals provided by the faulty punctuation in the first sentence and interprets the basic message to be *a waiter gets generous tips,* he or she will recognize this as a false statement. Generally, waiters do not get generous tips unless they give good service. The subordinate clause is essential to the meaning because it *restricts* the category of waiters to those who give good service. The clause *should not* be set off with commas.

Conversely, the subject of the second sentence designates a particular waiter who gets generous tips. The proper noun *Max* restricts the category to one individual. The subordinate clause merely supplies additional but nonessential information. Consequently, the clause *should be* set off with commas.

CORRECT (RESTRICTIVE)	A waiter *who gives good service* gets generous tips.
CORRECT (NONRESTRICTIVE)	Max, *who gives good service,* gets generous tips.

As you can see, a reader may eventually be able to figure out the meaning in spite of faulty comma usage. Nevertheless, writers who fail to follow the punctuation conventions that signal whether a sentence element is restrictive or nonrestrictive run the risk of confusing their readers—or, at the very least, of annoying them and thus detracting from the contents of the message.

Now analyze the preceding sentence, containing the subordinate clause *who fail to follow* . . . , and decide why that clause is restrictive (not set off by commas). If you determined that without the clause (i.e., *writers run the risk of confusing their readers*) we won't know *which* writers—and surely *not all* writers confuse their readers—then you are well on your way toward understanding the difference between nonrestrictive and restrictive elements.

Be sure to use *two* commas to set off a nonrestrictive element unless it begins or ends a sentence.

NOT That restaurant, specializing in Cuban cooking is one of my favorites.

BUT That restaurant, specializing in Cuban cooking, is one of my favorites.

OR Specializing in Cuban cooking, that restaurant is one of my favorites.

Typical nonrestrictive sentence elements are clauses, prepositional, verbal, and absolute phrases, appositives, and elements that slightly interrupt the structure of a sentence. Of these, clauses, prepositional and verbal phrases, and appositives may also be restrictive.

NONRESTRICTIVE CLAUSE	Key West, *where my brother lives,* is semitropical.
RESTRICTIVE CLAUSE	The city *where my brother lives* is semitropical.
NONRESTRICTIVE PREPOSITIONAL PHRASE	His boat, *on its side,* needs repairs.
RESTRICTIVE PREPOSITIONAL PHRASE	A boat *with a hole* is sure to sink.
NONRESTRICTIVE VERBAL PHRASE	The tourists, *tired and sunburned,* crowded the dock.
RESTRICTIVE VERBAL PHRASE	A woman *wearing sunglasses* dipped her feet in the water.
NONRESTRICTIVE APPOSITIVE	The tour guide, *a perspiring matron,* herded her charges.
RESTRICTIVE APPOSITIVE	"The novelist Ernest Hemingway once lived in Key West," she said.

An **appositive**, shown in the last two examples, is a noun or group of words functioning as a noun substitute. An appositive renames another noun and usually follows immediately after the noun. Most appositives of more than a word or two are nonrestrictive. Restrictive appositives, like other restrictive sentence elements, limit, define, or designate the noun they follow in such a way that their absence would change the basic meaning of the sentence.

Absolute phrases are always nonrestrictive; they provide explanatory detail rather than essential information. An absolute phrase is a noun or pronoun followed by a present participle or past participle verb form. The phrase modifies the entire main clause rather than specific words in the clause. Because they are nonessential and therefore nonrestrictive, absolute phrases are always set off by commas.

Thousands of refugees came ashore at Key West in 1980, *Fidel Castro having allowed them to leave Cuba.*

Interrupting expressions—words, phrases, or clauses that slightly disrupt the flow of a sentence—are sometimes called **parenthetical elements**. These elements should be set off by commas because they are not integral to the grammatical structure of the sentence. Words of direct address, mild interjections, transitional words and expressions, phrases expressing contrast, and words such as *yes* and *no* are usually considered interrupting expressions.

Other sentence elements also fall into the category of interrupting expressions if they are inserted out of their normal grammatical order. When they disrupt a sentence's grammatical flow (see Section 5), they require commas.

DIRECT ADDRESS	Please let us know, *Dad,* when you will arrive.
MILD INTERJECTION	*Well,* I had better get some sleep.
TRANSITIONAL WORDS	*Despite the storm, however,* the plane landed on time.
CONTRASTED ELEMENTS	Dogs, *unlike cats,* usually love to play in the water.
DISRUPTED SENTENCES	Promptness, *my mother always said,* is a virtue.
	The package, *battered and dented,* had been labeled "fragile."

One final category of sentence elements needs to be discussed: clauses and phrases that follow the main clause. In Section 30, we examined punctuation for introductory subordinate clauses and phrases that precede the main clause. These usually require a comma to prevent misreading and to signal the start of the main clause. But what about a subordinate clause or lengthy phrase that follows the main clause? Here, again, you must decide whether the information provided by the clause or phrase is restrictive or nonrestrictive.

If the information is essential to the meaning of the main clause, then the sentence element is restrictive and does not need a comma. If the information is nonessential and does not restrict the main clause's meaning, then the sentence element is nonrestrictive and should be separated from the main clause by a comma. Such phrases and clauses usually explain, amplify, or offer a contrast to the main clause, but the main clause does not depend on them for its meaning. Consider the following examples:

RESTRICTIVE	We cannot leave on vacation *unless the airline strike ends.*
NONRESTRICTIVE	I should pick up our tickets, *before I get busy and forget to do it.*

In the first example, the subordinate clause presents a condition for leaving on vacation. The meaning of the main clause depends on the qualification presented in the dependent clause. In the second example, the subordinate adverbial clause adds a kind of afterthought—an explanation, but not a condition that is essential to the meaning of the main clause. Consequently, a comma is necessary in the second sentence, but not in the first.

Usually subordinate clauses and phrases that follow the main clause are so closely tied to its meaning that they are considered restrictive. Using a comma after the main clause is generally the exception rather than the norm.

A good guide to whether or not a clause, phrase, or other sentence element is restrictive is the pitch and pause of your voice when you read the sentence. If your voice dips and hesitates before and after reading an expression, the element is likely to be nonrestrictive and require commas. If you read the sentence fairly even-toned and even-paced, the element is probably restrictive and does not need commas.

Remember that your readers will pause where you insert commas. Readers depend on you to provide the appropriate signals for meaning and emphasis.

Practice: Punctuating restrictive and nonrestrictive sentence elements   *Some of the following sentences use commas correctly; some do not. Examine the sentences and determine whether they are correct or incorrect as punctuated. The answers are listed next.*

[1] George Crum an American Indian working as a chef in Saratoga Springs invented the potato chip. [2] A guest, who complained about the French fried potatoes, had Crum slice a new batch for him. [3] The old batch apparently was simply too thick, for the guest's gourmet taste. [4] Crum, dutifully, sliced the new batch. [5] The guest sent them back for, once again, being too thick. [6] Crum, by this time really exasperated, sliced the third batch into paper-thin slices. [7] These were then fried, to a crisp. [8] The guest, to Crum's total amazement, loved the third batch. [9] The new way, of cooking potatoes, became more popular, every year. [10] Crum called them "Saratoga Chips" and served them, every night, at the posh resort.

Answers to the Practice   [1] incorrect   [2] incorrect   [3] incorrect   [4] incorrect
[5] incorrect   [6] correct   [7] incorrect   [8] correct   [9] incorrect
[10] incorrect

EXERCISE 31-1, COMMAS: NONRESTRICTIVE AND RESTRICTIVE SENTENCE ELEMENTS   (20c–f)

Although the following sentences are not punctuated to indicate the presence of nonrestrictive elements, many of them should be. In the blanks following the sentences, indicate whether the expressions set off or preceded by asterisks are restrictive (*R*) or nonrestrictive (*NR*).

Example	Those of us * on diets * stayed to hear the speaker.	*R*
	Ms. Grey * who spoke to the group * seemed well prepared.	*NR*

1. Ms. Grey said intelligent marketing * in today's economy * is often the difference between success and failure. _____

2. Wally Amos developed a new way * of marketing chocolate chip cookies. * _____

3. The cookie * with its random pieces of chocolate * was found in almost every kitchen. _____

4. Most of the chocolate chip cookies * eaten in the U.S. * were sold in supermarkets. _____

5. These cookies * which often were bought on the basis of price * cost about 89¢ per bag. _____

6. Some specialty bakeries had versions * that were slightly better. * _____

7. If you wanted a cookie * that had lots of chips and nuts * you had to bake it at home. _____

8. *Having gained experience as a Hollywood press agent * Wally Amos knew he could promote a product. _____

9. *Working from an aunt's recipe * Wally made cookies rich with pecans and chocolates. _____

10. He opened a cookie stand * on Sunset Boulevard * in Los Angeles. _____

11. Suddenly he was "Famous Amos" * with his picture on T-shirts and posters. * _____

12. He turned the chocolate chip cookie * which everyone took for granted * into a luxury. _____

13. *With his cookies selling for $4.00 a pound * Famous Amos was quickly selling a million dollars' worth of cookies every year. _____

14. Henry G. Parks * a Black entrepreneur who founded Parks Sausage * took a different route to success. _____

15. *An honor student in marketing at Ohio State * Parks was advised at one time to learn Spanish and to pretend to be from South America if he wanted a job. _____

16. Parks refused and landed a job which eventually made him a national sales representative for Pabst Brewing * responsible for market development among Blacks. _____

17. In 1951 Parks began making sausages * as a small business sideline.* _____

18. *Making sausage each morning and selling it in the afternoon * Parks quickly dominated the inner-city market in Baltimore. _____

19. Parks had perfected his product and showed * no doubt about it * that customers would buy his sausage. _____

20. Parks then began * through food-store chains * marketing his sausage to all ethnic groups. _____

Expand each of the following core sentences with nonrestrictive and restrictive clauses or phrases, using commas correctly.

Example   All employees are urged to make suggestions.

(nonrestrictive) *All employees, who will be affected by the strike, are urged to make suggestions.*

(restrictive) *All employees who will be affected by the strike are urged to make suggestions.*

21. The suggestions poured in.

(nonrestrictive) _____

(restrictive) _____

22. The solution was found.

(nonrestrictive) _____

(restrictive) _____

23. The insurance business is good nowadays.

(nonrestrictive) _____

(restrictive) _____

24. An unpopular decision was made by the manager.

(nonrestrictive) _____

(restrictive) _____

25. I've just gone on a diet.

(nonrestrictive) _____

(restrictive) _____

EXERCISE 31-2, COMMAS: NONRESTRICTIVE AND RESTRICTIVE SENTENCE ELEMENTS   (20c–f)

Insert commas when they are needed for nonrestrictive elements or interrupting expressions in the following sentences. If a sentence contains a restrictive element and needs no additional punctuation, write *NP* after it.

Example   For years‚ people have thought the U.S. did not have its own distinct foods.

1. However many foods that sound as if they have been of foreign origin actually were invented in America.

2. Vichyssoise for example was invented in 1910 by a French chef.

3. But that French chef who was named Louis Diat lived and worked in America.

4. Vichyssoise which is made from leeks and potatoes was first served cold by Diat.

5. Diat who used a recipe he learned from his mother worked at the Ritz Carlton Hotel in New York City.

6. Lebanon bologna which sounds as if its origins are in the Middle East is a smoked beef sausage made in Lebanon, Pennsylvania.

7. Spaghetti and meatballs was in point of fact first served in Brooklyn.

8. Cioppino which is a fish stew may have an Italian name.

9. It was however invented in Monterey and made popular in San Francisco restaurants.

10. Even Baked Alaska which should have some connection with Eskimos or the Great North was invented in 1867 by a New York chef.

11. Chop Suey was developed as a matter of fact by a Chinese diplomat.

12. However the inventor of Chop Suey Li Hung Chang was in New York when he invented it.

13. The dish which was an attempt to recreate authentic Chinese food with available ingredients and utensils caught on quickly.

14. The name is a combination of the words for chop sticks and soya sauce into *chop soya* which eventually became chop suey.

15. Even chow mein that other staple of Chinese restaurants was first made by Chinese railroad workers in San Francisco.

16. There are only two cheeses that have been invented in the United States.

17. One is Brick cheese which was supposedly developed by a Swiss-American John Jossi.

18. The other American cheese is Liederkranz a rather pungent cheese in the same group as Limburger.

19. The inventor Emil Frev tested his cheese on a choral society who liked the cheese so much they gave it the name of their group Liederkranz.

20. Despite its German-sounding name Liederkranz was developed in Monroe, New York.

As you have seen from the preceding text and exercises in Section 31, nonrestrictive and restrictive sentence elements are modifiers used to expand core sentences with additional information. At each number here, write a core sentence. Then expand that core sentence by adding modifying words: subordinate clauses, phrases, and interrupting elements. Make sure that at least two of your expanded sentences contain nonrestrictive modifying elements and at least two contain restrictive modifying elements. Set off nonrestrictive or interrupting elements appropriately with commas. Be ready to explain why you consider the modifying elements you have added restrictive or nonrestrictive.

Example (core sentence) *Limburger cheese smells terrible.*

If you ask me, Limburger cheese, a very soft white cheese, smells terrible.

21. (core sentence) _____

_____

_____

22. (core sentence) _____

_____

_____

23. (core sentence) _____

_____

_____

24. (core sentence) _____

_____

_____

25. (core sentence) _____

_____

_____

32
COMMAS: ITEMS IN A SERIES   (20g–i)

Commas are used to separate **three or more coordinate words, phrases, or clauses in a series.** Items in a series are coordinate if they are of approximately equal grammatical rank or importance.

> Artesians are an ethnic group of *unknown origin, undetermined ancestry, and mysterious habits.* [Three nouns modified by adjectives]
>
> No one knows for sure *who they are, where they came from, or how they got here.* [Three dependent clauses]

You have probably seen sentences in newspapers and magazines that omit the comma before the final element in a series: *The candidate offered a platform that Democrats, Republicans and Independents could support.* Although omitting the final comma is not incorrect, doing so can lead to confusion for the reader. Consider the following sentence, for example:

> It is known that Artesians like bowling, beer, pickles and ice cream with fudge sauce.

A reader may be unsure as to whether Artesians like pickles *and* also like ice cream with fudge sauce or whether they like a weird concoction of pickles and ice cream, both ingredients covered with fudge sauce. To prevent such confusion, establish the habit of always using a comma to signal the final element in a series.

> It is known that Artesians like bowling, beer, pickles, and ice cream with fudge sauce.

Commas are used to separate coordinate adjectives in a series, but they are **not used between adjectives that are not coordinate.** Adjectives are coordinate if each one separately modifies the noun—that is, (1) if *and* can be placed between each of the adjectives without distorting the meaning; and (2) if the order of the adjectives can be changed without distorting the meaning.

> Artesians are said to be quiet, peaceful, law-abiding folks. (Artesians are said to be quiet and peaceful and law-abiding folks. Artesians are said to be peaceful, law-abiding, quiet folks.)

Adjectives in a series are not always coordinate; sometimes they are **cumulative,** as the following sentence shows:

> Some people claim Artesians dislike congested suburban shopping centers.

Clearly, the adjectives cannot be moved around without reducing the sentence to nonsense. *Shopping* modifies the noun *center,* but we ordinarily use the two words together in such a way that they really constitute a single concept and function together as a compound noun—like *baseball* or *timekeeper. Suburban,* in fact, modifies the whole concept formed by the two words taken together. Of the three adjectives, *congested* is the most independent and loosely attached. We could say *congested and suburban shopping centers* without destroying the sentence's meaning.

Coordinate adjectives are rather like the spokes of a wheel, each one focused on the noun at the hub, each one separated from the others by a spacing comma. Adjectives in series that are not coordinate are more like funnels tightly stacked one inside the other, each one often modifying a word or words ahead of it and the last one modifying the noun itself.

The same principles governing punctuation for adjectives in a series apply when only two modifiers precede the word being modified. If the two modifiers are coordinate but not joined by a conjunction, use a comma between them. If they are cumulative rather than coordinate, do not use a comma.

> Apparently Artesians are shy, retiring types, but they are rumored to be fantastic poker players.

Commas are also used to set off **items in dates** following the series order month, day, and year. Commas are not used if just the month and year are given or if the series order is day, month, and year.

> An Artesian was seen publicly on July 4, 1981, but at no time since then.
> Before May 1903 only four Artesian sightings were recorded, two of them occurring on 21 June 1902 at a local pub.

Commas are used to set off **items in addresses and geographical names**. A comma should be placed after the last item if the geographical name or address appears within a sentence. No comma is used before a zip code.

ADDRESS	The pub was located at 212 Happy Hollow Road, Short Order, Oregon, and still stands at that address today.
GEOGRAPHICAL NAME	Other Artesians have been seen in Moffat, Scotland, and Cromwell, New Zealand, during the last decade.

Commas are also used to set off **titles that follow names**. In addition, commas are used in **numbers** to indicate thousands, but not in social security numbers, telephone numbers, zip codes, and so forth.

> According to Professor George Arcane, Ph.D., who is an authority on the subject, Artesians have a terrific sense of humor. He claims to have interviewed 11,405½ of them and says they all share the same telephone: Olympia 555-7426.

EXERCISE 32–1, COMMAS: ITEMS IN A SERIES   (20g–i)

After each of the following sentences, write *C* if the sentence is punctuated correctly and *NC* if it is punctuated incorrectly.

Example   By the age of 21, Paul Anka had sold over 3 million records earned over a million dollars, and written over 200 songs. *NC*

Anka is of Lebanese ancestry, and was born in Canada. *NC*

1. Patti, Laverne and Maxine were the singing Andrews Sisters.

2. They had several "ethnic crossover" hits, including "Beer Barrel Polka," "Rum and Coca-Cola," and *"Bei Mir Bist Du Schön."*

3. Of Greek, and Norwegian ancestry, they were born in Minnesota.

4. Many people think *"Bei Mir Bist Du Schön"* is German, Swedish or Danish, but the language is actually Yiddish.

5. "My Way" was written by Claude François translated by Paul Anka and sung by Frank Sinatra.

6. Fabian Forte, Bobby Rydell, and Frankie Avalon were all Italian-American rock stars.

7. Irving Berlin never attended school past the second grade, never learned to read music and never learned to play the piano in any key except F sharp.

8. Berlin's father, a rabbi, fled a pogrom in Russia, immigrated to America and settled in New York.

9. Leonard Bernstein, who writes musical scores for films, ballets, and operas, is the son of Russian-Jewish immigrants.

10. He is equally famous as the musical director of the New York, Philharmonic, Symphony Orchestra.

11. Sammy Cahn has been named Cohen, Kahn and Cahn.

12. Cahn has collaborated with Saul Chaplin, Jule Styne and Jimmy Van Heusen.

13. Cahn, a German-Jewish song writer, is famous for his rhythmic, surprising refrains.

14. Perry Como had a career as a barber, another as a successful, band singer, and yet another as a television personality.

15. Ray Charles dropped his last name when he began appearing professionally, to avoid being confused with "Sugar" Ray Robinson the boxer.

Insert commas at all points where they are required in the following sentences. (Use a pen or pencil which writes in a color other than black.) Write *NC* if the sentence needs no commas.

Example   George M. Cohan was not Jewish, was not born on July 4, and was not a "Yankee Doodle Dandy."

16. Cohan was a full-blooded Irish-American.
17. His original family name was Keohane.
18. Duke Ellington became famous as a band leader composer and pianist.
19. George Gershwin composed his first song in about fifteen minutes introduced it to Al Jolson and watched it sell two million records and one million copies of sheet music.
20. His famous Black folk opera *Porgy and Bess* has been produced in many stage screen and recorded versions.
21. Benjamin David Goodman was born on May 30 1909 in Chicago Illinois to impoverished Russian-Jewish parents.
22. Benny learned clarinet at his synagogue and was the first white band leader to employ Black musicians in his band.
23. Benny's synagogue musical training his Black band members and the arrangements of a Black musician named Fletcher Henderson helped to make Goodman the "King of Swing."
24. Oscar Hammerstein helped write *Oklahoma Show Boat* and *Carousel.*
25. His grandfather ran away from his home in Berlin Germany sold his violin and worked on a ship bound for America.
26. He made a fortune in tobacco bought two German-language theaters in New York and finally sold them to the Metropolitan Opera.
27. Arthur Fiedler was the son of Austrian-Jewish immigrant violinists.
28. Radio television and concert artists know him as the white-haired orchestra conductor of the Boston Pops.
29. In 1911 he was accepted into the Berlin Royal Academy in 1926 he conducted his first performance with the Boston Pops Orchestra and in 1930 he became its permanent conductor.
30. Fiedler was one of America's most popular best-known beloved conductors of his time.

EXERCISE 32–2, ALL KINDS OF COMMAS   (20)

Insert commas where they are required in the following sentences. (Use a pen or pencil which writes in a color other than black.)

Example   As a matter of fact, America's multiethnic society may be most obvious in its music industry.

1. In collaboration with Richard Rodgers Lorenz Hart wrote almost 400 songs and twenty-nine musicals.

2. Hart was born on the Upper East Side of New York City to German-Jewish parents Frieda and Max Hertz.

3. Like many immigrants the Hertzes "Americanized" their last name.

4. Whether it was called syncopated rhythm ragged time or ragtime Scott Joplin's music is some of the most popular music of all time.

5. Joplin was born on November 24 1868 in Texarkana Texas and began playing piano professionally at the age of 14.

6. He was known as the "King of the Ragtime Composers" but he never really enjoyed public acclaim in his own lifetime.

7. After the failure of his ragtime opera *Treemonisha* he suffered a nervous breakdown.

8. In 1917 he died in a New York mental hospital.

9. Sixty years later Joshua Rifkin recorded Joplin's rags.

10. "The Entertainer" one of Joplin's rags that was used in the film *The Sting* sold over 2000000 copies.

11. Charlie Mingus who was nicknamed "Jazz's Angry Man" grew up in the Watts ghetto.

12. Mingus played bass on which he backed Lionel Hampton Charlie Parker and Duke Ellington.

13. Mingus said that jazz is the American Black's tradition and he further claimed that whites had no right to play jazz.

14. Despite such controversial remarks Mingus often hired white musicians for his bands.

15. He referred to them however as "colorless."

16. Eubie Blake until his death in 1983 played the piano every day.

17. When he was 95 years old he saw a retrospective of his career open on Broadway.

18. As a pianist and composer Blake has had an amazing longevity.

19. Despite his wealth, Blake lived in Brooklyn's Black neighborhood Bedford-Stuyvesant.

20. Buffy St. Marie who rose to fame as a protest singer in the 1960's is a Cree Indian.

21. Since the 1970's Buffy has appeared regularly on *Sesame Street.*

22. Unless you have young children you may never have heard of Buffy's colleague Joe Raposo.

23. Raposo whose parents taught him piano violin viola and guitar is a Portuguese-American from Fall River Massachusetts.

24. Urged to study medicine by his parents Raposo found he couldn't stand the sight of blood.

25. He went to Harvard to study law but he became side-tracked by his love of music.

26. In 1959 he abandoned law school to concentrate on composing music.

27. Besides the musical themes for *Sesame Street* and *The Electric Company* Raposo's big hits have been songs for the Muppets.

28. *Sesame Street Fever* a disco album for children sold almost one million copies.

29. Some of Raposo's songs have also been hits in the adult world however.

30. "Being Green" "Sing" and "You Will Be My Music" have been Raposo's biggest sellers among adult audiences.

33
SEMICOLONS (21)

A **semicolon** is used to separate main clauses not joined by a coordinating conjunction. (See also Sections 17 and 30.)

> One thinks of cathedrals as creations of medieval Europe; one does not associate them with twentieth-century New York City.

Like a period, a semicolon marks the end of a complete, grammatically independent statement. Although it can be substituted for a period, a semicolon is most effectively used between two independent clauses that are closely related in thought. Whereas a period is a "full stop," marking a complete break between sentences, the semicolon separates and stops but does not fully break the flow of thought between grammatically independent statements.

> Work on Manhattan's Cathedral Church of St. John the Divine stopped in 1941; construction began again in 1979.

This close relationship of thoughts is underscored by another of the semicolon's uses: to separate main clauses joined by a conjunctive adverb. Conjunctive adverbs, words such as *however, moreover, therefore,* and *consequently,* carry a thought from one main clause to the next. (See Section 7 for additional discussion of conjunctive adverbs and a more extensive list of them.)

> Much of the cathedral had been completed by 1941; *however,* the church's two towers had not been built.

Conjunctive adverbs are easy to distinguish from coordinating and subordinating conjunctions if you remember that, unlike the other connectives, they can be moved from the beginning of their main clauses without destroying the sense.

> Work was suspended because of the Japanese attack on Pearl Habor; *consequently,* the church stood without towers for twenty years.
> Work was suspended because of the Japanese attack on Pearl Harbor; the church stood, *consequently,* without towers for twenty years.

Coordinating and subordinating conjunctions cannot be moved around in this way. *Work was suspended, and the church stood without towers* makes sense, but *Work was suspended, the church and stood without towers* does not.

Note that when a conjunctive adverb comes within the second main clause instead of at the beginning, the clauses still must be separated by a semicolon and the conjunctive adverb set off by a pair of commas.

A semicolon is also used to separate main clauses joined by a coordinating conjunction if the clauses are exceptionally long or contain internal commas. This use of the semicolon helps the reader to see clearly where one main clause stops and another starts. When you compare the following sentences, you will appreciate a reader's relief at finding a semicolon among the welter of commas:

Building a cathedral is like putting together an enormous, multiton, three-dimensional jigsaw puzzle, and it requires not an afternoon, but decades, even centuries, to finish.

Building a cathedral is like putting together an enormous, multiton, three-dimensional jigsaw puzzle; and it requires not an afternoon, but decades, even centuries, to finish.

Similarly, semicolons are used in place of commas to separate items in a series if the items themselves contain internal commas.

At the Cathedral of St. John the Divine, the stonecutters have included Poni Baptiste, a sculptor from Harlem; James Jamieson, an ex-butcher from the Bronx; and D'Ellis Kincanon, who is part Chickasaw Indian.

Practice: Using semicolons   *The following sentences are punctuated with commas and periods. Underline those punctuation marks that you think could be replaced by semicolons. The answers are listed next.*

[1] The Eskimo pie is neither a pie nor an Eskimo invention. [2] In fact, the Eskimo pie was invented by a Danish school teacher from Iowa, Christian Nelson. [3] Nelson managed a candy store after school. [4] One day he watched a young boy trying very hard to decide whether he should buy a candy bar or an ice cream sandwich. [5] After watching this agonizing decision, Nelson realized that a product combining the boy's alternatives would probably sell well. [6] After months of experimentation, Nelson came up with the right combination. [7] A heavy concentration of cocoa butter allowed the chocolate to stick to the ice cream. [8] Nelson called his invention "I Scream," and it was a big success. [9] However, once he sold the rights to candy-maker Russell Stover, who changed the name to "Eskimo Pie," Nelson's invention began netting him over $30,000 each week in royalties.

Answers to the Practice   [1-2] invention; in fact   [4-5] sandwich; after
[6-7] combination; a   [8-9] success; however

178

Name ——————————————— Date ——————— Score ———

EXERCISE 33, SEMICOLONS   (21)

Insert semicolons where they are needed in the following sentences. (Use a pen or pencil that writes in a color other than black.)

Example   Bing cherries are the sweetest type of cherry grown in America;they were developed by a Chinese immigrant known only as Bing.

1.   Bing was following in his ancestor's footsteps cherries were first grown in China.

2.   The first cherries west of the Rockies were brought to Oregon by Henderson Luelling it was this first wagonload of stock from which Bing developed the Bing cherry.

3.   The Bing cherry is sweet, firm, and juicy its skin color ranges from deep red to black.

4.   The Dutch contribution to America's menus is a roll-call of fattening foods for some reason most Dutch foods in America are breakfast foods.

5.   Dutch foods eaten here include waffles, which are served dripping in butter, crullers, which must drip sugary grease, hot cocoa, buckwheat cakes, which have made many a cold morning bearable, cookies, and chocolate bars.

6.   The Dutch invented the doughnut later an American put a hole in the middle.

7.   The Dutch called doughnuts "oilycake" their recipe was brought to America by the Pilgrims.

8.   The Pilgrims shaped their oilycake dough into round balls the size of walnuts hence their name for the dessert was "doughnuts."

9.   One problem with the early doughnut was its soggy middle however this problem was solved by a New England sailor named Hanson Gregory.

10. He decided that if the soggy middle were punched out, the hot oil would fry the cakes more evenly today a plaque in Rockport, Maine, honors the man who invented the doughnut hole.

Combine or repunctuate the following sentences, substituting semicolons for periods and commas where appropriate and changing capitalization if necessary.

Example   The hamburger has a long history. It probably began with the Russian dish, Tartar steak. Tartar steak is raw beef topped with a raw egg.

The hamburger has a long history ; it probably began with the Russian dish, Tartar steak, which is raw beef topped with a raw egg.

11. Russian sailors probably introduced Tartar steak to the German city of Hamburg. There German cooks improved the dish immensely by cooking it.

_____

_____

_____

12. They probably served the dish to a diner who found the original raw ingredients distasteful. Then after cooking the beef and egg, the Germans found the new dish irresistible.

_____

_____

_____

13. Obviously such a popular dish needed a name. It was called "Hamburger steak" after the city where it was first cooked.

_____

_____

_____

14. Hamburger steak was first served in America by German immigrants. However, the dish did not begin to resemble its modern version until 1904.

_____

_____

_____

15. At the St. Louis Exposition in 1904, hamburger steak was one of the most popular foods offered. In fact one vendor reportedly ran out of plates because so many people were being served in his cafe.

_____

_____

_____

16. The vendor began serving the hamburger steak on buns. Within hours, everyone decided to have their hamburgers served on these rolls.

_____

_____

_____

17. Other foods brought to America by Germans include pretzels, without which beer drinkers would have to hold a beer in both hands, beer itself, used to wash the pretzel down, sausages, noodles, sauerkraut, which tops the frankfurter in a hot dog, and the frankfurter, too.

_____

_____

_____

18. Of course, the frankfurter comes from Frankfurt, Germany. The first frankfurter sausage was made there in 1852.

_____

_____

_____

19. Germans coming to America brought with them their love of sausages bratwurst, liverwurst, and all the other specialty sausages became as popular here as they had been in Germany.

_____

_____

_____

20. Two German immigrants claim to have invented the frankfurter sandwich. Clearly, their strategy was to make the sandwich more popular by making it more portable.

_____

_____

_____

21. Antoine Feuchtwanger, a Bavarian, claimed to be the man who introduced the frankfurter sandwich to St. Louis in the 1880's. Charles Feltman also claims the honor, however.

_____

_____

_____

22. Feltman pushed a cart around Coney Island in the 1890's, and he sold, he said, his frankfurters in toasted rolls for 10¢.

_____

_____

23. The sentimental favorite to win here is Feltman. His story seems more historically accurate.

_____

_____

_____

24. Frankfurter sandwiches are still called "Coney Islands" in some parts of the country, and they were called "dime red hots" before they were "hot dogs."

_____

_____

_____

25. The Germans, with their hot dogs and hamburgers, seem to have specialized in portable food. It was also a German-American who first thought of putting ice cream on a stick. Harry Burt registered his patent on the Good Humor Ice Cream Sucker in 1920.

_____

_____

_____

_____

34
COLONS, DASHES, AND PARENTHESES (22–23)

The **colon** has some characteristics similar to the semicolon and some similar to the dash. In fact, from time to time you may be unsure about whether to use a colon or one of the other two punctuation marks. In this section, we examine the distinctions that will help you determine the appropriate punctuation to use.

Like a semicolon, a colon can be used between main clauses that lack a coordinating conjunction. However, whereas the semicolon indicates a stop, the colon indicates an addition or expectation. The colon separates main clauses, the second of which explains, illustrates, or amplifies the first.

> Stonecutting is not something you can learn in a day: it requires a four-year apprenticeship.

A colon can also be used to set off a long final appositive (words that rename a nearby noun or noun substitute) or to set off a long summary. A dash is used to set off a short final appositive or short summary.

LONG APPOSITIVE USING COLON	Medieval cathedrals were built by apprentices: young workers learning their trade under a master craftsman.
SHORT APPOSITIVE USING DASH	Medieval masters paid their apprentices not with money but with subsistence—food and lodging.
LONG SUMMARY USING COLON	The apprentices working on the Cathedral of St. John the Divine today are an unusual bunch: They have come from New York's ghetto to learn a medieval European craft.
SHORT SUMMARY USING DASH	They receive not only wages but also a place in history for their work—a kind of immortality.

A colon can be used to introduce examples, a series, or a list. When it introduces a list, the colon may be preceded by the phrases *as follows* or *the following,* or these phrases may be only implied.

COLON PRECEDED BY *THE FOLLOWING*	Some of the world's great cathedrals are in the following cities: Chartres, Amiens, Canterbury, Cologne, Barcelona, and Milan.
COLON USED WHERE *AS FOLLOWS* IS IMPLIED	Two architectural styles dominate European cathedrals: the Romanesque and the Gothic.

It is not necessary to use a colon after the linking verb *are* or after the participle *including*.

> Several features distinguish Gothic cathedrals, including pointed arches, ribbed vaults, and buttresses.

A colon is used to introduce a formal quotation. Also, established convention requires a colon to separate items in biblical citations, titles with subtitles, and divisions of time.

FORMAL QUOTATION	In 1170 four knights murdered Archbishop Thomas à Becket in Canterbury Cathedral, acting upon the words of King Henry II: "Will no one rid me of this priest?"
BIBLICAL CITATION	Ecclesiastes 3:1–8
TITLE WITH SUBTITLE	*Poets and Pilgrims: Chaucer's Canterbury Tales*
DIVISION OF TIME	11:55 P.M.

The **dash** is best used for emphasis and clarity to indicate shifts in sentence structure or thought or to set off parenthetical elements that might be confusing if punctuated with commas.

SHIFT IN SENTENCE STRUCTURE	A cathedral in New York City—its presence seems almost an anachronism—sets a bit of the Old World down in the New World.
SHIFT IN THOUGHT	The stonecutters at St. John the Divine—the best go to Bath, England, for special training—work from scale drawings of the structure.
EMPHASIS ON PARENTHETICAL ELEMENT	James Robert Bambridge—a master builder from England—is directing the construction of the cathedral's gallery and two towers.
INTRODUCTORY LIST OR SUMMARY	Measuring, marking, and chiseling—these are the steps in "tapping stone."
INTERRUPTION OR HESITATION IN SPEECH	"The feeling I get from working here is like—like soaring. It makes me want to—" "To sing," says another stonecutter, finishing the sentence for his friend.

The dash is also used for clarity to set off internally punctuated appositives. Remember that a semicolon can be used between items in a series containing internal commas (see Section 33). Using dashes to set off an appositive made up of an internally punctuated series serves a similar clarifying purpose.

A cathedral's architectural elements, gables, turrets, pinnacles, and spires, reach heavenward, designed as a celebration of glory to God.

A cathedral's architectural elements—gables, turrets, pinnacles, and spires—reach heavenward, designed as a celebration of glory to God.

The dashes quickly signal to the reader that the words following *elements* are a series of appositives and that *elements* is not part of the series.

When typing a dash, use two hyphens with no space beside or between them.

Parentheses are used to set off nonrestrictive parenthetical information, explanation, or comment that is incidental to the main thought of a sentence. Parentheses used instead of dashes downplay the importance of the information, whereas dashes emphasize it. Parentheses are also used to enclose numerals or letters that label items listed within a sentence.

PARENTHETICAL INFORMATION	The Cathedral Church of St. John the Divine will take a great deal of money ($21 million) and thirty years to finish.
NUMBERED OR LETTERED ITEMS	Other modern cathedrals built according to medieval architectural styles are (1) St. Patrick's Cathedral in New York City; (2) the National Cathedral in Washington, D.C.; and (3) the Anglican cathedral in Liverpool, England.

EXERCISE 34, COLONS, DASHES, AND PARENTHESES   (22–23)

Insert carets at the points in the following sentences where dashes or colons are required. Then write the dashes or colons above the lines.

Example   Plastic cups, plastic bags, plastic spoons all these are the work of
Leo H. Baekelandt.

1. Baekelandt immigrated to the United States from Ghent that is one of the largest cities in Belgium in 1889.

2. He worked as a research chemist for a small development laboratory the Ansco Company.

3. Baekelandt's first invention he sold the rights to Kodak for $1 million was Velox photographic paper.

4. In 1909 Baekelandt developed Bakelite the first insoluble plastic material that would keep its shape.

5. Early attempts resulted in plastic materials with one disadvantage they could be melted and reshaped at relatively low temperatures.

6. Bakelite once it had been formed under heat and pressure could not be melted or reformed.

7. Bakelite the name was clearly formed from Baekelandt's own name made its inventor an even wealthier man.

8. The first plastic had to be called by its trade name since its chemical name was quite complex oxybenzylmethylene glycol anhydride.

9. Bakelite started a manufacturing revolution more than 2,000 plastic resins were developed in the forty years after 1909.

10. Bakelite was used to manufacture all manner of things pot handles, automobile parts, even false teeth.

11. What had been a technical chemist's term plastic became a household word.

12. Chester Carlson, the son of Swedish immigrants, had a very dissimilar experience with his first invention nobody wanted it.

13. Both as a law student who couldn't afford textbooks and as a young patent lawyer, Carlson grew bored with the one constant problem of law practice waiting for copies.

14. As a student remember he couldn't afford to buy textbooks Carlson copied them by hand.

15. As a lawyer in the early 1930's even then copies were made by hand, by carbon, or by the slow process of photostatic copying Carlson felt he wasted valuable time waiting while copies were being made.

16. He began experimenting his undergraduate training was in physics in the back room of a Long Island beauty salon.

17. In 1937 he invented the dry copy machine the Xerox machine.

18. RCA, IBM, General Electric all the major electronics corporations in America turned Carlson's invention down.

19. So, Carlson started the company that gave a name to this process of copying Xerox.

20. The copying machine produced so much income that Carlson became a philanthropist in his later years the inventor of the Xerox machine couldn't give money away fast enough.

Insert carets at the points in the following sentences where dashes, colons, or parentheses are required. Then write the dashes, colons, or parentheses above the lines.

Example   Peter Goldmark invented the long-playing (33 1/3 RPM) record.

21. Goldmark invented the long-playing record he loved classical music so he could listen to an entire symphony without changing records.

22. Old record albums 78 RPM held only about five minutes of music on each side.

23. Listening to classical music Brahms's Second Piano Concerto, to be precise inspired Goldmark to concentrate on improving the quality of recordings.

24. Within a very short time he finished his work on the long-playing record in 1948 Goldmark no longer had to jump to change records.

25. The new records had 250 grooves per inch the old ones had only eighty grooves per inch.

26. The 33 1/3 records had twenty minutes not five of music on each side.

27. Goldmark further improved the new records by making them from unbreakable plastic the old shellac 78's broke quite easily.

28. The new records saved space a one-foot stack of new records could hold all the music on a ten-foot stack of 78 RPM records.

29. Goldmark's other inventions are a long list in themselves color television, the sapphire phonograph needle, a lightweight tone arm, and even a knee-activated automobile horn.

30. Goldmark emigrated to the United States from Hungary other Hungarian scientists include Teller, Wigner, and Von Neumann.

35
SUPERFLUOUS INTERNAL PUNCTUATION   (24)

If you have not provided enough internal punctuation to guide your readers, they may have to go over your sentences several times to understand the meaning. But using too many internal punctuation marks can be just as confusing. If punctuation is inserted where it is not necessary, or if it separates words that belong together, readers will have to struggle to untangle your message. Punctuation should aid meaning, not detract from it. The following guidelines discuss some common instances of superfluous (unnecessary) internal punctuation:

1. Do not separate a single or final adjective from a noun.

INCORRECT	The magnificent, unchanging, ceaseless, restless, surge of the sea.
CORRECT	The magnificent, unchanging, ceaseless, restless surge of the sea.

2. Do not separate a subject from a verb unless there are intervening words that require punctuation.

INCORRECT	My car, is at the service station.
CORRECT	My car is at the service station.
	My car, which is at the service station, requires repair.

3. Do not separate a verb from a complement or an object unless there are intervening words that require punctuation.

INCORRECT	My car is, a beautiful automobile.
CORRECT	My car is a beautiful automobile.
	My car is, unlike many cars of its type, a beautiful automobile.

4. Do not separate two words or phrases that are joined by a coordinating conjunction. A comma is used to separate independent clauses joined by a coordinating conjunction; however, if constructions other than independent clauses are involved, a comma does not precede the coordinating conjunction.

INCORRECT	She was captain of the swim team, and president of the class.
CORRECT	She was captain of the swim team and president of the class.

5. It is not necessary to separate an introductory word, brief phrase, or short clause unless such a separation is necessary for clarity or emphasis.

CORRECT	In my opinion, he will not win.
OR	In my opinion he will not win.
CORRECT	In brief, bathing suits can help or hinder competitive swimmers. [The comma is necessary after *In brief* to prevent a momentary misreading.]

6. Do not separate a restrictive modifier from the main part of a sentence. (See Section 31.)

| INCORRECT | All men, who want to volunteer, report to the adjutant. |
| CORRECT | All men who want to volunteer report to the adjutant. |

7. Do not separate indirect quotations, or single words or short phrases in quotation marks, from the rest of the sentence.

INCORRECT	She said, she could go no further.
CORRECT	She said she could go no further.
INCORRECT	He was voted, "most popular teacher" by the senior class.
CORRECT	He was voted "most popular teacher" by the senior class.

8. Do not separate a preposition from its object with a comma.

| INCORRECT | I went to, the grocery store, the dry cleaners, and the shoe repair shop. |
| CORRECT | I went to the grocery store, the dry cleaners, and the shoe repair shop. |

9. Do not use a semicolon to separate a main clause from a subordinate clause, a phrase from a clause, or other parts of unequal grammatical rank.

INCORRECT	I rode my bicycle; although it was raining.
CORRECT	I rode my bicycle although it was raining.
INCORRECT	My glasses got raindrops on them; making it very hard to see clearly.
CORRECT	My glasses got raindrops on them, making it very hard to see clearly.
	My glasses got raindrops on them; I found it very hard to see clearly. [Equal rank: two main clauses]

10. Do not use a semicolon before a direct quotation or before a list.

INCORRECT	She asked; "What's for dinner?"
CORRECT	She asked, "What's for dinner?"
INCORRECT	The back yard was full of junk; an old washing machine, a pile of inner tubes, and four overflowing garbage cans.
CORRECT	The back yard was full of junk: an old washing machine, a pile of inner tubes, and four overflowing garbage cans.

11. Do not use a colon between a verb and its object or complement or between a preposition and its object—even if the objects or complements are in series (see also Section 34).

INCORRECT	The back yard also contained: three dog houses, a beat-up car, and a lot of rats.
CORRECT	The back yard also contained three dog houses, a beat-up car, and a lot of rats.
INCORRECT	Rats are: unsightly, unclean, and unhealthy.
CORRECT	Rats are unsightly, unclean, and unhealthy.
INCORRECT	The Health Department ordered the owners to: clean up the trash and spray for: rodents, mosquitoes, and roaches.
CORRECT	The Health Department ordered the owners to clean up the trash and spray for rodents, mosquitoes, and roaches.

EXERCISE 35, SUPERFLUOUS INTERNAL PUNCTUATION   (24)

Write out each of the following sentences, correcting any superfluous internal punctuation. If the sentence is correctly punctuated, write *correct* in the blank.

Example   The country of Yugoslavia, was created in 1918 out of several Balkan states.

The country of Yugoslavia was created in 1918 out of several Balkan states.

1.   These Balkan countries had previously been ruled by, the Hapsburg Empire.

_____

_____

2.   Serbia, Croatia, Montenegro, Herzegovina—all these countries, are nonexistent now.

_____

_____

3.   The first, Croatian immigrants came to America in 1698.

_____

4.   They settled in Ebenezer, Georgia; and introduced silkworm cultivation to the American South.

_____

_____

5.   Their colony was destroyed by an early, Civil War battle which occurred on the outskirts of Savannah.

_____

_____

6.   Before World War I; almost 700,000 Croatians alone emigrated to the United States.

_____

_____

7. Most of these Croatians eventually settled in large industrial centers; such as Pittsburgh, Chicago, and New York.

_____

_____

8. After World War I, and the subsequent formation of Yugoslavia, over 200,000 Croatians returned to Europe.

_____

_____

9. Michael Pupin, a Serbian inventor, developed much of the hardware, necessary for long-distance telegraph communication.

_____

_____

10. Nikola Tesla, another Yugoslav, held a patent, for the rotating-field motor; he sold his patent to George Westinghouse.

_____

_____

11. There are, an estimated million Yugoslav-Americans in the population today.

_____

_____

12. The Swiss, on the other hand, are the smallest group of foreign-born, in the United States.

_____

_____

13. The Swiss, or Swiss-Americans, comprise only 0.7 percent of the foreign-stock, population.

_____

_____

14. Swiss immigrants and their descendants, gave America Swiss chard, the leafy green vegetable; dotted Swiss, a curtain and dress fabric; and the Brown Swiss cow, a dairy breed raised primarily in New England.

_____

_____

15. In addition, Swiss immigrants have given us: Hershey's milk chocolate, the Chevrolet, Waldorf salad, Lobster Newburg, and the Lincoln Tunnel.

_____

_____

16. Two U.S. Presidents, Hoover, and Eisenhower, were of Swiss-German ancestry.

_____

_____

17. A few, scattered, Swiss were among the earliest Europeans in America.

_____

18. Diebold von Erlach, a Swiss mercenary soldier, fought, in the service of Spain, in Florida, in 1562.

_____

_____

19. The first, Swiss, colony was built near Charleston, South Carolina, in 1670.

_____

_____

20. Thirteen years later, Swiss immigrants, were invited to settle in Pennsylvania, where William Penn promised them religious freedom.

_____

_____

21. The Swiss brothers Peter and John Delmonico opened their famous restaurant in, New York in, 1827.

_____

_____

22. It was at Delmonico's, that Americans first tasted elegant European dishes.

_____

_____

23. Lobster Newburg was called Lobster Wenburg when a Delmonico descendant first prepared, it in 1876.

_____

_____

24. He named it in honor of, Ben Wenburg, who first had the idea of preparing lobster with: egg yolks, heavy cream, sherry, and cognac.

_____

_____

25. After an argument with Ben, Delmonico changed the menu so his ex-friend could claim no credit for the inspiration for Lobster Newburg.

_____

_____

36 INTERNAL PUNCTUATION REVIEW I (20-24)

Insert correct internal punctuation marks where they are needed in the following sentences.

Example Lacrosse, which is more popular in Canada than in the United States, is one of the few games native to North America.

1. The Ojibwa name for the game is *baggataway* the Ojibwa had been playing the game for hundreds of years before Europeans came to America.
2. The Indian version of lacrosse was a rough bloody test of endurance.
3. The Cherokee called lacrosse "the little brother of war" and they often arranged games between tribes.
4. As a matter of fact these games must have looked like wars.
5. There was no playing field the game simply followed the ball and the players sometimes for miles and as many as 2,000 men may have played in a single game.
6. The objective of the game which was to disable as many opponents as possible made lacrosse good combat training.
7. The single game if the Indian version could really be considered a game could last three days.
8. In 1763 to celebrate King George III's birthday the Ojibwa and Sac tribes played a demonstration game in front of the gates of a British fort in Michigan.
9. The King's birthday was in June and the French and Indian War had ended in February.
10. The British had forgotten about the hostilities between themselves and the Indians but the Indians had not forgotten.
11. As the lacrosse game went on British troops left their posts to watch.
12. The British relaxing and enjoying the spectacle even opened the gates to the fort in a gesture of peace.
13. One of history's cruelest massacres was the result the lacrosse players stormed through the gates produced hidden weapons and killed all but twenty of the British.
14. Given that horrible beginning it is hard to understand the Canadian and American fondness for lacrosse.
15. As early as 1867 lacrosse became the national sport of Canada.
16. In modern America lacrosse is played mostly by college teams mainly in the Northeast and Northwest.

17. A Canadian Dr. W. George Beers popularized the game and wrote down the rules and regulations he is known in Canada as the father of lacrosse.

18. A French priest gave the game its name he thought the lacrosse stick or weapon if you prefer looked like a Bishop's crozier *la crosse* in French.

19. Indians still play the game and in fact still supply all college teams with the only authentic equipment the equipment made on the St. Regis reservation.

20. Indian lacrosse sticks are made from a tough flexible hickory grown on the reservation.

21. It takes a year to shape wire and cure the sticks before they are shipped to lacrosse teams.

22. Most of the other sports played in America actually almost all have their origins in other countries.

23. Bowling for example was first practiced by the Germans and introduced to America by the Dutch.

24. Handball invented in Ireland in the tenth century was brought to America by the Irish in the nineteenth century.

25. Badminton was discovered in India by British soldiers the Indians who played the game called it *poona*.

26. It was introduced to England where it was popular but nameless by returning soldiers.

27. The Duke of Beaufort popularized the sport at his country home Badminton in Gloucestershire England and the name stuck.

28. The first U.S. badminton match was played in New York in 1878 but the sport did not become popular immediately.

29. It finally caught on when soldiers returning from World War I some of them had been stationed in England took up the game.

30. Even polo the sport of the rich "horsey set" has its origins like badminton in India.

Name _____ Date _____ Score _____

37 INTERNAL PUNCTUATION REVIEW II (20-24)

Expand the following core sentences, adding the constructions that are indicated in parentheses. Be sure to use correct internal punctuation.

Example The farmers hoped for a good year.

(beginning participial phrase) *Wistfully, looking at the clouds, the farmers hoped for a good year.*

(nonrestrictive appositive) *The farmers, who had borrowed heavily, hoped for a good year.*

(a brief introductory phrase) *After last spring's rain, the farmers hoped for a good year.*

(two independent clauses) *It had been a rainy spring, so the farmers hoped for a good year.*

1. The lecture had begun.

(appositive) _____

_____

(items in series) _____

_____

(two independent clauses) _____

_____

(coordinating conjunction) _____

_____

2. The lecturer reacted strangely.

(subordinate clause) _____

_____

195

(beginning participial phrase) _____

_____

(nonrestrictive element) _____

_____

(interrupting expression) _____

_____

3. The audience was spellbound.

    (expressions in series requiring commas) _____

_____

    (expressions in series requiring semicolons) _____

_____

    (a date and an address) _____

_____

    (short final summary) _____

_____

4. He was a man for all seasons.

    (long introductory expression) _____

_____

    (nonrestrictive modifier) _____

_____

    (long final appositive) _____

_____

    (two independent clauses) _____

_____

5. He became a renowned inventor.

    (restrictive modifier) _____

_____

(abrupt interruption of the sentence) _____

_____

(items in series requiring no punctuation within items) _____

_____

6.   I listened carefully.

(beginning participial phrase) _____

_____

(brief introductory phrase) _____

_____

(two independent clauses) _____

_____

7.   She seems to know her material.

(a date) _____

_____

(long introductory expression) _____

_____

(an appositive) _____

_____

8.   Margaret likes all kinds of food.

(two independent clauses) _____

_____

(coordinating conjunction) _____

_____

(subordinate clause) _____

_____

9.   This car doesn't suit my needs.

(nonrestrictive modifier) _____

_____

(subordinate clause) _____

_____

(two independent clauses) _____

_____

(items in series requiring no punctuation within items) _____

_____

_____

(items in series requiring punctuation with semicolons) _____

_____

_____

10. The next lecture is tomorrow.

(brief introductory phrase) _____

_____

(two independent clauses) _____

_____

(subordinate clause) _____

_____

38

QUOTATION MARKS, BRACKETS, ELLIPSIS AND SLASH MARKS (25–26)

Quotation marks signal to the reader that you are writing someone else's words rather than your own. If you decide to insert your own words within a quotation, those words are set off with brackets to let the reader know they are not part of the original, quoted material. If you omit any of the quoted words, ellipsis marks are used to indicate the omission. These three types of punctuation marks enable the reader to distinguish between your words and those of another source.

Double quotation marks are used to enclose a direct quotation from either a written or a spoken source. Commas or periods that occur at the end of the quoted matter are always placed within the quotation marks. Colons and semicolons are always placed outside, after the quotation marks.

> She answered very shortly, "I don't want to."
>
> The boys' leader replied, "The driver of the yellow car was driving recklessly," and the others in the group agreed with him.
>
> He answered very shortly, "I don't want to"; this was not the answer we had expected.
>
> She said, "There are several reasons for my actions": One was that she was tired, a second was that she was bored, and a third was that she didn't know the guest of honor.

A dash, question mark, or exclamation point belongs inside the quotation marks when it applies only to the quotation; it belongs outside the quotation marks when it applies to the entire statement.

> She asked, "When may I see you again?"   Did she say, "I'll probably see you again"?

A comma is used to separate an opening quotation from the rest of the sentence unless the quotation ends in an exclamation point or a question mark.

> "This is the book I'm looking for," he said.
>
> "Drat it!" he roared.
>
> "When do we leave?" she asked.

When a quotation is broken to designate the speaker, a comma should be used after the first part of the quotation. The quotation following the interrupting construction should be punctuated as would any phrase or clause.

> "I don't believe," said Ms. Wicket, "that I understand you."
>
> "I don't believe it," said Ms. Wicket. "There are just too many reasons why it can't be true."
>
> "I don't believe it," said Ms. Wicket; "you really can't mean it."

Although a comma ordinarily follows the designation of the speaker, as the foregoing examples show, the comma may be omitted if the quotation is grammatically closely related. When the quotation is fairly long or formally introduced, a colon may precede it.

CLOSELY RELATED: NO PUNCTUATION	He growled "Now you just wait a minute" and barred the door.
	I remember the words "Four score and seven years ago," but I can't remember the rest of the speech.
FORMAL INTRODUCTION: COLON	My mother's disciplinary lectures always began: "When I was your age, I had funny notions, too. But I outgrew them."

Quotation marks are used to set off poems and song titles and also to indicate titles of articles, short stories, and parts of longer works.

"The Death of the Hired Man" is one of Robert Frost's best poems.
Glenn Miller's theme song was "Moonlight Serenade."

You can use quotation marks to set off words in a special sense, but do not use them around common nicknames, slang, colloquialisms, trite expressions, or for emphasis or apology. If a word is appropriate, it will stand on its own.

This is what I call a "foppish" metaphor.
"Silly" means "stupid" or "foolish," according to the dictionary.

BUT NOT In these supposedly "modern" times, I feel "out of it."

When words ordinarily placed within quotation marks appear within another quotation, use single quotation marks to set them off. Single quotation marks should never be used for anything but a quotation within a quotation.

She told the class, "Please read 'The Tell-Tale Heart' for Monday."

BUT NOT I said, 'Where did you put my notebook?'

A prose quotation more than four lines long should be displayed—that is, set off from your own words with each line indented from the left margin. A displayed quotation does not take quotation marks at its opening and close; setting it off serves to signal the reader that it is a quotation. If quotation marks occur within material you intend to use as a displayed quotation, include them as they appear in the original material.

As Hayes says in *The Crane Papers*:
Part of the distinctly American tradition is a belief in the New World. America was the land fondly dreamed of as the New Eden, a second chance for men and women to begin again on virgin shores. They could build a new civilization— and this time do it right. It is this tradition that the poet Hart Crane inherits and expounds in his poem "The Bridge" (254).

Quoted poetry and song lyrics should be enclosed in quotation marks and run into the text if three or fewer lines are being quoted. Indicate the end of a run-in line of poetry with a **slash mark** (/).

Crane is sure unity is possible. He writes, "The stars have grooved our eyes with old persuasions / O, upward from the dead."

If you are quoting more than three lines of poetry, display them. Like displayed quotations of prose, displayed quotations of poetry do not take quotation marks at opening and close unless they occur in the original. Displayed lines of poetry are not run on and consequently do not need slash marks.

Use **brackets** to set off editorial remarks in quoted material and to enclose *sic* ("thus it is") to indicate that a mistake in a quotation is that of the original writer and not that of the quoter.

"He [Tennyson] was poet laureate of England for several years."
The dispatch continued: "It was a climatic [*sic*] battle. Everyone knows the end is near."

Ellipsis marks (three spaced periods) show you have deliberately omitted a word or words from the material you are quoting. If you omit words at the end of a quotation, use four periods: the first is the usual sentence period, and the last three are the ellipses. The closing quotation mark encloses all the periods.

"Part of the distinctly American tradition is a belief in the New World. America was . . . the New Eden . . . a second chance to begin again. . . ."

EXERCISE 38-1, QUOTATION MARKS   (25)

Rewrite the following indirect quotations as direct quotations.

Example   Janice said that she was happy about the meeting.

Janice said, "I am happy about the meeting."

1. She told us that today's speaker was from the Board for Certification of Genealogists.

_____

2. The speaker indicated that professional genealogists will research your family's background for a fee.

_____

3. Did he ask how we can find out about these people?

_____

4. [Make a split quotation out of the following.] Yes, the board, according to the speaker, will mail a list to anyone who's interested.

_____

5. One of the students remarked that the Board provides a valuable service.

_____

6. She said that she had heard of many people who had been victimized by companies claiming to do genealogical research.

_____

7. The speaker answered that the Certification Board exists to help people avoid unscrupulous researchers like those.

_____

8. Many people, according to the lecture, still perform their own research.

_____

9. He asked the lecturer what the best way to get started was.

_____

10. [Make a split quotation out of the following.] There are, he was told by the speaker, many books, libraries, and other sources of information that should help you.

_____

Rewrite the following sentences to punctuate each correctly. In addition to other changes, be sure to capitalize where necessary.

Example   Do you know what I think she asked I think I'll start my research at home.

"Do you know what I think?" she asked. "I
think I'll start my research at home."

11. That way Marge said all I'll need are a pen and some paper.

_____

12. There was an article entitled Tracing Your Ancestry in this morning's paper Marge said.

_____

13. The first thing you should do said Professor House is talk to your relatives.

_____

14. You may be surprised she said sometimes tracing your ancestry is easier than you thought.

_____

15. Most families keep wills diaries birth and marriage certificates she said.

_____

16. Since 1820 Professor House added records of passengers traveling by ship have been kept in every major port.

_____

17. It has long been customary in many families Marge said to keep an informal genealogy in the family Bible.

_____

18. Yes the speaker said those can be invaluable.

_____

19. It is relatively easy said Marge to track down church and government records in the United States.

_____

20. Parish records in other countries also record births deaths and marriages Ernest said but very few people really have to travel abroad to consult them.

_____

EXERCISE 38-2, QUOTATION MARKS, BRACKETS, ELLIPSIS AND SLASH MARKS   (25-26)

Punctuate the following sentences by inserting punctuation marks where they are necessary. Circle any letters that should be capitalized. If a sentence is correct, write *C* after it.

Example   "Here we are, the librarian said. (T)his is the records section."

1. We are taking a course we explained that requires us to use these records.
2. This week we're studying the chapter Getting Started in *A Basic Course in Genealogy* by D. E. Gardner.
3. Our instructor claims that over a million people actively pursue genealogical research.
4. Mr. Bole stated categorically no specific education is required to perform this kind of research.
5. Are you sure asked Liza.
6. The text I had read as follows correspondent sic courses are helpful.
7. I know I said but no courses or licenses are required just to use the material.
8. Surely Liza said training will make you a better researcher.
9. Who wrote the chapter Public Records in *Tracing Your Civil War Ancestor*?
10. Our instructor said authoritatively all researchers hope to find a royal ancestor.
11. I know everyone might enjoy that but I think he may be overstating his case Alex maintained.
12. The dictionary says that the word genealogy doesn't mean the same as ancestry.
13. I'm not interested in finding a noble ancestor aren't there other things to be discovered asked Judy.
14. One saying that turns out to be good advice for a genealogist is he who hesitates is lost.
15. Many sources of information Judy informed us are really quite permanent.
16. She also told us that board-certified genealogists are in demand at many institutions.
17. A professional genealogist Mr. Bole said also maintains record collections.
18. But he continued professional genealogists rarely started as amateurs.
19. Many people in this field Bole said are trained first as librarians or archivists.
20. However he explained literally thousands of publications are designed to aid the amateur.

Using the verse printed here, write two paragraphs. In the first paragraph show (1) how to quote three lines or less of poetry and (2) how to use ellipsis marks to show the omission of word(s) from a quotation. In the second paragraph, show (1) how to quote more than three lines of poetry and (2) how to insert editorial remarks into quoted material. For your editorial remarks, you might want to indicate that the author, Emma Lazarus, was a Jewish poet who donated her sonnet, from which these lines are taken, at a fund-raising auction for the Statue of Liberty in 1883. These words are, of course, engraved on a plaque inside the statue's pedestal.

> Give me your tired, your poor
> Your huddled masses yearning to breathe free
> The wretched refuse of your teeming shore,
> Send these, the homeless, tempest-tossed, to me;
> I lift my lamp beside the golden door.

(Paragraph 1) _____

_____

_____

_____

_____

_____

_____

_____

(Paragraph 2) _____

_____

_____

_____

_____

_____

_____

_____

_____

39
ITALICS   (27)

Word punctuation signals that a word has a special use or particular grammatical function. Italics, capitals, apostrophes, and hyphens are the punctuation marks used to signal special word uses and functions. For example, when you write a word with an apostrophe, you are signaling that the word is either a possessive form or a contraction because convention has led readers to recognize possessives and contractions by means of the apostrophe.

Italics are letters sloped to the right in print. In handwritten or typewritten manuscripts, italics are indicated by underlining. This word punctuation is used for titles of books, newspapers, magazines and journals, computer programs, and all works that are published separately—that is, not published as part of another work.

An item such as a short story, article, chapter, or poem that is published as part of a larger work is set off by quotation marks (see Section 38). For example, John Milton's lengthy poem about creation and the fall of Adam and Eve is punctuated *Paradise Lost* when it appears as a separate publication; it is punctuated "Paradise Lost" when it appears in the collection *John Milton: Complete Poems and Major Prose.*

Be sure to italicize the word *The* only if it is actually part of a specific title:

> *The New York Times*

BUT

> the *Reader's Digest*

The names of plays, movies, record albums and tapes, television or radio programs, and works of art, as well as the names of ships and aircraft, are italicized.

Hamlet	*Superman II*
Hill Street Blues	the *U.S.S. Nimitz*
Hard Day's Night	the *Concorde*

Italics are used to set off foreign words and expressions that have not yet been adopted into English. They are also used to indicate letters, words, and numbers used as words. Quotation marks are also used to set off words used in a special sense (Section 38), but if your subject requires you to refer to words as words frequently, italics are the more scholarly convention. Finally, italics can be used to give special stress to a word. However, don't overuse italics for stress or emphasis. Otherwise, your writing will seem shrill and immature sounding.

He graduated *magna cum laude.*

I cannot distinguish your *n*'s from your *u*'s.

The word *empathy* does not mean the same as *sympathy.*

That was *her* suggestion, not mine.

EXERCISE 39, ITALICS (27)

In the following sentences, indicate by underlining the words or expressions that should be italicized.

Example Was the <u>Mayflower</u> the first ship to visit American shores?

1. Anyone doing historical research should watch his or her p's and q's.
2. The television miniseries Centennial was very well researched.
3. In the word receive does the i go before or after the second e?
4. The word algebra is borrowed from Arabic.
5. So are alcohol and assassin.
6. Caviar and shish kebab are words English borrowed from Turkish.
7. Sometimes the a in shish kebab is replaced by an o.
8. The word robot comes from the Czech word for work.
9. Robot was first used in Karel Capek's play, R.U.R., in 1923.
10. The Oxford English Dictionary says the word jazz is of Black origin.
11. Webster's New International says the word is a Creole word from West Africa.
12. Up until the 1880's Black was considered a slave term; Blacks used the word colored to refer to their race.
13. By 1919, The Negro Year Book stated that the word Negro was acquiring a dignity it had previously lacked.
14. On June 7, 1930, The New York Times announced that in the future the n in Negro would be capitalized.
15. In 1933 the U.S. Government Printing Office began to capitalize Negro.
16. Many people, including leaders such as W.E.B. DuBois and Adam Clayton Powell, continued to use the word Black.
17. DuBois wrote The Souls of Black Folk and Black Folk Then and Now.
18. In 1967, the Amsterdam News, the leading Black newspaper, announced that its writers would no longer use the word Negro.
19. Today the publishing industry uses Black almost exclusively, often capitalizing the word in the same manner as references to other racial and ethnic groups such as Indian, Chicano, or Caucasian.
20. Most book indexes use the word Black as a heading rather than Negro or Afro-American.

Write sentences including the information called for in parentheses. Be sure to use correct word punctuation.

Example   (word used as word and letter used as word) _It is difficult to remember the second a in Parliament._

21.   (title of magazine and title of magazine article) _____

_____

_____

22.   (title of work of art and word punctuated for emphasis) _____

_____

_____

23.   (title of book and title of short story or poem) _____

_____

_____

24.   (title of movie, television program, or play) _____

_____

_____

25.   (foreign expression or word used as word) _____

_____

_____

26.   (title of record album or computer program) _____

_____

_____

40
CAPITALS (28)

A century or more ago, writers commonly capitalized almost all nouns. Today conventions governing capitalization have changed so that we capitalize only proper nouns, their derivatives and abbreviations, and common nouns used as part of proper nouns. A proper noun is one that names a particular person, place, or thing rather than a general category: *Chrysler* versus *car*.

We also always capitalize the first word of a sentence or a line of poetry as well as the pronoun *I* and the interjection *O*.

The following guidelines illustrate uses of capitals for categories of proper nouns:

1. Specific persons, races, nationalities, languages, ethnic or religious groups.

Robert	African	Chicanos	Gypsies
Liz	Cuban	Quakers	Eskimos
Thomas G. Brown	Chinese	Moslems	French

2. Specific places.

Miami	Iceland	Rockefeller Center	Saturn
Delaware	Lake Michigan	Nile River	U.S.S.R.

3. Specific organizations (including widely used abbreviations), historical events, and documents.

Knights of Columbus	NAACP
World War II	Declaration of Independence
Gray Panthers	New York Philharmonic Orchestra

4. Days of the week, months, holidays.

Monday	Christmas	Ramadan
May	Passover	Memorial Day

5. Sacred religious terms.

the Virgin Mary	Allah	the Torah
the Savior	the Creation	Mass

6. Titles of books, plays, magazines, newspapers, articles, and poems. Capitalize the first word and all other words except articles, conjunctions, and prepositions of fewer than five letters.

Mutiny on the Bounty	*Newsweek*	*The Wall Street Journal*
Fiddler on the Roof	*King Lear*	*Ms.*

7. Titles when they precede a proper noun.

President Reagan	Mr. John Doe	the Reverend Paul Mills
General Bradley	Dr. Hilda Vail	Treasurer Jean Ritchie

8. Common nouns used as part of a proper name.

Fifth Street	Yale University	First National Bank
Atlantic Ocean	Shedd Aquarium	Exxon Corporation

Avoid unnecessary capitalization. The following items are usually *not* capitalized:

1. Directions. *North, east, south,* and *west* are capitalized only when they occur at the beginning of a sentence or when they refer to specific geographical locations.

He drove south for ten miles.   the Middle East
He liked the Deep South.   the northern states

2. Seasons. *Fall, autumn, winter, spring,* and *summer* are not capitalized.

3. Family Relationships. Capitalize nouns indicating family relationships only when they are used as names or titles or in combination with proper names.

I hoped to hear from Mother soon.   My sister Harriett is a lawyer.
I have great regard for my mother.   I received a letter from Uncle Carl.

4. Common nouns and adjectives used in place of proper nouns and adjectives.

| | He graduated from high school. |
| BUT | He graduated from Cedar Falls High School. |

| | He traveled by car. |
| BUT | He traveled by Delta Airlines. |

| | She enjoyed sociology and statistics. |
| BUT | She registered for Sociology 235 and Mathematics 201, Statistical Analysis. |

Sometimes it is difficult to decide whether a word is a proper noun or a common noun. For example, if you write *The wedding was held at a Lutheran church.*, should *church* be capitalized or not? In this case, no, it should not be capitalized. However, if you write *The wedding was held at the Lutheran Church.*, you need to capitalize *Church*. In the first instance, the word *church* is a general term (common noun) rather than a reference to a specific church (proper noun), as is the case in the second instance. It may help you to think of proper nouns as being like formal titles or given names.

One indicator to help you decide whether or not to capitalize is the article used with a word. If the article is *a* or *an,* the word is probably a common noun: *a board of directors.* Sometimes, but by no means always, the article *the* will indicate that a word is a proper noun: *the Board of Directors of General Motors.* Your best bet is to determine if a word belongs to a collective category or if it refers to a "titled" person, place, or thing.

A second issue is whether or not to capitalize nouns that refer to and are the same as proper nouns—for example, *The Mulberry City Council met Tuesday, and the council voted to deny the rezoning request.* When the complete title of a person, place, or thing is not used, ordinarily the repeated words are treated as common nouns (as in category 4 under "Unnecessary Capitalization"). Sometimes, however, the shortened form of a proper noun will be capitalized to signify respect, as in *The Reverend Joseph West will deliver Sunday's sermon; the Reverend is a well-known member of the clergy.* Of course titles shortened to just proper names are always capitalized: *Visit Custom Upholstery Company for your upholstery needs because Custom guarantees satisfaction,* not . . . *because custom guarantees satisfaction.* The following sentences provide further illustrations of capitalization:

He traveled by Delta Airlines because, he said, the airline's staff was courteous and Delta flights are usually on time.
My favorite lake is Lake Louise.
The school board president attended a meeting of the National Association of Public School Boards.
Columbiana County is a county in eastern Ohio.

EXERCISE 40, CAPITALS   (28)

Rewrite the following sentences, correcting all errors in capitalization.

Example   Many native north american plant and animal names were borrowed by english from indian languages.

Many native North American plant and animal names are borrowed by English from Indian languages.

1.   There are over 500 indian words in english now.

_____

2.   The algonquians of the eastern woodlands provided the most.

_____

3.   Some words, like *chile* and *tomato,* were borrowed from mexican indians.

_____

4.   Other words came directly from spanish.

_____

5.   The carib indians of the west indies used open-pit fires to preserve meat.

_____

6.   The spanish word for this outdoor cooking is *barbacoa.*

_____

7.   Even george washington enjoyed barbecues.

_____

8.   His diary entry for september 18, 1773, notes that he attended a barbecue.

_____

9.   The american version of english began to diverge from the british version as soon as the pilgrims stepped off the *mayflower.*

_____

10. In 1783, noah webster published the *american spelling book* and in 1806 he published his *compendious dictionary of the english language.*

___

11. What would halloween or the u.s. senate be without the dutch words *spook* and *filibuster?*

___

12. American english borrowed words from every european language every new group of immigrants brought to america.

___

13. Even asian and african languages have been raided for their useful vocabulary.

___

14. The hooligans, as the english tell the story, were an irish family living in london.

___

15. The word *boycott* is formed from the name of captain charles boycott, a retired british officer whose tenants refused to work for him.

___

___

16. Most of the french words in american english came by way of the louisiana french.

___

17. The name of the famous violin maker, stradivarius, is one of the italian words added to our language.

___

18. The word *coach,* without which the story of cinderella could not be told, is a reference to the village of kocs in hungary, where the coach was invented.

___

___

19. Other than english, the languages most commonly claimed as primary languages by americans were spanish, german, and italian.

___

20. The menderes river, which twists and turns throughout western turkey, gave english the verb *meander.*

___

41
APOSTROPHES AND HYPHENS   (29–30)

APOSTROPHES

An **apostrophe** signals the possessive case of nouns and indefinite pronouns. The following guidelines illustrate its use in forming the possessive case:

1. Words not ending in *s* add an apostrophe and *s* to form the possessive.

the man's suitcase   the women's suitcases

2. Singular words ending in *s* add an apostrophe and *s* unless the second *s* makes pronunciation difficult.

James's bike   Euripides' plays

3. Plural words ending in *s* add only the apostrophe.

the dogs' food   the babies' shoes   the Browns' mailbox

4. With compounds, only the last word is made possessive.

my father-in-law's chair   someone else's locker

5. With nouns of joint possession, only the last noun is made possessive.

George and John's bedroom

6. With nouns of individual possession, both nouns are made possessives.

Beth's and Bart's swimsuits

Do not use an apostrophe with the possessive form of personal pronouns *his, hers, its, ours, yours, theirs,* and *whose.*

An apostrophe indicates the omission of a letter or number.

you are	you're
cannot	can't
it is	it's
would not	wouldn't
of the clock	o'clock
class of 1978	class of '78

An apostrophe is also used to form the plurals of letters, numbers, and words used as words. Note that these are the *only* instances in which apostrophes are used in forming plurals. Apostrophes are *never* used to form the plurals of proper names or other nouns.

Mind your *p's* and *q's.*
The *'30's* were called the Jazz Age.
Don't put too many *and's* in one sentence.

HYPHENS

The **hyphen** has two different uses. It is used to indicate that a word is continued from one line to the next (see "Syllabication," Section 27), and it is used to punctuate compound words. The following guidelines give the conventions for using hyphens in compound words:

1. To form compound words that are not accepted as single words. Since there is no general rule that can be applied to such compounds, the best way to determine whether a compound word is hyphenated is to consult the dictionary.

2. To join two or more words serving as a single adjective before a noun.

a well-liked person   an ill-fitting suit

Omit the hyphen when the first word is an adverb ending in *-ly*.

a rapidly fired pistol   a slowly sinking ship

Do not hyphenate adjectives that follow the verb as predicate adjectives.

	They were well-known actors.
BUT	The actors were well known.

3. To avoid an awkward union of letters such as *bell-like*.

4. To form compound numbers from twenty-one through ninety-nine and to designate spelled-out fractions.

twenty-two   three-fourths

5. In conjunction with prefixes *self-*, *all-*, and *ex-*, and the suffix *-elect*.

self-confidence	all-important	ex-President Carter
vice president-elect	Governor-elect Orr	ex-champion

EXERCISE 41-1, APOSTROPHES   (29)

In the blanks, write the singular possessive for the following nouns.

Example   *lioness*   _lioness's_

1. *Jim*   _____   2. *Kansas*   _____

3. *Honda*   _____   4. *Jane*   _____

5. *anyone*   _____   6. *nobody*   _____

7. *business*   _____   8. *Janis*   _____

9. *Moses*   _____   10. *Pericles*   _____

In the appropriate blanks, write the singular possessives and the plural possessives for the following nouns.

		Singular	*Plural*
Example	*class*	_Class's_	_Classes'_
11.	*sheep*		
12.	*cat*		
13.	*cash*		
14.	*mother-in-law*		
15.	*chief*		
16.	*waiter*		
17.	*acrobat*		
18.	*night*		
19.	*bus*		
20.	*lady*		
21.	*treasurer*		

		Singular	Plural
22.	football	_____	_____
23.	man	_____	_____
24.	life	_____	_____
25.	town	_____	_____
26.	match	_____	_____
27.	baby	_____	_____
28.	file	_____	_____
29.	Jones	_____	_____
30.	camera	_____	_____
31.	watch	_____	_____
32.	neck	_____	_____
33.	statue	_____	_____
34.	hero	_____	_____
35.	city	_____	_____
36.	woman	_____	_____
37.	secretary	_____	_____
38.	car	_____	_____
39.	jazz	_____	_____
40.	pie	_____	_____

Form the correct contractions for the following words.

Example   we have   _*we've*_

41.	I will	_____	42.	they are	_____
43.	do not	_____	44.	I am	_____
45.	were not	_____	46.	you are	_____
47.	it is	_____	48.	they will	_____
49.	was not	_____	50.	who is	_____

216

EXERCISE 41-2, APOSTROPHES AND HYPHENS   (29-30)

Insert apostrophes, 's, and hyphens where they are needed in the following sentences.

Example   Some of America's most famous works of literature were written by
immigrants or their descendants.

1.   Some of the best loved works in literature and in journalism have been written by or
for ethnic Americans.

2.   Ted Morgan is the "Americanized" name of a French American author.

3.   Morgans original name was Sanche de Gramont.

4.   When Morgan became an American, he decided that having a French aristocrats name
was no longer appropriate.

5.   He formed his new name from his old names letters.

6.   William Peter Blatty is a Lebanese immigrants youngest child.

7.   Blattys first book after his success was about his Lebanese family.

8.   His best seller, which enabled him to do this, was *The Exorcist.*

9.   When the movie version opened, it attracted record breaking crowds.

10. John Dos Passos was the son of a well to do lawyer, himself the son of an immigrant
Portuguese shoemaker.

11. Dos Passos trilogy, *U.S.A.,* is considered by some to be the best American novel.

12. In 1959, when he might have been considered an ex novelist, Dos Passos received
a patent for a toy pistol which blew bubbles.

13. Will Durant was a famed historian of French Canadian ancestry.

14. The first six volumes of Durants *Story of Civilization* are his work alone; he and his
wife collaborated on the rest of the volumes.

15. The Durants work is a monumental history and a great literary achievement.

16. Not many people know that Kahlil Gibran was actually a Lebanese American.

17. Gibrans most famous book, *The Prophet,* was written after he had lived in Boston
for twenty eight years.

18. Gibran had emigrated to Boston in the 1890s.

19. *The Prophet* is one of the best sellers of all time.

20. With no advertising except word of mouth it has caused a never ending Gibran cult.

21. Ironically, considering her last name, Marilyn Frenchs family is of Polish ancestry.

22. Isaac Asimov is the son of Russian Jewish immigrants who lived in Brooklyn.

23. Asimov is an ex chemist who writes science fiction and science nonfiction.
24. By the late 1970s, Asimov had published over 200 books.
25. Jerzy Kosinski is a Polish born novelist whose work is highly regarded.
26. Kosinski was the first foreign born writer to receive the National Book Award.
27. H. L. Menckens satire and social criticism made him famous.
28. This "lighter" work made him famous in the 1920s.
29. His most lasting contribution, however, was his three volume language study, *The American Language.*
30. Mencken, whose father was a German American businessman, began his career in journalism on Baltimores leading paper, the *Sun.*

42 PUNCTUATION REVIEW (19–30)

Revise the following sentences, providing necessary end, internal, and word punctuation. Also correct any errors in capitalization and italicization.

Example   Did you know that Maria Tallchief the ballerina is an Osage indian

Did you know that Maria Tallchief, the ballerina, is an Osage Indian?

1. Isn't Dan Rather the great grandson of an Indian woman

2. I wonder whether Burt Reynolds has a Cherokee grandmother

3. Donald Duncan modified an old design for the yo-yo then he introduced it to America as a childrens toy

4. Although philippine hunters used the yo-yo as a weapon they might still recognize the modern version

5. Used since the sixteenth century the Philippine yo-yo was a long rope with heavy weights at each end

6. When it was correctly thrown the yo-yo caught an animal around the neck or legs

7. Fleeing their homeland many Cubans were airlifted to America between 1965 and 1973

8. Many of these immigrants were professional people well educated and highly skilled

9. Juanita Castro Fidel Castros avidly anticommunist sister arrived in 1964

10. She has she says "nothing to discuss" with her brother

---

11. The most recent Cuban immigrants those immigrating in 1980 left Cuba by boat

---

12. These boats many of them small and overloaded ferried refugees on a voyage that was often extremely dangerous

---

---

13. The U.S. government which at first considered the refugees to be illegal aliens granted them political asylum

---

---

14. The earliest Cuban immigrants who arrived in the 1830s settled in Miami Tampa and other cities in southern Florida

---

---

15. Because french culture was dominant for centuries in Europe french cooking has been admired and imitated all over the world

---

---

16. French cooking schools have been attended by many cooks including the star of televisions The French Chef Julia Child Diana the Princess of Wales and middle class housewives from Kansas and new jersey

---

---

17. Many french words that are associated with food have been borrowed into english some of these words that refer particularly to elegant food are gourmet menu and cuisine

---

---

18. We have also borrowed the words hors d'oeuvre an appetizer entrée the main course and even dessert which is formed from an old French word that meant "clear the table"

_____

_____

_____

19. Few people remember that the french came to america before the english the first french colony was at Parris Island now in South Carolina

_____

_____

20. The colony survived two years it had to be abandoned in 1564

_____

21. Many french immigrants were Huguenots who were fleeing religious persecution they came to america from England Holland or Germany

_____

_____

22. One French Huguenot Priscilla Molines arrived on the Mayflower

_____

23. In Longfellows poem The Courtship of Miles Standish she is a character named Priscilla Mullins

_____

_____

24. The U.S. government purchased the Louisiana Territory in 1803 consequently the French living there automatically became U.S. citizens

_____

_____

25. Many patriots were of French ancestry including John Jay the Marquis de Lafayette who commanded American troops during the american revolution and of course Paul Revere

_____

_____

_____

26. Vincennes, Indiana Maine Vermont and Lake Champlain all these were named by French explorers

_____

27. Americans have always loved French things even French names

_____

28. We prefer perfumes with French names Arpege, Chanel

_____

29. We like clothing with the names of French designers Cardin St. Laurent Sasson sewn on

_____

30. Apparently a French name suggests high style sophistication and sex appeal

_____

Insert punctuation where it is needed in the following sentences. (Use a pen or pencil that writes in a color other than black.)

31. Popcorn is a native American food apparently it was brought to the first Thanksgiving by the Indians
32. F. W. Rueckheim a German American inventor experimented with popcorn trying to make it even more popular
33. By adding sugar syrup and peanuts Rueckheim created a new candy which he called Cracker Jack
34. It was first offered for sale in the late 1800s
35. Cracker Jack is made even today according to Rueckheims original recipe
36. Rueckheim developed the idea of putting a prize in each box and he coined the Cracker Jack advertising slogan "The more you eat the more you want"
37. Doesnt everybody paw through the box to find the prize first
38. The sailor boy on the box Jack was modeled after Rueckheims grandson Jack who died at the age of eight
39. Another German American horticulturist Orville Redenbacher experimented for years with hybrid popcorn seeds
40. He turned popcorn growing into a science but he was able to grow a superior popcorn
41. Redenbacher's hybrid makes a larger lighter fluffier kernel when it is popped
42. His "gourmet" popping corn as he calls it has made him rich
43. Americans eat almost 400 million pounds of popcorn every year that figure works out to about two pounds per person
44. Almost half the total consumed 200 million pounds is cooked at home
45. Popcorn in all its forms eaten plain strung on a string coated with syrup or pressed into syrup-covered balls has become a part of many of America's festive occasions

43

EFFECTIVE SENTENCES: COORDINATION AND SUBORDINATION (31)

Sections 6 through 8 on phrases, clauses, and sentence types introduced some ideas we now need to review. As you discovered in those earlier sections, phrases enable a writer to elaborate, amplify, and qualify the information provided in the core of the sentence—in the simple subject and simple predicate. Clauses enable a writer to combine several related ideas into one sentence. Using coordination and subordination, a writer can express related thoughts in one sentence, instead of having to write a separate sentence for each thought. By using different types of sentence patterns, a writer can achieve greater sentence variety and emphasis.

In the next four sections, we explore these techniques in detail, techniques that can give you more control over your writing and thus improve your ability to express your meaning in interesting and effective ways.

COORDINATION

The simplest kind of coordination involves joining words, phrases, or clauses with the coordinating conjunctions *and, but, or, nor, for, so,* and *yet.* Coordination establishes relationships of approximately equal rank or importance between ideas. Coordination also allows you to condense and compress information. Notice how the information in the following series of sentences is compressed and smoothed when it is combined into one sentence using coordinating conjunctions:

> Peas are harvested in the spring. They cannot tolerate hot weather. Pumpkins need hot weather to mature. They are harvested in the fall.

> Peas cannot tolerate hot weather *and* are harvested in the spring, *but* pumpkins need hot weather to mature *and* are harvested in the fall. [Two independent clauses coordinated by the conjunction *but,* showing contrast; verbs within clauses coordinated by the conjunction *and.*]

You have probably also noticed that the coordinated sentence makes more sense than the four separate sentences—because the relationships among ideas have been clearly expressed by the conjunctions, rather than left for the reader to figure out.

In addition to the coordinating conjunctions previously mentioned, parts of sentences can be joined by correlative conjunctions—coordinating conjunctions that work in pairs—such as *both . . . and, either . . . or, neither . . . nor, not . . . but, not only . . . but also.* For example: *I **not only** planted peas **but also** spread mulch around the strawberries.*

Conjunctive adverbs such as *however, nevertheless, therefore,* and *furthermore* do not connect words, phrases, and clauses but, when used with a semicolon, link whole sentences: *A late frost killed the tender seedlings; **therefore,** we will have to replant the peas this weekend.*

SUBORDINATION

Another effective method of combining and relating ideas is subordination. Coordination will not provide the focus you need if, for example, two ideas are not of equal importance or one depends on the other for its meaning. Consider the following pair of sentences:

IDEAS COORDINATED	The rain ended, *and* the sun came out.
IDEAS SUBORDINATED	*When* the rain ended, the sun came out.

In the first sentence the two events are given equal importance and rank by the coordinating conjunction *and*. The second sentence, however, expresses a more specific relationship, a time relationship, which establishes the dependence of one event upon the other: first the rain ended; then the sun came out.

If you combine too many ideas—or illogically combine ideas—with coordinating conjunctions, your writing will reflect what is known as "primer style," parts of sentences monotonously and unemphatically connected by *and* or *but*: *The rain ended, and the sun came out, and we went back to the garden, but it was too muddy to work.*

Another form of primer style is successive, short, choppy sentences: *The ground was soaked. Everything had turned to mud. The water ran down the gutters. Children played in the puddles.*

Subordinating details, qualifications, and ideas of lesser importance indicates your focus to the reader. Subordinating conjunctions include *although, because, if, when, since, before, unless,* and *after,* as well as the relative pronouns *who, which,* and *that* (see Section 7 for a more complete list).

Remember that because a subordinate clause is of lesser importance, the information in it should not contain your main idea. The main idea belongs in the main clause. You do not want to mislead your reader by illogically burying the most important idea in a dependent clause.

ILLOGICAL SUBORDINATION OF MAIN IDEA	When the sun came out, the storm ended.
LOGICAL SUBORDINATION OF QUALIFYING IDEA	When the storm ended, the sun came out.

In many cases, of course, only you know for sure which idea is your primary focus and which is a modifier. The following examples show how subordination can affect meaning by changing the focus in the same collection of information:

Because they raise gardens, many people save money on food bills.
[Stresses saving money in main clause]

Many people raise gardens because doing so saves money on food bills.
[Stresses raising a garden in main clause]

APPOSITIVES, PARTICIPIAL PHRASES,
AND ABSOLUTE PHRASES

Besides subordinate clauses, three other types of constructions can be used to subordinate ideas and economically add details to core sentences.

An **appositive** is a word or phrase that renames or further identifies another word, usually a noun or pronoun. In the sentence *The potato, a tuber, is characterized by its swollen underground stem.,* the words *a tuber* are the appositive renaming *potato*. An appositive can often be substituted for a subordinate clause or even several subordinate clauses or sentences, thus providing a more streamlined way of supplying details. Notice how the following examples proceed from separate ideas in separate primer-style sentences, to sentences combined using clauses, to sentences combined using an appositive:

PRIMER-STYLE SEPARATE SENTENCES	The potato is a tuber. A tuber is characterized by a swollen underground stem.
SENTENCES COMBINED WITH CLAUSE	The potato is a tuber *that is characterized by a swollen underground stem.*
SENTENCES COMBINED WITH AN APPOSITIVE	The potato, *a tuber,* is characterized by a swollen underground stem.

A **participle** is a verb form ending in *-ing* (present participle: *moving, eating, sleeping*), ending in *-ed* or *-en,* or having another irregular form (past participle: *moved, eaten, slept*). Participles, together with their objects and modifiers forming participial phrases, can function as adjectives. They offer another alternative to subordinate clauses for combining ideas in sentences, as the following examples show:

SEPARATE SENTENCES	The potato was probably first grown in the Andes region of South America. It was transported to Europe by the Spanish. It became a staple of the northern European diet.
SENTENCES COMBINED WITH CLAUSES	The potato, *which was probably first grown in the Andes region of South America,* was transported to Europe by the Spanish *where it became a staple of the northern European diet.*
SENTENCES COMBINED WITH PARTICIPIAL PHRASES	The potato, *probably first grown in the Andes region of South America and transported to Europe by the Spanish,* became a staple of the northern European diet.
	Probably first grown in the Andes region of South America and transported to Europe by the Spanish, the potato became a staple of the northern European diet.

Participles are fairly flexible in their placement, as the previous examples show. However, be careful not to create misplaced or dangling modifiers when you use participles to combine ideas (see Sections 22 to 23).

An **absolute phrase** is an especially compressed modifier that, because it modifies the whole sentence rather than any single word, can be placed effectively at many locations in a sentence. An absolute phrase consists of a subject (usually a noun or pronoun), a participle, and any modifiers of the participle. Almost any sentence containing a form of the verb *be* followed by a present or past participle can be transformed into an absolute phrase by omitting the *be* form of the verb. Absolute phrases can also be formed by changing a main verb into its *-ing* form.

SENTENCE	The potatoes were mashed, so I put them into a bowl.
ABSOLUTE	*The potatoes mashed,* I put them into a bowl.
SENTENCE	The food was tasty, and the guests asked for second helpings.
ABSOLUTE	*The food being tasty,* the guests asked for second helpings.

These different ways of subordinating information and combining ideas allow you to construct denser, more compact and streamlined sentences. You can also vary the structure of your sentences and achieve a tighter focus on ideas you want to emphasize.

Practice: Identifying subordinated modifiers   *Underline the appositives, participial phrases, and absolute phrases in the following sentences. The answers are listed next.*

[1] Bowling, considered by many a purely American sport, actually originated in Germany. [2] Knocking down the heathens represented by the clubs, a strike proved the bowler's religious virtue. [3] The practice abandoned by the Church, bowling's popularity continued to grow. [4] The game finally secularized, innovation was quick. [5] Eventually, wooden balls, forerunners of today's bowling balls, were substituted for rounded rocks, the rocks having been first used as the bowler's primary equipment. [6] Taking the place of the clubs originally used, slender pins like those used today were introduced.

Answers to the Practice   [1] considered . . . sport [participial phrase, appositive] [2] Knocking . . . clubs [participial phrase]   [3] The . . . Church [absolute phrase] [4] The . . . secularized [absolute phrase]   [5] forerunners . . . balls [appositive]; the . . . equipment [absolute phrase]   [6] Taking . . . used [participial phrase]

EXERCISE 43-1, COORDINATION AND SUBORDINATION   **(31a–b)**

Revise the following sentences using coordinating conjunctions, subordinating conjunctions, and relative pronouns to combine ideas and eliminate primer style.

Example   Everybody thinks of football as an American game. It has English forerunners.

Although everyone thinks of football as an American game, it has English forerunners.

1.   Many games around the world are known as football. The American game of football is merely one of these games.

2.   No player in England plays a game called "soccer." The citizen of Yorkshire or London refers to soccer as football.

3.   The British national sport attracts huge crowds of fans. The games are televised frequently. American tourists are confused to hear soccer referred to as football.

4.   No football fan misses the World Cup football finals. In the World Cup matches, each participating country is eliminated as its team loses.

5.   A huge audience around the world watches the match on television. The last game of the finals decides who is the world champion team.

6.   Soccer stadiums are huge. They are much larger than the football stadiums Americans are used to seeing. Thousands of fans crowd into the stadium to watch the World Cup games.

7.   The audience is very emotional. The spectators sometimes take their frustrated emotions out on each other.

8.   There have often been riots after World Cup games. In fact, injuries or deaths are far too common.

9. European "football" fans are much more serious about their game than American fans are. The teams in World Cup soccer games are national teams.

10. Rugby is another sport that is related to American football. Rugby is an English game. It is played by athletes of all ages.

11. Tackling the opponent or touching the ball with the hands is not allowed in soccer. In rugby carrying the ball and tackling are both legal.

12. Footwork and "heading" the ball are the primary ways to advance the soccer ball. Rugby allows the use of both the hands and the feet.

13. Rugby and football look similar. No pads or helmets are allowed in rugby. Injuries, cuts, and bruises are frequent.

14. It has been said that the rugby team that survives longest is the winner. There have been many attempts to ban football in England. These attempts started in the Middle Ages.

15. Soccer has been called a gentleman's game played by ruffians. Rugby is a ruffian's game played by gentlemen.

16. Rugby players are called "ruggers." The players prefer to play without pads. They think human nature would encourage players to hit harder if their competitors wore pads.

17. The players wear heavy gym shorts, thick jerseys, socks, rugby shoes, and mouthpieces. Other equipment or pads are used only if an injury requires protection. Their gear seems suicidally simple.

18. Rugby games are played in two halves. Each half lasts forty minutes. Teams meet to play two games, back-to-back.

19. The very physical, demanding game is played for 160 minutes. Very short rest periods are allowed. A rugby player must be in top physical condition.

20. American football developed from rugby. Rugby is catching on again in America in its own right. It has all the appeal of football. It is much simpler and less expensive.

EXERCISE 43-2, PARTICIPLES, ABSOLUTES, AND APPOSITIVES   (31c-d)

Combine the following sentences, expressing what you believe to be the most important idea in the main clause and using participial phrases, appositives, or absolute phrases to subordinate other ideas. Be sure to avoid dangling or misplaced modifiers in your revisions.

Example   Basketball is a truly American sport. Basketball is played in no other country as widely as it is played in the United States.

Basketball, a truly American sport, is played in no other Country as widely as it is played in the United States.

1. Basketball was developed in 1891. You might think that it was developed by a "native" American. That is not the case.

    _____

2. The inventor of basketball was James Naismith. Naismith was born in Canada.

    _____

3. His team needed a sport they could play indoors. Football was played in the autumn. Baseball season started in the spring.

    _____

4. Naismith wanted an activity to keep his football and baseball players in shape during the winter. The winter weather made outdoor athletic work impossible.

    _____

5. Football and baseball require running and throwing. The gymnastic exercises performed in the winter did not allow practice in running and throwing.

    _____

6. Naismith's invention solved this problem. He simply developed a game that involved running and throwing.

    _____

7. The first basketball game was played in 1892. It was played at the International YMCA Training School.

    _____

8. Naismith did not recognize that his first game of basketball would be an historic occasion. His players did not recognize that this was a new national sport.

    _____

9. A basketball squad performed in an exhibition game in the 1904 Olympics. The game drew a large crowd. It made a less than lasting impression on the Olympic Committee.

_____

10. The popularity of the game increased. There was pressure to make basketball an Olympic sport. In 1936 the Olympic Committee decided to include basketball as an official Olympic sport.

_____

11. Naismith died three years later. He had lived to see the game he invented added to the Olympics and to college sports programs all across the country.

_____

12. Girls were also given the opportunity to play basketball. For years, girls' games were played by a different set of rules.

_____

13. A team's guards and forwards played on opposite sides of the court. They could not cross the court's center line.

_____

14. Now girls' basketball rules allow a team to use the full court. High school and college girls' teams use the same rules as the boys' teams use.

_____

15. In some states basketball is the most popular collegiate sport. People in Indiana call their love of basketball "Hoosier hysteria."

_____

16. James Naismith nailed first cardboard boxes and later peach baskets to his gymnasium wall. He could not have known how popular "basket" ball was going to become.

_____

17. (Write your own sentence using a participial phrase to combine ideas.)

_____

18. (Write your own sentence using an appositive to combine ideas.)

_____

19. (Write your own sentence using an absolute phrase to combine ideas.)

_____

20. (Write your own sentence using coordinating conjunctions and subordinating conjunctions to combine ideas.)

_____

44
PARALLELISM   (32)

If successive parts of a sentence, or successive sentences, use the same grammatical construction, they are parallel. Parallel constructions emphasize coordinate relationships, stressing equal importance or rank by means of the repeated grammatical patterns.

You can create parallel structures in just about any part of a sentence by using coordination.

SUBJECTS	*Art, music, and dance* are virtually international languages.
VERBS	These forms of expression *attract and captivate* audiences everywhere.
DIRECT OBJECTS	Audiences understand *art, music, and dance* without translation.
INFINITIVE PHRASES	They only need *to see and hear* to understand and appreciate the message.
PARTICIPLES MODIFYING NOUNS	*Dancing feet or singing voices* communicate across political barriers.
ADJECTIVE COMPLEMENTS	Art forms are both *universal and personal* at the same time.
NOUN COMPLEMENTS/ PREPOSITIONAL PHRASES	They are *importers of cultural exchange and exporters of human understanding.*

The equal emphasis stressed by parallel form provides you with yet another tool for indicating and reinforcing meaning in your sentences. Rather than having to say "this is ranked the same as that," you can indicate the ranking through sentence structure. Consequently, parallel structures are particularly useful for combining sentences, as the following examples show.

SUCCESSIVE SENTENCES	Music is a good cultural ambassador. Dance is another effective international communicator.
SENTENCES COMBINED USING PARALLELISM	Music and dance are good cultural ambassadors as well as effective international communicators.

Because parallel structures are formed with coordinators—either coordinating conjunctions (*and, but, or, nor,* etc.) or correlative conjunctions (*either, or; neither, nor; not only, but also; both, and; whether, or*), you must be careful to avoid faulty parallelism which would destroy the sameness of structure and thus the equality of emphasis on each side of the coordinator. If you use a noun phrase on one side of the conjunction, for example, be sure to use a noun phrase on the other side as well. If you use *and who, and which,* or *and that* in the second half of a parallel structure, you must be sure to introduce the same type of structure in the first half, too.

CORRECT	That is Wolfgang Steinmetz, who is a great pianist and who is also an excellent mathematician.
FAULTY	That is Wolfgang Steinmetz, a great pianist and who is also an excellent mathematician.
CORRECT	That is Wolfgang Steinmetz, a great pianist and an excellent mathematician.
	That is Wolfgang Steinmetz, who is a great pianist and an excellent mathematician.
FAULTY	You are either wrong or I am wrong. [Adjective *wrong* is not really parallel with clause *I am wrong.*]
CORRECT	Either you are wrong or I am. [Two parallel clauses.]
FAULTY	They not only have insulted me but everyone. [Verb *have insulted* is not properly parallel with pronoun *everyone.*]
CORRECT	They have insulted not only me but everyone. [Pronouns *me* and *everyone* are parallel.]

EXERCISE 44, PARALLELISM   (32)

Revise the following sentences to express coordinate ideas in correct parallel form.

Example   Records of Chinese immigration to the U.S. were incomplete and not able to be trusted until the middle of the nineteenth century.

Records of Chinese immigration to the U.S. were incomplete and untrustworthy until the middle of the nineteenth century.

1. Some historians claim Chinese shipbuilders were working in America as early as 1751; other historians say the American West had a small population of Chinese laborers by 1788.

2. In 1820, records show that only one Chinese immigrant came to America, and between 1821 and 1830 America attracted two more.

3. Later mass immigration was stimulated by the long droughts in China and the fact that gold had been discovered in California in 1848.

4. Early Chinese immigrants called America "Beautiful Land," but it was named "Mountain of Gold" by the later immigrants.

5. These later immigrants came here looking for gold, yet hard work was what they found.

6. At first, the Chinese were welcomed and cheap labor for railroad construction was the kind of work they were given.

7. The completion of the Union Pacific railroad threw thousands of Chinese laborers out of work and the "native American" working class felt threatened by them.

8. By 1870, over 100,000 Chinese lived in America, and California was the state where most of them lived.

9.   Many of these immigrants, most of them in fact, were unskilled and lacked an education.

_____

10. They had hoped to work, save their money, and eventually to send a "nest egg" of savings back to their families in China.

_____

11. Despite the discrimination they faced and the way they endured through hardships, these Chinese stayed in America and had to begin to call it home.

_____

12. When Americans went to work in the mines, they traveled light and women had been left behind.

_____

13. They considered laundry, tailoring, and to prepare meals "women's work."

_____

14. In fact few of the men in the mining camps were willing or were practiced at the skills to do these sorts of chores.

_____

15. The Chinese had been barred from many jobs, so these chores were seen by the Chinese as golden opportunities.

_____

16. Laying railroad ties and to dig tunnels were dangerous jobs.

_____

17. Washing and having to iron were difficult chores, but at least they were safe.

_____

18. The iron, ironing board, and the board you wash clothes on were the keys to escape from "coolie" wages.

_____

19. The laundry industry was a business in which a Chinese laborer could quickly change from hired hand to owning his own business.

_____

20. Like the European immigrants, the Chinese were able to turn a despised or neglected trade and make it something they could use as a steppingstone to higher status.

_____

45
EMPHASIS   (33)

As you learned in Section 43 on coordination and subordination, the structure of a sentence plays a key role in focusing a reader's attention on the ideas you want to emphasize. If the most important idea appears in the main clause and information of lesser importance is subordinated, the reader has received valuable signals about the emphasis you intend. Parallel arrangements of information also provide emphasis, as Section 44 explained. Emphatic positioning, use of loose, periodic, and balanced sentences, and appropriate use of active and passive voice verbs also help you achieve emphasis in your writing.

One of the hazards of combining sentences, as you did for the exercises in Section 43, for example, is that emphasis can disappear as you join phrases and clauses together. Even though sentence combining helps to establish relationships between ideas and reduces unnecessary repetition, if you put too many ideas in a sentence that is not constructed with a clear emphasis, readers won't know where to focus their attention. First of all, don't be tempted to pile too much information into a single sentence. Secondly, be sure to structure your sentences for emphasis.

UNFOCUSED SENTENCE CONTAINING TOO MUCH DETAIL	The car with the broken axle and the smashed front end had turned over in the ditch after being hit by the train, but the tow truck began to right the wrecked vehicle because miraculously no one was injured.
SENTENCE REVISED FOR EMPHASIS	After being hit by the train, the car turned over in the ditch, its axle broken and its front end smashed. Miraculously, no one was injured, so the tow truck began to right the wrecked vehicle.

EMPHATIC POSITIONS WITHIN SENTENCES

Generally, the most emphatic place in a sentence is the ending. The next most emphatic place is the beginning. The middle of the sentence receives the least amount of emphasis. A good writer achieves forcefulness by inserting the strongest points either at the ends or at the beginnings of sentences.

WEAK	Most politicians can be trusted, in my opinion.
STRONGER	In my opinion, most politicians can be trusted.
	Most politicians, in my opinion, can be trusted.
WEAK	We will have a picnic if it does not rain.
STRONGER	If it does not rain, we will have a picnic.

Naturally, you are the one who must decide which information merits emphasis. In the first example, the writer has decided in one case that *In my opinion* should be stressed. In the second case, *in my opinion* becomes the least important information in the sentence and so is inserted parenthetically in the middle. The point is that you should not inadvertently structure a sentence to destroy the emphasis you intend.

LOOSE, PERIODIC, MIDBRANCHING, AND BALANCED SENTENCES

A **loose** or **right-branching sentence**, sometimes called a **cumulative sentence,** is a sentence that concerns itself with its main idea first and its subordinate details later. The **periodic** or **left-branching sentence** has an exactly opposite arrangement: its subordinate details come first and its main idea comes last. Thus, the periodic sentence often achieves an effect of drama and suspense. Although it provides forcefulness and a sense of climax, the periodic sentence must be used judiciously since its overuse may result in a loss of the very effect you want to achieve. A **midbranching sentence** places modifying details between the subject and the verb. Like the periodic sentence, it must be used carefully because it varies from readers' expectations—from ordinary, cumulative thought patterns and sentence patterns. A midbranching sentence can either emphasize or deemphasize subordinate details, depending on whether it is punctuated with dashes or commas.

A **balanced sentence** is a compound sentence in which the independent clauses are exactly, or very nearly, parallel in all elements. Balanced sentences are useful for showing contrasts.

LOOSE, RIGHT-BRANCHING	The dog came home with its collar gone, its fur full of burrs, and its tail between its legs.
PERIODIC, LEFT-BRANCHING	Its collar gone, its fur full of burrs, and its tail between its legs, the dog came home.
MIDBRANCHING EMPHASIZED	The dog—its tail between its legs—came home.
MIDBRANCHING DEEMPHASIZED	The dog, its tail between its legs, came home.
BALANCED	The dog came home with burrs in its fur, but it came home without its collar.
	An undisciplined puppy is "disobedient"; an undisciplined dog is a menace.

ACTIVE AND PASSIVE VOICE

The **active voice** places emphasis upon the performer of the action, whereas the **passive voice** places emphasis upon that which receives the action. For the most part, you should utilize the active voice since the effect is more forceful. The passive voice results in a slower movement of context and in impersonal and colorless writing. Use it only if you wish to place emphasis upon the recipient of an action rather than to emphasize the action itself. In some instances, the performer of the action may not be known. In this case the passive voice is often used. (See Section 13 for more discussion of active and passive voice.)

ACTIVE	John broke the news to her at midnight.
PASSIVE	The news was broken to her by John at midnight.
PASSIVE	He was murdered between ten and eleven o'clock last night.
ACTIVE	Someone murdered him between ten and eleven o'clock last night.

In the second example here, the passive voice is probably preferable since the important aspect is the murder. With active voice and the emphasis that "someone did it," self-evident information gets the emphasis.

EXERCISE 45-1, EMPHASIS   (33a–b)

Revise the following sentences to achieve greater emphasis. Decide which elements are more important and which are less important and position the sentence elements to reflect your choice.

Example   The most popular Chinese holiday is New Year's Day, probably.

Probably the most popular Chinese holiday is New Year's Day.

1. Chinese-Americans who follow Chinese traditions number years differently than is done in America, as a matter of fact.

    _____

2. For example, the year 1984 is the year 4682 on the Chinese calendar.

    _____

3. As a matter of fact, it is on February 2 that the Chinese New Year begins.

    _____

4. Each year is also named for one of twelve animals, as well.

    _____

5. For example, the year of the rat was 1984.

    _____

6. The year of the rat requires a special celebration, according to the Chinese.

    _____

7. The rat was the first animal to report to the emperor of the universe, and that is why the year of the rat begins the twelve-year cycle, according to legend.

    _____

8. Ambition and honesty are the characteristics of people born in the year of the rat, along with an inability to save money or form lasting relationships.

    _____

9. People born in the year of the monkey or the year of the dragon are the signs most compatible with people born in the year of the rat.

    _____

10. The year of the horse is when people are born who are least compatible with people born in the year of the rat.

    _____

Revise the following sentences, making them periodic.

Example   On New Year's Day, Chinese families pour wine over the ground to commemorate the families' ancestors.

To commemorate the families' ancestors, on New Year's Day Chinese families pour wine over the ground.

11. The Chinese New Year's celebration actually varies, to fall precisely on the day the first new moon enters Aquarius.

_____

12. The celebrations actually begin seven days earlier to allow a full week for the more important parts of the festival.

_____

13. Most of the earlier preparations are unknown to outsiders, because these ceremonies are quieter than the parades and fireworks.

_____

14. This week is a lucky week for housewives because the week is devoted to physical and spiritual purification of the home.

_____

15. Physical cleaning and spiritual cleaning are sometimes indistinguishable since the Chinese identify household dirt with "evil influences."

_____

16. Other special ceremonies during the week are held to pay homage to the household gods which protect the home.

_____

17. Old images of these gods are burned and new ones brought home to honor the gods for protecting the home during the year.

_____

18. New Year's customs vary slightly from one Chinese community to the next, which reflects the regional diversity of religious customs in China.

_____

19. Some Chinese-Americans fast on the day before New Year's Day, to prepare themselves to appreciate the New Year's feast, in some parts of the country.

_____

20. Unmarried people are given gifts on New Year's Day during the Chinese celebration, just as other Americans receive Christmas gifts from their friends and relatives.

_____

Using your own paper, write a paragraph containing at least two loose sentences, two periodic sentences, one midbranching sentence, and one balanced sentence. Label your sentences according to type.

238

EXERCISE 45-2, ACTIVE AND PASSIVE VOICE   (33e)

Where appropriate, revise the following sentences using the active voice. If you believe that the passive voice is preferable in a sentence, write *correct* in the blank.

Example   Wang Laboratories were founded by An Wang, an electronics specialist, in 1955.

An Wang, an electronics specialist, founded Wang Laboratories in 1955.

1. The Manhattan Fund, a mutual stock fund, was started by Gerald Tsai, Jr., who was born in Shanghai.

_____

2. Over 150,000 investors were brought together by Tsai to start his mutual fund.

_____

3. All in all, $270 million was put into the fund by optimistic investors.

_____

4. Fellowships for advanced students are provided by the Li Foundation.

_____

5. The Foundation was established by K. C. Li for this worthy purpose.

_____

6. The world's largest tungsten refinery, the Wah Chang Corporation, is also owned by Mr. Li.

_____

7. A national discount-store network, National Dollar Stores, was begun by Joe Shoong and his family in 1907.

_____

_____

8. By 1928, a total of fifty-three stores had been added to their original holdings of one store and a warehouse.

_____

_____

9. An early program to recruit Chinese students for American universities, the Chinese student movement, was initiated by Yung Wing.

10. Wing came to America in 1847 and Yale University was attended by him.

11. Naturalized American citizenship was granted to Wing in 1849.

12. The first Chinese newspaper in America was published in San Francisco in 1854.

13. Dr. Mary Stone, the first Chinese woman to graduate from an American medical school, was trained by the University of Michigan faculty.

14. In 1940, the number of "Chinatowns" in the United States was put at twenty-eight.

15. Fifteen years later, the "Chinatowns" had been numbered at sixteen.

16. The increasing Americanization of the Chinese-American population is illustrated by this decrease in separate Chinese communities.

17. The first Chinese-American to serve as an elected official was Wing F. Ong, who was elected to the Arizona legislature in 1946.

18. A seat on the New York Stock Exchange was first purchased by a Chinese-American in September, 1979.

19. In 1959, the first Chinese-American U.S. Senator was sent to Washington by Hawaii's citizens.

20. The first Chinese-American to serve as a judge was Delbert E. Wong, who was appointed by California Governor Edmund Brown.

46
VARIETY (34)

Throughout the preceding three sections of this text, we have been considering various ways to achieve effective expression in sentences. Coordination and subordination, parallelism, emphatic positioning of sentence elements, a mixture of loose, periodic, midbranching, and balanced sentences, proper use of active and passive voice are all means for adding variety to your writing.

Even though you may feel satisfied if you can simply put your ideas into grammatically correct sentences, your ideas will lose much of their impact if they are always presented in the same types of sentence constructions. If you rely too heavily on short, simple sentences, always use subject-verb-object sentence patterns, or begin every complex sentence with a subordinate clause, your writing may become monotonous and predictable. Consequently, the reader can be lulled, almost hypnotized, by the unvarying sentence style and may pay less attention to the meaning. Learn to vary the length, type, and pattern of your sentences to fit your meaning, to establish emphasis, and to keep your reader's attention engaged.

SENTENCE LENGTHS AND PATTERNS

Section 45 discussed the advantages and disadvantages of combining a series of short sentences into a larger sentence that relates ideas. The best writing uses a mixture of short sentences and long ones. Readers appreciate having related ideas combined into compound and complex sentences, because then they do not have to work at and guess about connections between thoughts. On the other hand, if you wish to establish a point dramatically, a short sentence will emphatically break the rhythm of a paragraph and draw the reader's attention. Compare the following two paragraphs, and notice how sentence variety helps to achieve emphasis in the second one.

> We could hear the wind howling above us. We huddled in the storm shelter. The tornado roared through the neighborhood like a freight train. It was quiet suddenly, so we climbed the stairs carefully. Our knees were shaking. Father opened the door, and our house was gone.

> We could hear the wind howling above us as we huddled in the storm shelter. Sounding like a freight train, the tornado roared through the neighborhood. Suddenly it was quiet. Our knees shaking, carefully we climbed the stairs, and Father opened the door. Our house was gone.

The second paragraph gains much of its dramatic effect from careful sentence construction. The writer has combined sentences in the first part of the paragraph, piling details together to reinforce the sense of chaos associated with the storm. The use of the participial phrase *Sounding like a freight train* and the absolute phrase *Our knees shaking* vary the subject-verb-object arrangement established in the first sentence. The free adverbial modifiers (ones that can be moved to several positions in the sentence) *suddenly* and *carefully* have been located near the front of their sentences for contrast and emphasis. A short sentence has been used to draw the attention to the contrast between the storm's noise and the ominous silence after it had passed. Finally, to emphasize the shock, the writer has used a short, blunt statement to say the house had been destroyed. As a result, the reader can participate in the feelings the writer experienced during the incident—from fear to shock—partially because of the varied sentence lengths and patterns.

Varying the beginnings of sentences often achieves effective expression. Note the revisions of the following sentence:

Little trouble developed in the beginning, and the manager looked forward to a harmonious future.

BEGINNING WITH A PREPOSITIONAL PHRASE	In the beginning, little trouble developed, and the manager looked forward to a harmonious future.
BEGINNING WITH AN ABSOLUTE PHRASE	Little trouble having developed in the beginning, the manager looked forward to a harmonious future.
BEGINNING WITH A PARTICIPIAL PHRASE	Having little trouble in the beginning, the manager looked forward to a harmonious future.
BEGINNING WITH AN EXPLETIVE	There was little trouble in the beginning, and the manager looked forward to a harmonious future.
BEGINNING WITH A SUBORDINATE CLAUSE	Because little trouble developed in the beginning, the manager looked forward to a harmonious future.
BEGINNING WITH A COORDINATING CONJUNCTION	But little trouble developed in the beginning, and the manager looked forward to a harmonious future.

Varying the position of free modifiers (those that can be moved from one place to another in sentences) can also be effective. Adverbs, adverb phrases and clauses, and some participial phrases and absolute phrases can be moved, giving you a choice of effects. Note, for example, the following sentences:

Struggling for a foothold, the mountain climber clung to the cliff.
The mountain climber, *struggling for a foothold,* clung to the cliff.
The mountain climber clung, *struggling for a foothold,* to the cliff.

The basic sentence pattern in English is subject-verb-object. We have already seen that opening a sentence with modifiers changes the effect of this pattern. But **inverting the pattern** can also provide variety, although you should use inversion judiciously because it often strikes readers as somewhat abnormal. You can invert the subject and the object; or you can open with a modifier, inverting the subject and verb.

These delays we would not tolerate. [object-subject-verb]
Next to the newstand on the corner stood the police officer. [modifier-verb-subject]

Finally, **various types of sentences** can be used to create effects. Although you most often write declarative statements, an occasional question, command, or exclamation may better achieve the effect you desire. Notice how the changes in the following paragraph, from question to command to statement to exclamation to statement, lend variety and emphasis to the message:

Is it true that people will settle for trash on television? Believe it. Studies show viewers will watch almost any type of garbage as long as it isn't obscene. But if they consider a program to be pornographic, watch out! Then there is an uproar about "filth" on television.

242

EXERCISE 46-1, CHANGING SENTENCE PATTERNS
AND TYPES FOR VARIETY   (34)

Revise each of the following sentences to begin with the listed types of constructions. Invent details as necessary to create these constructions.

Example   Ethnic actors now appear in many television programs.

In the United States, ethnic actors now appear
(prepositional phrase) *in many television programs.*

Formerly denied work, ethnic actors now ap-
(absolute) *pear in many television programs.*

1. Ethnic groups have received much network attention in the last fifteen years, and Blacks have increasingly been spotlighted.

    A. (prepositional phrase) _____

    B. (participial phrase) _____

    C. (expletive) _____

    D. (subordinate clause) _____

    E. (coordinating conjunction) _____

2. *The Jeffersons* showed life in an upwardly mobile Black family, and depicted the Black family's relations with both Black and white neighbors.

    A. (subordinate clause) _____

    B. (expletive) _____

    C. (prepositional phrase) _____

    D. (absolute) _____

    E. (participial phrase) _____

3. For years, *Hawaii Five-O* was the only television show to offer regular work for Chinese-American actors.

    A. (subordinate clause) _____

    B. (participial phrase) _____

C. (absolute) _____

D. (expletive) _____

4. The comedies probably helped people through laughter to see the similarities as well as the differences between ethnic groups.

   A. (prepositional phrase) _____

   B. (participial phrase) _____

   C. (absolute) _____

   D. (subordinate clause) _____

5. *Star Trek* was another program which featured several ethnic characters.

   A. (subordinate clause) _____

   B. (absolute) _____

   C. (prepositional phrase) _____

   D. (coordinating conjunction) _____

   Revise each of the following sentences as indicated.

   Example   Ethnic actors are now common on television programs.

   (Invert subject and verb.) _Now common on television programs are ethnic actors._

6. All kinds of programs employ ethnic actors now, including police and detective dramas.

   (Reposition participial phrase.) _____

   _____

   _____

7. Television now is a medium that illustrates America's ethnic presences.

   (Invert subject and verb.) _____

   _____

   _____

EXERCISE 46-2, SENTENCE COMBINING FOR VARIETY
AND COHERENCE   (34)

On your own paper, use the techniques we have reviewed in this unit on effective sentences to revise the following paragraph. Strive for sentence variety and emphasis while achieving paragraph coherence. Your revision should contain at least one example of each of the following:

1. Short sentences combined into a complex sentence (subordinating conjunction).

2. Short sentences combined into a compound sentence (coordinating conjunction).

3. Parallel construction.

4. Absolute phrase.

5. Participial phrase.

6. Inverted order—verb preceding subject.

7. Appositive.

8. Verbs in both the active and passive voices.

9. Question or command.

10. Effective subordination.

Potatoes are not native to North America. They were exported, then imported. Finally, the potato was responsible for huge numbers of immigrants' coming to America. Spanish explorers found the potato used as a food in South America. They took potatoes home to Spain. Potatoes were easy to grow. They became an inexpensive food source. Soon the potato became a staple in the diet of almost all northern Europeans. The potato was introduced to North America by European settlers. They brought the potato, a familiar food by that time, in their ships to the new settlements in America. The potato's spread into North America was circuitous, to say the least. Back in Europe, the Irish particularly relied on the potato. Poor Irish peasants often ate little else. In 1845 and 1846, a blight struck the Irish potato crop. The blight turned the potatoes black. It destroyed them. Thousands of poor Irish farmers starved. There was no disaster-relief system in 1846. If they stayed in Ireland, these peasants would have starved to death. Nearly a million Irish people left their homes. They immigrated to America. In America they could find jobs and they could eat.

Revise each of the following sentences as indicated.

Example   Savoring every bite, Jean ate the potato salad.

(Reposition free adverbial modifier.) *Jean, savoring every bite, ate the potato salad.*

1. The influence of the potato spread quickly.

   (Reposition free adverbial modifier.) _____

   _____

2. The potato came to North America by way of Europe from South America.

   (Reposition prepositional phrase.) _____

   _____

3. Poor people greeted such a low-cost food with enthusiasm, the potato being an inexpensive source of carbohydrates.

   (Invert subject and verb.) _____

   _____

   (Reposition absolute.) _____

   _____

   (Reposition prepositional phrase.) _____

   _____

4. The peasants planted the potato; the potato grew with little care; happily the peasants added the potato to their diets.

   (Reposition free adverbial modifiers.) _____

   _____

   (Invert subject and verb.) _____

   _____

   (Reposition prepositional phrases.) _____

   _____

   (Create parallel construction.) _____

   _____

246

47
THE DICTIONARY   (36a)

Most people use a dictionary mainly for checking spelling and meaning, but a writer can use a good dictionary for aid in many other ways as well. A dictionary also records a word's pronunciation, origin (etymology), part of speech, principal parts and plurals or other forms, and frequently its synonyms, antonyms, and level of usage. Often a dictionary also includes lists of abbreviations, spelling, capitalization, and punctuation rules, biographical and geographical information, vocabularies of rhymes and given names, and a list of U.S. colleges and universities.

Rather than just using your dictionary in the usual way—to look up spelling and meaning—familiarize yourself with the whole volume. Begin by reading the **front matter.** Read the user's guide or explanatory notes, which will tell you what each part of a dictionary entry means and what special information it contains.

Then read the pronunciation guide and the explanation of the abbreviations your dictionary uses. The purpose of the various type faces, labels, abbreviations, symbols, and other conventions found in a dictionary's entries is to achieve compactness and comprehensiveness. Unless you understand their meaning and use, you will miss a great deal of the information your dictionary has to offer. Several of the exercises in this section require information from various parts of dictionary entries, so you will have to read the front matter in your dictionary before you can answer them correctly.

The **back matter** can provide a wealth of information you probably never even knew your dictionary contained. Look it over so that you will know where to find rules for capitalization, for instance, the next time you need them.

Contrary to popular belief, dictionaries do not "define" words. Rather, they record meanings of actual usage, past and present. Some dictionaries record the general, most current meaning first. Others, such as *Webster's Collegiate Dictionary,* list a word's meaning in historical order, the oldest meaning first. Check the front matter in your dictionary to see which type of order it uses.

Language constantly changes. Over time, meanings that once were current may be superseded by newer ones that have achieved wide usage and acceptance. New words enter a language, and other words disappear. For example, thirty years ago you would not have been able to find the word *astronaut* in any dictionary. Dictionaries are periodically revised to take such changes into account. Although you do not need to replace your dictionary every time a new edition is published, you will probably find that by the time you reach middle age the dictionary you used in high school or college will no longer suit your needs. The dictionary is a writer's best resource; be sure you have one that serves as a good working partner.

Practice: Using your dictionary   Read the user's guide at the front of your desk dictionary. Then answer the following questions.

1.   What does the "order of definitions" or "order of senses" section say about the way meanings are listed within an entry?

2.   What symbol does your dictionary use to indicate the beginning and ending of a word's etymology?

3.   How many different usage labels are used in your dictionary, and what are they?

4. What does your dictionary say about cross-references?

5. What does your dictionary say about synonyms?

Title of your desk dictionary: _____

_____

EXERCISE 47, THE DICTIONARY   (36a)

In the blanks, identify the language from which each word was borrowed; give only the earliest given source. Since the term *borrowing* refers to languages other than English, the answers *Middle English (ME)*, *Old English (OE)*, and *Anglo-Saxon (AS)* are not correct.

1. resile	_____	6. sidereal	_____	11. xylem	_____
2. retort	_____	7. sitar	_____	12. bravado	_____
3. retail	_____	8. stearic	_____	13. carnelian	_____
4. sanguine	_____	9. tattoo	_____	14. deckle	_____
5. sastruga	_____	10. trauma	_____	15. largesse	_____

In the blanks, indicate the original or etymological meaning of each word—that is, give the meaning within the brackets in the dictionary, not the meaning in the definition of the word itself. For example, the etymological meaning of the word *animism* is "soul."

16. badinage	_____	21. hypocrite	_____	26. pedigree	_____
17. ghoul	_____	22. janitor	_____	27. respond	_____
18. germ	_____	23. matador	_____	28. sinus	_____
19. finance	_____	24. memoir	_____	29. swindler	_____
20. harbinger	_____	25. peignoir	_____	30. umbrage	_____

All the following words are derived from the name of a person or a place. In the blank after each word, indicate the name of the person or place from which that word is derived.

31. roentgen _____	36. bangalore torpedo _____
32. Baedeker _____	37. camellia _____
33. balmoral _____	38. jackanapes _____
34. Doppler effect _____	39. paisley _____
35. bouvardia _____	40. palace _____

After referring to the user's guide in your dictionary, describe how it indicates the plural form of nouns.

_____

_____

_____

_____

_____

Consult your dictionary and in the blanks list all the plural forms it gives for the following nouns.

41. sister-in-law _____   46. wolf _____

42. datum _____   47. appendix _____

43. hippopotamus _____   48. focus _____

44. alumna _____   49. deer _____

45. sheep _____   50. criterion _____

After referring to the user's guide in your dictionary, explain how it indicates the principal parts of verbs.

_____

_____

_____

_____

Consult your dictionary and in the blanks list all the past tenses and past participles it gives for the following verbs.

51. hang (suspend) _____   56. bear (carry) _____

52. shrink _____   57. rise _____

53. lie (recline) _____   58. bear (give birth to) _____

54. swim _____   59. dive _____

55. lay (place) _____   60. shine _____

48
VOCABULARY   (36b)

Just as a variety of sentence patterns or methods of paragraph development can make your writing more interesting for a reader, so a varied and appropriate use of language can improve your writing. Your choice of vocabulary can be extremely important to many aspects of your writing. Not only do the most accurate and expressive words convey your meaning best, but vocabulary choices can improve coherence within paragraphs. Synonyms, for example, can help your reader see the connections between ideas, as well as add variety to sentences.

On the other hand, you must be careful when selecting synonyms. Many words are loosely synonymous, but each word has its own connotations or shades of meaning. If you consult a thesaurus, synonym dictionary, or the synonym entries in your desk dictionary, also be sure to look up the meaning of the synonym in the dictionary. You want to be certain that the connotations of the word fit the context in which you intend to use it. Some words may not be appropriate to the tone of your paragraph, even though they are synonymous.

A word's etymology can help you decide if it is an appropriate synonym. Suppose you are looking for an alternative to the word *famous* to describe the research on pickles at Dill University. You have narrowed the synonyms down to *reputed* and *renowned,* words you found listed under *famous* in the thesaurus. The dictionary defines *repute* to mean "to assign a reputation to." Its origin is a Latin word that loosely means "to be considered." *Renowned* means "being widely honored and acclaimed." Its origin is an Old French word that means "to name again." Although the shades of meaning are subtle, you may decide that *reputed* has less positive connotations and that its etymology suggests subjective opinion, whereas *renowned* seems more forceful and carries connotations that more exactly fit your sentence's meaning.

The previous example illustrates another important point about vocabulary: Thousands of words we use regularly have been borrowed or adapted from other languages. *Renowned* can be traced to the Old French word *renomer.* As the etymology indicates, the root form of the word means "name." The prefix *re-* means "again": hence the word's meaning, "to name again."

If you study common prefixes and suffixes (attachments added to a word's beginning or ending) as well as learn to recognize common word roots, you will be able to increase your vocabulary considerably. Just by knowing the meaning of a word's parts, you can often decipher its approximate meaning even if you have never seen the word before. The following lists of prefixes, suffixes, and combining forms taken from the *Prentice-Hall Handbook for Writers,* Ninth Edition, can help you increase your vocabulary.

PREFIXES

PREFIX	MEANING	EXAMPLE
ab-	away from	absent
ad-*	to *or* for	adverb
com-*	with	combine
de-	down, away from, *or* undoing	degrade, depart, dehumanize
dis-*	separation *or* reversal	disparate, disappoint

PREFIX	MEANING	EXAMPLE
ex-*	out of *or* former	extend, ex-president
in-*	in *or* on	input
in-*	not	inhuman
mis-	wrong	mistake
non-	not	non-Christian
ob-*	against	obtuse
pre-	before	prevent
pro-	for *or* forward	proceed
re-	back *or* again	repeat
sub-*	under	subcommittee
trans-	across	transcribe
un-	not	unclean

*The spelling of these prefixes varies, usually to make pronunciation easier. *Ad* becomes *ac* in *accuse*, *ag* in *aggregate*, *at* in *attack*. Similarly, the final consonant in the other prefixes indicated is assimilated by the initial letter of the root word: *colleague (com + league); divert (dis + vert); evict (ex + vict); illicit (in + licit); offend (ob + fend); succeed (sub + ceed).*

SUFFIXES

Noun suffixes denoting *act of, state of, quality of*

SUFFIX	EXAMPLE	MEANING
-dom	freedom	*state of* being free
-hood	manhood	*state of* being a man
-ness	dimness	*state of* being dim
-ice	cowardice	*quality of* being a coward
-ation	flirtation	*act of* flirting
-ion	intercession	*act of* interceding
-sion	scansion	*act of* scanning
-tion	corruption	*state of* being corrupt
-ment	argument	*act of* arguing
-ship	friendship	*state of* being friends
-ance	continuance	*act of* continuing
-ence	precedence	*act of* preceding
-ancy	flippancy	*state of* being flippant
-ency	currency	*state of* being current
-ism	baptism	*act of* baptizing
-ery	bravery	*quality of* being brave

Noun suffixes denoting *doer, one who*

SUFFIX	EXAMPLE	MEANING
-eer	auctioneer	*one who* auctions
-st	fascist	*one who* believes in fascism
-or	debtor	*one who* is in debt
-er	worker	*one who* works

Verb suffixes denoting *to make* or *to perform the act of*

SUFFIX	EXAMPLE	MEANING
-ate	perpetuate	*to make* perpetual
-en	soften	*to make* soft
-fy	dignify	*to make* dignified
-ize, ise	sterilize	*to make* sterile

Adjectival suffixes

SUFFIX	MEANING	EXAMPLE
-ful	full of	hateful
-ish	resembling	foolish
-ate	having	affectionate
-ic, ical	resembling	angelic
-ive	having	prospective
-ous	full of	zealous
-ulent	full of	fraudulent
-less	without	fatherless
-able, -ible	capable of	peaceable
-ed	having	spirited
-ly	resembling	womanly
-like	resembling	childlike

COMBINING FORMS (Appearing Generally, But Not Always, as Prefixes)

COMBINING FORM	MEANING	EXAMPLE
anthropo	man	*anthropo*logy
arch	rule	*arch*duke, mon*arch*
auto	self	*auto*mobile
bene	well	*bene*ficial
eu	well	*eu*logy
graph	writing	*graph*ic, bio*graphy*
log, logue	word, speech	mono*logue*
magni	great	*magni*ficent
mal	bad	*mal*ady
mono	one	*mono*tone
multi	many	*multi*plication
neo	new	*neo*classic
omni	all	*omni*bus
pan, pant	all	*pan*hellenic
phil	loving	*phil*osophy
phono	sound	*phono*graph
poly	many	*poly*gamy
pseudo	false	*pseudo*nym
semi	half	*semi*formal
trans	across	*trans*continental

Practice A: Prefixes   Add the appropriate prefix to each of the following words to indicate a negative meaning. The answers are listed at the end of this section.

[1] loyal   [2] justice   [3] emotional   [4] enchant   [5] impeachable
[6] eluctable   [7] believer   [8] proportionate   [9] credible   [10] flattering

Practice B: Suffixes   Add the appropriate suffix to each of the following words to indicate act of, state of, or quality of. Check the spelling of the new words since the addition of a suffix may change the spelling of the word. The answers are listed at the end of this section.

[1] wise   [2] appease   [3] state   [4] friendly   [5] competent   [6] erupt
[7] administer   [8] execute   [9] secede   [10] existential

Answers to Practice A   [1] dis-   [2] in-   [3] un-   [4] dis-   [5] un-   [6] in-
[7] un- (or non-)   [8] dis-   [9] in-   [10] un-

Answers to Practice B   [1] wisdom   [2] appeasement   [3] statehood
[4] friendliness   [5] competence (or competency)   [6] eruption   [7] administration
[8] execution   [9] secession   [10] existentialism

EXERCISE 48–1, PREFIXES, SUFFIXES, AND COMBINING FORMS   (36b)

Add the appropriate prefix to each of the following roots to form a word that will fit in the sentence at the right.

Example   -descript   The building was utterly *nondescript*.

1.   -act   The rest will _____ the stress of the last few days.

2.   -own   I don't want him to _____ his own family and friends.

3.   -ordinary   She deserves the award for her _____ services.

4.   -curricular   She presented a long list of _____ activities she has conducted.

5.   -sensitive   He seems to be _____ about criticism of his record.

6.   -noble   That really is rather _____ of him.

7.   -adjusted   Do you think it indicates a _____ personality?

8.   -vene   Possibly the authorities will _____ and force a settlement.

9.   -collegiate   Even though she works in public relations, she has done nothing to help _____ cooperation between the schools.

10.   -filtrate   Well, we tried to _____ her office, but we were not successful at all.

11.   -poly   Does the library have a _____ on genealogical records?

12.   -spect   In _____ , I see that our search elsewhere was foolish.

13.   -durately   The reference librarian will never _____ refuse to help.

14.   -tract   I'll _____ my criticism when the staff is more helpful.

15.   -meate   Your negative attitude will _____ all your research.

16.   -jointed   Your research paper may seem _____ .

17.   -standard   Some instructors would consider it _____ .

18.   -applied   You don't think they've _____ their funds, do you?

19.   -thesis   You need a more general idea, to provide a _____ of your research.

20.   -stain   I will _____ from further criticism.

Form verbs and adjectives by adding suffixes to the following words. Adjust spelling as necessary.

		VERB	ADJECTIVE
Example	civility	*Civilize*	*civil*
21.	mystic	_____	_____
22.	sum	_____	_____
23.	false	_____	_____
24.	difference	_____	_____
25.	origin	_____	_____
26.	type	_____	_____
27.	familiarity	_____	_____
28.	veneration	_____	_____
29.	person	_____	_____
30.	mobility	_____	_____

Write two words constructed from each of the following combining forms.

Example	com	*Combat*	*Common*
31.	in	_____	_____
32.	pro	_____	_____
33.	re	_____	_____
34.	pre	_____	_____
35.	ism	_____	_____
36.	ate	_____	_____
37.	ance	_____	_____
38.	ous	_____	_____
39.	ment	_____	_____
40.	dom	_____	_____

On your own paper, write a sentence for each word of the pairs you constructed in items 31 through 40.

EXERCISE 48–2, WORD MEANING   (36c)

Circle the number of the word closest in meaning to the italicized word in each given phrase.

Example   an *august* person ((1)) notable   (2) month   (3) omen   (4) perforator

1.   an *execrable* meal   (1) vigorous   (2) excusable   (3) enjoyable   (4) very bad

2.   a *vitriolic* debate   (1) hardened   (2) transparent   (3) bitter   (4) vocal

3.   a *diurnal* cycle   (1) different   (2) daily   (3) circuitous   (4) poetic

4.   a *surreptitious* act   (1) belittling   (2) unusual   (3) secretive   (4) illogical

5.   *apotheosis*   (1) pardon   (2) charm   (3) theory   (4) deification

6.   *attenuate*   (1) rub   (2) make slender   (3) absorb   (4) enlarge

7.   *bedizen*   (1) adorn   (2) inhabit   (3) two-footed   (4) alien

8.   a *captious* person   (1) spacious   (2) fickle   (3) fault-finding   (4) slanderous

9.   the *nascent* plants   (1) tasteless   (2) final   (3) emerging   (4) vocal

10.   *perfidy*   (1) deception   (2) completeness   (3) pierced   (4) hasty

11.   *repast*   (1) history   (2) confutation   (3) meal   (4) hobby

12.   *divagation*   (1) wandering   (2) amusement   (3) navigation   (4) stray

13.   a *brazen* remark   (1) insolent   (2) cast   (3) bronzed   (4) ornate

14.   *whim*   (1) sharp   (2) former   (3) weep   (4) fancy

15.   *abjure*   (1) renounce   (2) servile   (3) displace   (4) agree

16.   *ostentatious*   (1) plausible   (2) showy   (3) correlated   (4) hardening

17.   *protuberance*   (1) bulge   (2) lavish   (3) angry   (4) division

18.   *immure*   (1) imprison   (2) reward   (3) protect   (4) harden

19.   *subterfuge*   (1) infernal   (2) deception   (3) diminution   (4) body of an airplane

20.   an *obdurate* person   (1) submissive   (2) erase   (3) stubborn   (4) cover

21.   the *epitome* of taste   (1) letter   (2) typical representation   (3) land   (4) apex

22.   *gratis*   (1) free   (2) cheese sauce   (3) gift   (4) fine

23.   *novice*   (1) beginner   (2) split   (3) end   (4) old-timer

24.   *solace*   (1) comfort   (2) addition   (3) solicit   (4) impropriety

25.   *ludicrous*   (1) careful   (2) profitable   (3) laughable   (4) gloomy

26.   *cortege*   (1) rhyme   (2) flower   (3) procession   (4) chat

27. *conundrum* (1) particles (2) pipe (3) puzzle (4) boredom

28. a *condign* reward (1) kindly (2) assert (3) well-deserved (4) related

29. *concupiscent* (1) running together (2) lustful (3) eccentric (4) hopeless

30. *cognate* words (1) related (2) thoughtful (3) convincing (4) unlike

31. an *eclectic* decor (1) specific (2) military (3) selective (4) severe

32. a *droll* remark (1) amusing (2) elf (3) sour (4) waste

33. a *dolorous* face (1) financial (2) sorrowful (3) humorous (4) fatal

34. *disingenuous* (1) uncommon (2) immature (3) pleasant (4) not straightforward

35. *diffidence* (1) greed (2) controversy (3) disguise (4) timidity

36. *decorous* (1) ornamental (2) proper (3) harmful (4) old

37. *deciduous* (1) final (2) decisive (3) leaf-shedding (4) deadly

38. a *cursory* glance (1) profane (2) superficial (3) greedy (4) roomy

39. *credulous* (1) believable (2) corrupt (3) gullible (4) irrational

40. *craven* behavior (1) molded (2) bird (3) cowardly (4) profane

41. *excoriate* (1) denounce (2) disembowel (3) atone (4) furnish

42. to *expiate* one's guilt (1) explain (2) spit (3) destroy (4) atone

43. *extant* (1) complete (2) existing (3) search (4) praise

44. *feckless* (1) ineffective (2) careless (3) punctual (4) foul

45. *flagitious* (1) nonviolent (2) elaborate (3) necessary (4) vicious

46. *emollient* (1) lit (2) soothing (3) timid (4) secret

47. *envenom* (1) bite (2) embitter (3) subjugate (4) trap

48. *ergo* (1) besides (2) therefore (3) scholar (4) convent

49. *erotic* (1) strange (2) extreme (3) amatory (4) worn

50. *esoteric* knowledge (1) artistic (2) confidential (3) denounced (4) evident

51. *innocuous* (1) lazy (2) harmless (3) foul (4) harmful

52. *indolent* (1) poor (2) lazy (3) energetic (4) encouraging

53. *impotent* (1) all-powerful (2) incapable (3) beg (4) curse

54. *hyperbole* (1) exaggeration (2) assumption (3) instrument (4) platform

55. *histrionic* (1) historical (2) hairy (3) theatrical (4) scientific

56. *heinous* (1) atrocious (2) pleasurable (3) wolf (4) unorthodox

57. *gregarious* (1) free (2) distorted (3) sociable (4) derived

58. *gnostic* (1) atheist (2) wise (3) glandular (4) spiritual wisdom

59. *germane* (1) European (2) verbal noun (3) pertinent (4) flowery

60. *garrulous* (1) talkative (2) free (3) greedy (4) flowery

49
APPROPRIATENESS (37)

The appropriateness of your word choice directly affects the way readers respond to your writing. Inappropriate words will confuse readers and ultimately may irritate them. The words you choose set the tone of your writing; they tell the readers the attitude you are taking toward your subject and toward them as well.

What constitutes appropriate language? That depends to some extent on your topic, your purpose, and your audience. A letter to a close friend will have a much more informal style and will probably contain several slang expressions that would not be appropriate in a research report written for a college psychology class. The research report would undoubtedly contain some social-science jargon understood by people in psychology but possibly unfamiliar to the general public.

Although appropriateness is a somewhat relative matter, several guidelines do apply to all but the most informal writing:

1. Avoid **slang expressions** and **nonstandard English** unless you are recording actual conversation that uses them. Although slang is colorful and often lively, it is usually understood by a relatively small group of people. Furthermore, slang expressions quickly lose vigor. Today's slang may be meaningless to most readers in a year or two. Nonstandard English is normally associated with provincialism and lack of education; you should avoid it in your writing.

SLANG	That prof hit us with a really heavy number.
REVISION	That professor gave us a very difficult assignment.
NONSTANDARD ENGLISH	They wasn't on time, so let's don't wait for them.
REVISION	They weren't on time, so let's not wait for them.

2. Avoid **jargon** when writing for a general audience, and replace **artificial diction** with more straightforward words. Like slang, jargon is a vocabulary well known only to those in a particular group or discipline. Computer programmers, for example, are quite familiar with terms such as *byte* and *baud-rate*; general readers are not. Unless you are writing for a special audience, use jargon sparingly and define terms you think your readers might not know.

Artificial diction, on the other hand, never adds anything desirable to writing. Choose simple, direct words instead of elaborate, pompous-sounding ones. The person who writes *Males of advanced years fail to maintain their recollective faculties.* gains nothing; the one who writes *Old men forget.* makes an effective point.

EXERCISE 49, SLANG AND NONSTANDARD ENGLISH   (37)

Revise the following sentences to rid them of slang or nonstandard expressions.

Example   I was wasted after that all-nighter.

I was exhausted after studying all night.

1. The governor looks like a shoo-in again this year.

_____

_____

2. I shouldn't ought to have toted that poke.

_____

_____

3. The new restaurant we visited was the pits.

_____

_____

4. They were getting water from a spigot in the front yard.

_____

_____

5. I don't mean to put it down, though.

_____

_____

6. If they had any gumption, they would of found a place with a kitchen.

_____

_____

7. That fruitcake of a waiter almost drove me bananas.

_____

_____

8. The service out there was really gross.

_____

_____

9. Scarcely none of us got our main courses at the same time.

_____

_____

10. Our evening was fouled up good.

_____

_____

11. I had borrowed money for the bill off of my sister.

_____

_____

12. I hear it's for sale, on account of business being so poor.

_____

_____

13. They need to red up the whole building if they want to sell it.

_____

_____

14. The partners in that business must don't have much business sense.

_____

_____

15. They'll be lucky if they can get theirselves out of this mess.

_____

_____

Revise the following sentences using more straightforward language to correct artificial diction or jargon and any other inappropriate wording.

Example My nasal passages are congested.

_____ *My nose is stopped up.* _____

16. Woody Allen's comedic style is infinitely more naturalistic than Steve Martin's.

---

17. Allen's persona is lent verisimilitude by that very natural style.

---

18. One's perceptions of Martin's characterizations are dominated by the conviction that he is merely acting out a thespian role.

---

19. Martin's characters seldom possess genealogy, marriage, or other relationships that typify life in the phenomenal world.

---

20. In *The Jerk,* for example, the audience knows only that his character is a Caucasian foundling raised by a Black family.

---

21. Statistically the possibility of this happening is at a less than .05 probability.

---

22. Therefore the audience never experiences a willing suspension of disbelief.

---

23. The personae adopted for the cinema by Woody Allen, on the contrary, accrue innumerable naturalistic details.

---

24. Allen, né Konigsberg, always portrays a character of Jewish ethnicity and the audience possesses an awareness of the character's inner life.

---

25. The ethnic characteristics of Allen's characters do not allow the characters to spring at us from an existential void.

_____

_____

26. An explosive device being found in the suspect's place of habitation, the law-enforcement personnel maintained surveillance for his arrival there.

_____

_____

27. If our intergrader reliability coefficient can't be improved, we'll have to discontinue use of this instrument.

_____

_____

28. The superficiality of outward appearances is often incongruent with reality.

_____

_____

29. These days, it seems as if everything is a carcinogenic.

_____

_____

30. The lunar excursion module has contacted the surface.

_____

_____

50
EXACTNESS   (38a–c,e–g)

If a reader is to understand what you mean, your word choice needs to be as exact as possible. Selecting correct words and appropriate synonyms, avoiding invented words and improprieties, and using concrete and specific words are ways to achieve exactness in your writing.

The previous section on vocabulary briefly discussed synonyms. Synonyms are two or more words that mean essentially, but not exactly, the same thing. Desk dictionaries discriminate between word meanings by means of **synonymies**. These explanatory passages, labeled either *Synonyms* or *Syn.*, usually follow the definition of a main-entry word. The synonymy lists a group of synonyms for the main entry and explains the difference in meaning between the words listed. The following synonymy for the word *anger* is taken from *Webster's New World Dictionary of the American Language,* Second College Edition.

> **Syn.** *anger* is broadly applicable to feelings of resentful or vengeful displeasure: *indignation* implies righteous anger aroused by what seems unjust, mean, or insulting; *rage* suggests a violent outburst of anger in which self-control is lost; *fury* implies a frenzied rage that borders on madness; *ire,* chiefly a literary word, suggests a show of great anger in acts, words, looks, etc.; *wrath* implies deep indignation expressing itself in a desire to punish or get revenge.

When you consult a dictionary to locate the synonymy for a group of words, you may not always select the entry that contains the synonymy. In such a case, the dictionary will refer to the word where the synonymy occurs. In the case shown here, for example, had you first looked up the word *indignation,* you would have found the notation *Syn. see anger.*

In being exact it is also important not to confuse words. Some words give trouble because of similarities in spelling or pronunciation or similarities in both respects. One such group of words is **homonyms**, words that are identical in spelling and pronunciation but that have different meanings (*butter*—a spread; *butter*—a goat in action). Another group of words, called **homographs**, are identical in spelling but have different pronunciations and meanings (*wind*—one of nature's forces; *wind*—to coil the spring of). A third group of words, called **homophones**, are pronounced the same but are spelled differently and have different meanings (*red*—a color; *read* —the past tense of the verb *read*). Still a fourth group can be called **approximate homonyms**—that is, words that are pronounced or spelled approximately the same but have different meanings (*elicit*—to bring out; *illicit*—unlawful).

The best course of action when using words of these types is to look them up in the dictionary and learn their correct spellings and meanings.

Readers usually find words used in very unexpected ways to be troublesome because they do not fit convention and their meanings are therefore likely to be unclear. You should thus use invented words and improprieties with great care and only when you are sure their meanings will be clear.

Invented words can be grouped into three categories. One group is **neologisms**: either new words or, more commonly, old words with new meanings or usages. For example, the noun *shot* originally referred to bullets or pellets for firearms. Since the invention of the camera, *shot* can also mean a photograph or single cinematic view. Another group is **coined words**: deliberately invented creations which often achieve some degree of general use. *Smog* (smoke + fog), *motel* (motor + hotel), and *flak* (antiaircraft gunfire) are examples.

The third group is **noncewords**, words made up to fit special situations and generally not used more than once, as in *She committed final examicide because she didn't study for the chemistry test.*

Usually you should avoid invented words. When in doubt about whether a word is invented, consult the dictionary. If the dictionary does not list it or labels it as a substandard word, do not use the word in formal writing. In some instances in some contexts, your instructor may permit you to invent words yourself. Before doing so, however, you should determine his or her attitude toward such words.

Improprieties are legitimate words wrongly used: *The exits are signed clearly.* Sometimes you may wonder whether a word used as one part of speech can be used as another part of speech. English is fairly free in shifting words from one part of speech to another, a process called **functional shift.** For example, the noun *fire* is used as an adjective—as in *fire engine*—and as a verb—as in *fire the cannon.* However, convention dictates whether a word shifts or not. Unless a shift has generally been accepted, you would be wise to avoid it. Otherwise, the reader may find your usage inappropriate and confusing. If you are in doubt, consult the dictionary to ensure that the shift you want to use is not an impropriety.

Writing that captures the reader's interest and most effectively conveys the author's exact meaning usually relies on a high proportion of concrete and specific words to give it life and clarity. **Concrete words** name things we can perceive with our senses, things we can see, hear, touch, taste, and smell. **Abstract words,** on the other hand, name qualities, ideas, and concepts. *Honesty* is an abstraction. To say someone turned in a lost wallet at the campus police station is to show concretely what honesty means. **Specific words** refer to the individual members of a class or group. **General words** refer to all the members of a class or group. *Clothing* is general, but *shoes, shirts,* and *skirts* are specific. Using concrete and specific words in conjunction with abstract and general terms provides definition for your ideas and helps your reader to understand exactly what you mean.

Like concrete and specific words, **figurative language** can help readers understand your ideas. Fresh and appropriate figures of speech can be a very effective way of making meaning concrete. On the other hand, inappropriate figurative language will only obscure meaning. Replace **trite expressions** and **stereotyped** or **hackneyed phrases** with new or original expressions. Supply fresh figurative language instead of relying on tired clichés worn thin by constant use. But be careful not to "mix" metaphors or use figures of speech that are illogical, inept, or ludicrous.

When we read expressions such as "white as the driven snow" or "hot as the noonday sun," our reaction is likely to be "If I've heard it once, I've heard it a thousand times." As the last sentence indicates, we are apt to respond to a cliché with another cliché! Similes (comparisons introduced by the words *like, as, as if, as when*) that we have heard "a thousand times" obviously no longer stir our imaginations. Similarly, tired metaphors (implied comparisons—for example, *She riveted him to the wall with her piercing gaze.*) do not convince your readers that you have anything insightful to say about your topic. Illogical figures of speech not only fail to inform, they can be so absurd that readers may miss your point entirely or find your writing silly.

ILLOGICAL FIGURE OF SPEECH	His eyes, flashing like pools of flame, drowned me in their fire.
REVISION	His eyes, flashing like flames, seared me.

Name _____ Date _____ Score _____

EXERCISE 50-1, SYNONYMS   (38a)

In your dictionary, look up the synonymy that applies to each of the following groups of words. Write sentences in which you use and differentiate in meaning, according to the synonymy, each of the words in the group. You may change tense or part of speech in making up your sentences. The synonymies in this exercise are based on the *American Heritage Dictionary*, Second College Edition. If you are using a different dictionary, it may be necessary to look up some word meanings under the base entries for those words.

Example   misfortune *She had the misfortune to be standing in the wrong place.*

adversity *Adversity had forced him to sell his car to pay the rent.*

1. miscellaneous _____

    heterogeneous _____

    assorted _____

2. business _____

    industry _____

    commerce _____

    trade _____

    traffic _____

3. slow _____

    dilatory _____

    leisurely _____

    laggard _____

    deliberate _____

4. sly _____

    cunning _____

    tricky _____

    guileful _____

5. stupid _____

slow _____

dull _____

obtuse _____

dense _____

crass _____

6. mercy _____

leniency _____

clemency _____

forbearance _____

charity _____

7. effort _____

exertion _____

endeavor _____

application _____

strain _____

8. sad _____

depressed _____

dejected _____

desolate _____

9. area _____

region _____

district _____

10. decide _____

determine _____

settle _____

rule _____

conclude _____

resolve _____

**EXERCISE 50-2, SIMILAR WORDS, INVENTED WORDS,
IMPROPRIETIES   (38b, c)**

Construct sentences in which each of the following words is used correctly. In the case
of verbs, you may change the tense.

Example   accept _*I accept your offer.*_____

except *I would accept his invitation except that
I find him to be a bore.*

1. perspective _____

prospective _____

2. conscience _____

conscious _____

3. descent _____

decent _____

4. your _____

you're _____

5. precede _____

proceed _____

6. roll _____

role _____

7. waiver _____

waver _____

8. affect _____

effect _____

9. personnel _____

personal _____

10. principle _____

    principal _____

In the blanks, insert correct words for those italicized words that are substandard, invented words, or improprieties. Write *correct* if the italicized word is correct.

Example   He is *incredible* about my family history.   *incredulous*

11. Westside's team *thrubbed* Prep 61 to 3.   _____

12. We'll not do that *no how.*   _____

13. An immigrant can live *anywheres* he or she wants.   _____

14. Koreans in New York have specialized in *all-nite* grocery stores.   _____

15. Many immigrants have *combated* discrimination at first.   _____

16. The *premiere* Presley in America was Andrew Presley, Sr.   _____

17. Presley's *prodigy* have spread out across the United States.   _____

18. The history of the United States shows that it will *except* anyone.   _____

19. May I *infer* that you have proof of your remarks?   _____

20. Your behavior was simply *incouth.*   _____

21. The evidence in this case is *unrefutable.*   _____

22. We'll believe as we do, *irregardless* of the evidence.   _____

23. This whole process is highly *unregular.*   _____

24. The first step in making soup is to *seethe* some water.   _____

25. He *cogitated* that his position was unpopular.   _____

26. We *concluded* to go to the Chinese New Year's Day festival.   _____

27. I can *imply* from your actions that you're anthropology students.   _____

28. Many ethnic people feel safer *middle-of-the-roading* it.   _____

29. *Reclamation* of this land may take months.   _____

30. The laws of physics are not *unchanging.*   _____

EXERCISE 50-3, SPECIFIC AND CONCRETE WORDS   (38e)

Revise the following sentences, replacing nouns, verbs, and adjectives with more specific concrete words where appropriate. Invent details as needed.

Examples   I love Mexican food.

_____*I love tacos.*_____

He's nice.

_____*Sam, the janitor, always greets me with a smile.*_____

1.   I like casseroles.

_____

2.   Too many people have been absent.

_____

3.   The plane left.

_____

4.   She read a book.

_____

5.   Your paper was too general.

_____

6.   The class will write a research paper.

_____

7.   Some guy wants to see you.

_____

8.   I feel nervous.

_____

9.   The house is dilapidated.

_____

10. There is a man outside.

_____

11. Leonard is messy.

_____

12. We had an argument.

_____

13. We made a lot of noise.

_____

14. We attracted a crowd.

_____

15. He's not feeling well.

_____

16. I ate sparingly.

_____

17. British cars are expensive.

_____

18. Honesty always pays.

_____

19. The bank was busy.

_____

20. Your speech was a hit.

_____

21. This is a nice room.

_____

22. I've redecorated my room.

_____

EXERCISE 50-4, FIGURATIVE LANGUAGE, TRITENESS, CLICHÉS   (38f, g)

Revise the following sentences using figures of speech that are apt and logical.

Example   He was sweating like a fish out of water.

He was sweating like a jogger at noon.
He was gasping like a fish out of water.

1. He hit the deck to burn the midnight oil, so he could pass his senior exam.

2. Put your shoulder to the wheel and keep your ear to the ground to succeed.

3. Let's buckle down and rise to the occasion.

4. Like a raging ball of fire, the moonbeams danced on the water.

5. If everyone pitches in, we can keep the home fires burning.

6. Laura's Achilles heel is keeping her fingers in every pie.

7. The police have to stiffen their backbones before this case slips through their fingers.

8. I swept her off her feet by leaps and bounds.

_____

9. Like a lamb to the slaughter, she gave him the soft soap.

_____

10. We've got to turn over a new leaf if we don't want our marriage on the rocks.

_____

_____

11. The Ferrari had a real head of steam, feeding the flames of my lust to own one.

_____

_____

12. In the turns, the Porsche stuck to the pavement like flypaper.

_____

13. I was holding on to the steering wheel like glue.

_____

14. The recall movement was beginning to snowball, running madly forward out of control.

_____

_____

15. Let's massage this report and make sure none of our ideas drop through the cracks.

_____

_____

Revise the following sentences to eliminate all trite expressions, but be sure to preserve the ideas suggested by them.

Example   The mountainous waves towered over our boat.

_____ *The enormous waves rose over our boat.*

16. The view from this window is pretty as a picture.

_____

_____

17. The architect who built this was smart as a whip.

_____

_____

18. He took a hilly lot and made it flat as a pancake.

_____

_____

19. It's silent as the grave in this room because it's insulated so well.

_____

_____

20. Fearing that we'd never finish the house had me plunged into the depths of despair.

_____

_____

21. I knew we had to strike while the iron was hot to close the deal.

_____

_____

22. The last changes we asked for were the straw that broke the camel's back.

_____

_____

23. Now our architect is as mad as a wet hen.

_____

_____

24. We've changed our minds a thousand times.

_____

_____

25. We'll be warm as toast in here in the winter.

_____

_____

26. We could be moved in quick as a flash.

_____

_____

27. He promised us that the deal would go off without a hitch.

_____

_____

28. I thought you were a model of decorum throughout the ordeal.

_____

_____

29. When the going got rough, you were cool as a cucumber.

_____

_____

30. There was never any chance that I'd go to pieces.

_____

_____

51
IDIOMS   (38d)

An **idiom** is an expression peculiar to a given language—that is, it does not follow the normal pattern of the language, or it has a total meaning different from the one suggested by its separate words. In the previous sentence, the phrase *different from* is idiomatic: it does not follow the normal pattern of English. The expression *to lose one's head* exemplifies the second type of idiom: literally, the words indicate decapitation, but native speakers of English know the expression is not meant literally. To lose one's head is to become irrational or excessively emotional.

For any writer, the most troublesome idioms are those requiring a particular preposition after a given verb or adjective. The following list can help you know which idiomatic construction to use for a given meaning.

absolved by, from	I was *absolved by* the dean *from* all blame.
accede to	He *acceded to* his children's demands.
accompany by, with	I was *accompanied by* Louise. The terms were *accompanied with* a plea for immediate peace.
acquitted of	They were *acquitted of* the crime.
adapted to, from	This machine can be *adapted to* farm work. The design was *adapted from* an Indian invention.
admit to, of	He *admitted to* the prank. The plan will *admit of* no alternative.
agree to, with, in	They *agreed to* the plan but *disagreed with* us. They *agreed* only *in* principle.
angry with, at	They are *angry with* me and *angry at* the treatment they received.
capable of	She is *capable of* great kindness.
charge for, with	He expected to be *charged for* his purchase, but he didn't expect to be *charged with* stealing something.
compare to, with	He *compared* the roundness of the baseball *to* that of the earth. He *compared* the economy of the Ford *with* that of the Plymouth.
concur with, in	I *concur with* you *in* your desire to use the revised edition.
confide in, to	*Confide in* me. You *confided to* me that you had stolen the car.
conform to, with **conformity with**	The specifications *conformed to* (or *with*) my original plans. You must act in *conformity with* our demands.
connected by, with	The rooms are *connected by* a corridor. I am officially *connected with* this university.
contend for, with	Because she needed to *contend for* her principles, she found herself *contending with* her parents.
differ about, from, **with**	We *differ about* our taste in clothes. My clothes *differ from* yours. We *differ with* one another.

different from*	Our grading system is *different from* yours.
enter into, on, upon	She *entered into* a new agreement and thereby *entered on* (or *upon†*) a new career.
free from, of	He was *freed from* cultural assumptions by his education. He is *free of* prejudice.
identical with	Your reasons are *identical with* his.
join in, to, with	He *joined in* the fun *with* the others. He *joined* the wire cables *to* each other.
live at, in, on	She *lives at* 14 Neil Avenue *in* a Dutch Colonial house. She *lives on* Neil Avenue.
necessity for, of **need for, of**	There was no *necessity (need) for* you to lose your temper. There was no *necessity (need) of* your losing your temper.
object to	I *object to* the statement in the third paragraph.
oblivious of	When he works at the computer he is *oblivious of* the passing of time.
overcome by, with	I was *overcome by* the heat. I was *overcome with* grief.
parallel between, to, with	There is a *parallel between* your attitude and his. This line is *parallel to* (or *with*) that one.
preferable to	A leisurely walk is *preferable to* violent exercise.
reason about, with	Why not *reason with* them *about* the matter?
reward by, for, with	They were *rewarded by* their employer *with* a raise *for* their work.
variance with	This conclusion is at *variance with* your facts.
vary from, in, with	The houses *vary from* one another *in* size. People's tastes *vary with* their personalities.
wait for, on	They *waited for* someone to *wait on* them.
worthy of	That candidate is not *worthy of* your trust.

Different than is colloquially idiomatic when the object of the prepositional phrase is a clause:

This town looks *different from* what I had remembered. [Formal]
This town looks *different than* I had remembered it. [Colloquial]

†In many phrases, *on* and *upon* are interchangeable: *depend on* or *depend upon; enter on* or *enter upon.*

EXERCISE 51, IDIOMS   (38d)

Refer to Section 51, as necessary, to complete this exercise. In each blank, write the preposition that forms the correct idiomatic construction.

Example   He was relieved _____*of*_____ all further responsibility.

1. You must conform _____ the group if you are going to live with them.

2. She is capable _____ finishing her research.

3. Mr. Brown lives _____ 1112 Ash Street, on the reservation.

4. He is a man who has been oblivious _____ changes in the world.

5. Privacy is preferable _____ modern life, he decided.

6. We disagree _____ many things,

7. but we agree _____ each other about anthropologists.

8. They are worthy _____ your trust.

9. His informant was angry _____ him.

10. The necessity _____ your interview is in doubt.

11. The two anthropologists vary _____ each other in background.

12. You and I differ greatly _____ our objectives.

13. She was overcome _____ the fact that she had less than a year to finish the work.

14. The two sites were identical _____ each other.

15. The informant confided _____ the anthropologist all her family's squabbles.

16. He acceded _____ her demands for privacy.

17. The report must conform _____ the university's style sheets and research practices.

18. Never have there been two anthropologists whose methods varied _____ one another so much.

19. I was angry _____ the way I was evaluated.

20. I decided to enter _____ a new career.

In the following list, some expressions are idiomatically correct and some are not. In performing the exercise, refer either to Section 51 or to your dictionary, as necessary. Cross out any incorrect prepositions and write correct prepositions to the right of them. If an expression is correct, write *correct*.

Example   to compare one to the other   *Correct*

He is capable to change.   *of*

21. a recommendation to improvement   _____

22. different than we thought   _____

23. furnishing supplies for cattle ranchers   _____

24. If you need money, get it off the comptroller.   _____

25. not suitable to one of such eminence   _____

26. My quotation was of Margaret Mead.   _____

27. a great confidence with me   _____

28. overcome his surroundings   _____

29. a need to reappraise the project   _____

30. as different to each other as day and night   _____

31. embarrassed at my mistake   _____

32. ashamed at my bad mistake   _____

33. contend with the difficulties of the assignment   _____

34. the authority vested to me   _____

35. in regard of her wishes   _____

36. the only one objecting from the proposal _____

37. vary in several respects   _____

38. free of the chains that had bound them   _____

39. to refrain of further interference   _____

40. antithetical with our ethics as ethnologists   _____

52
DIRECTNESS   (39)

Your writing will be more effective if it is direct—if you use only those words that contribute to your meaning. Words and phrases that contribute nothing to meaning cause your readers to work hard at plowing through the language, but for no real payoff. Eventually readers become tired, bored, impatient, and unwilling to continue. The following guidelines can help you to remove wordiness from your writing:

1. Eliminate unnecessary nominals and weak verbs by recasting them as more vigorous and direct noun-verb combinations. A nominal is a noun formed by adding a suffix to a verb. Examples are *-ment, -tion, -ance,* or sometimes *-ity, -ize,* or *-ness: disagreement, substitution, deliverance.* Vague, weak verbs such as *make, give,* and *take* often occur with nominals as replacements for the stronger, more energetic verbs that have been changed into nouns.

NOMINAL/WEAK VERB	The *disagreement* about taxes *took* place between Brooks and Cortini.
REVISED	Brooks and Cortini *disagreed* about taxes.
WEAK/NOMINAL VERB	The coach *made* a *substitution* of Horwich for Brown.
REVISED	The coach *substituted* Horwich for Brown.

2. Prefer the active voice to the passive voice. Section 45 explained that active voice verbs make a sentence more lively and direct. They also use fewer words because active voice sentences require neither the helping verb used in a passive verb construction nor the prepositional phrase that identifies the agent of the action. Compare the following pair of sentences, and notice how much more economical and direct is the active voice sentence:

PASSIVE	The procedure was demonstrated by the lab technician.
ACTIVE	The lab technician demonstrated the procedure.

3. Eliminate words and phrases that do not contribute to meaning. Expressions such as *type of, in the case of, in the field of, aspect, factor, situation, I think, in my opinion* can often be cut from sentences. Expletives such as *there is, there are,* and *it is* can frequently be replaced by the true subject of the sentence to improve directness.

POOR	The best type of football team has the best quality of blockers.
IMPROVED	The best football team has the best blockers.
POOR	Pat majored in the field of engineering.
IMPROVED	Pat majored in engineering.
POOR	Another aspect of the situation that needs study, in my opinion, is the company's falling productivity.
IMPROVED	We should study the company's falling productivity.
POOR	There were four classes meeting on the third floor.
IMPROVED	Four classes met on the third floor.

4. Reduce clauses to phrases and phrases to single words when possible. Section 43 shows how economical and effective participles, appositives, and absolutes can be. These constructions frequently result from reducing whole clauses to phrase modifiers, as when *The train, which ran on time, pulled into the station.* is rewritten *The train, running on time,*

pulled into the station. Phrases and clauses can sometimes be reduced to one-word modifiers for further directness.

WORDY   The slipper, which was made of glass, fit the foot of Cinderella.

REVISED   The glass slipper fit Cinderella's foot. [The clause *which was made of glass* has been reduced to the single adjective *glass*; the prepositional phrase *of Cinderella* has been reduced to the single possessive noun *Cinderella's*.]

5. Avoid ineffective repetition and redundancy. Unintentional repetition, unlike repetition intended to create emphasis and coherence, often adds unnecessary—even silly-sounding—words to a sentence.

AWKWARD   Improved communication improved the staff's ability to satisfy
REPETITION   top management's expectations.

REVISED   Improved communication better enabled the staff to satisfy top management's expectations.

Redundant words say the same thing twice—for example, *visible to the eyes*. Note the following list of common redundancies and their revisions:

REDUNDANT	DIRECT
advance forward	advance
continue on	continue
refer back	refer
combine together	combine
close proximity	close
circle around	circle
small in size	small
few in number	few
disappear from view	disappear
throughout the whole	throughout
basic fundamentals	fundamentals
important essentials	essentials

**EXERCISE 52, WORDINESS, REDUNDANCY,
AND AWKWARD REPETITION   (39)**

Revise the following sentences to eliminate unnecessary words and phrases and
awkward repetition.

Example   Even ice cream is a foreign food from abroad.

Even ice cream is a foreign food.

1. Even the favorite food of many Americans, ice cream, was "imported" from another
    country.

2. According to *Time* magazine, in their opinion Americans eat more ice cream than
    anyone else in the world.

3. The Australians are in second place in the eating of ice cream.

4. Ice cream is not a native food to America.

5. The forerunner of ice cream in the field of dessert was flavored ice.

6. Nero, who was Emperor of Rome, was fond of flavored ice.

7. Marco Polo, who lived in the thirteenth century, brought back a recipe for a milky
    frozen dessert.

8. He had made the discovery of the recipe in the country of China.

9. In the year of 1533 Catherine de Medicis gave iced desserts an introduction to the
    French court.

10. The number of iced desserts available then was few in number.

11. There were only flavored ices and sherbets known until someone came up with the idea and thought to introduce frozen cream.

_____

12. To refer back in history, George Washington owned an ice-cream maker.

_____

13. It's reasonable to assume that Washington enjoyed ice cream, then.

_____

14. By the eighteenth century, devices for combining together the ingredients of ice cream were in almost every home.

_____

15. Until 1904 there were no ice-cream cones throughout the whole world.

_____

16. Ernest Hamwi, who was an immigrant from Damascus, Syria, rolled a thin, circular Persian pastry into the familiar cone shape and added a scoop of ice cream at the top.

_____

17. This improved way of handling ice cream improved Hamwi's business immensely.

_____

18. Hamwi invented his invention at the Louisiana Purchase Exposition in St. Louis.

_____

19. He called his invention the "World's Fair Cornucopia," which has become better known today as the ice-cream cone.

_____

20. In the field of ice cream there is a lot of government regulation.

_____

21. Despite these regulations, ice-cream makers continue on developing new products.

_____

22. The ingredients used in ice cream are few in number.

_____

23. In my opinion, I think butterfat content is the key factor in making ice cream taste rich.

_____

24. In the case of premium ice cream, it must contain less than 30 percent air.

_____

25. Most types of inexpensive ice cream have as much as 50 percent air.

_____

53
SPELLING   (40)

Many people, especially bad spellers, secretly believe good spellers are born, not made. There seem to be more exceptions than rules in spelling. Apart from correct pronunciation (which aids correct spelling), careful proofreading, and distinguishing between words that are similar in sound but different in meaning and spelling (such as *altar* and *alter*), the dictionary is your best resource. Learning spelling rules can also aid your spelling. Although there are exceptions to them, the following rules from the *Prentice-Hall Handbook for Writers,* Ninth Edition, provide general guidelines for correct spelling:

1. Avoid secondary and British spellings.

AMERICAN	BRITISH
encyclopedia	encyclopaedia
fetus	foetus
inquiry	enquiry
color	colour
center	centre
mold	mould
traveled	travelled
judgment	judgement

2. Distinguish between *ie* and *ei*: Write *i* before *e* except after *c* or when sounded like *a,* as in *neighbor* and *weigh.*

thief	conceive	sleigh
believe	ceiling	eight

3. Drop the final *e* before a suffix beginning with a vowel but not before a suffix beginning with a consonant.

please + ure = pleasure	sure + ly = surely
slide + ing = sliding	retire + ment = retirement

4. Change a final *y* to *i* before a suffix, unless the suffix begins with *i.*

defy + ance = defiance	cry + ing = crying
lively + hood = livelihood	rely + ing = relying

5. Double a final single consonant before a suffix beginning with a vowel when a single vowel precedes the consonant *and* the consonant ends an accented syllable or a one-syllable word. If both of these conditions do not exist, do not double the final consonant.

stop + ing = stopping	stoop + ing = stooping
admit + ed = admitted	benefit + ed = benefited

6. Usually you form the plurals of nouns ending in sounds that can be smoothly united with -*s* by adding -*s*. Form the third person singular of verbs ending in sounds that can be smoothly united with -*s* by adding -*s*.

SINGULAR	PLURAL	VERBS	
picture	pictures	blacken	blackens
radio	radios	criticize	criticizes

7. Form the plurals of nouns ending in sounds that cannot be smoothly united with -*s* by adding -*es*. Form the third person singular of verbs ending in sounds that cannot be smoothly united with -*s* by adding -*es*.

SINGULAR	PLURAL	VERBS	
porch	porches	tax	taxes
bush	bushes	collapse	collapses

8. Form the plurals of nouns ending in *y* preceded by a consonant by changing *y* to *i* and adding -*es*. Form the third person singular of verbs ending in *y* preceded by a consonant in the same way.

SINGULAR	PLURAL	VERBS	
pity	pities	deny	denies
nursery	nurseries	fly	flies

9. Form the plurals of nouns ending in *y* preceded by *a, e, o,* or *u* by adding -*s* only. Form the third person singular of verbs ending in *y* preceded by *a, e, o,* or *u* in the same way.

SINGULAR	PLURAL	VERBS	
day	days	play	plays
key	keys	employ	employs

10. Frequently you retain the plural of the original language in spelling plural nouns borrowed from French, Greek, or Latin, even though some of these nouns have been anglicized.

SINGULAR	PLURAL (foreign)	PLURAL (anglicized)
analysis	analyses	
crisis	crises	
appendix	appendices	appendixes
radius	radii	radiuses

EXERCISE 53-1, SPELLING   (40)

Some of the following words reflect preferred spellings. Others reflect British or secondary spellings. Write the preferred spelling of each word in the blank to its right.

Example   judgement   *judgment*

1. Barytone   _____   11.   gaol   _____

2. grey   _____   12.   realise   _____

3. catchup   _____   13.   councillor   _____

4. civilise   _____   14.   programme   _____

5. storey   _____   15.   fibre   _____

6. anaesthetic   _____   16.   cyder   _____

7. jeweller   _____   17.   plough   _____

8. enquiry   _____   18.   Pigmy   _____

9. labour   _____   19.   insure   _____

10. theatre   _____   20.   reflexion   _____

Draw a line through misspelled words in the following phrases and write them correctly in the blanks at the right. If no word is misspelled, write *correct* in the blank.

Example   the lonelyest person around   *loneliest*

21. loseing the case   _____

22. a candadate's speech   _____

23. a new devise for homeowners   _____

24. the principle idea to be learned _____

25. medeival history   _____

26. a cursury examination   _____

27. a member of Parliment   _____

28. an Elizabethan tradgedy _____

29. two paralell paths _____

30. a priviledge you earn _____

31. we practicly won _____

32. spend a nickle _____

33. you're quiet right _____

34. lacking in judgement _____

35. a morgage payment _____

36. the sophmore class _____

37. elected by acclimation _____

38. my roll in the class play _____

39. the high school principle _____

40. there exercises are strenuous _____

41. the student goverment _____

42. the lattitude and longitude _____

43. how's the whether _____

44. whether they win or loose _____

45. driving passed the street _____

46. the capitol gains tax _____

47. whose on first base? _____

48. our forth game of the season _____

49. taking seperate vacations _____

50. the event that occured here _____

51. a nuculear-powered submarine _____

52. the auxilary generator _____

53. a tempermental artist _____

54. accidently dropped the book _____

55. an iminent judge _____

56. a grievous mistake _____

57. new farm equippment _____

58. a contemptable way to behave _____

59. you probly will _____

60. the read section of the orchestra _____

To the right of each of the following sets of words, write the correct spelling of any misspelled words in the set. If no word is misspelled, write *correct* in the space.

Example	eclectic	droll	dolerous	mournful	*dolorous*
61.	circular	propheticaly	common	successful	_____
62.	riches	bordom	poverty	thickness	_____
63.	foul	greedyly	difficulty	loudness	_____
64.	widespread	threatening	all-powerful	obvioussly	_____
65.	sweet	political	noisy	oily	_____
66.	closeing	baritone	joining	opening	_____
67.	father	out-dated	noisy	disslike	_____
68.	proud	bowing	dully	servilaty	_____
69.	obece	bowing	confusion	prevention	_____
70.	annoying	soothing	foul-smelling	harmfull	_____
71.	congeniality	perplexed	offensive	ilogical	_____
72.	wicked	knew	nerveous	hazy	_____
73.	mythical	watery	sleazy	wicked	_____
74.	temple	miscellaneous	dress	fraudulant	_____
75.	dieing	biting	soft	sarcastic	_____
76.	irons	manners	distribution	couragous	_____
77.	food	plain	encounter	distributeion	_____
78.	lively	heavenly	mixed	naseating	_____

79.	flowing	lying	depresed	specific	_____
80.	gown	comparison	mixture	voracaty	_____
81.	verbal	stoppable	drowsy	concealed	_____
82.	proverb	most	mosque	spirit	_____
83.	imitative	belittling	adversion	abjure	_____
84.	wifes	canopy	text	mold	_____
85.	misuse	discomfort	satireical	generosity	_____
86.	native	poor	benificial	ill-bred	_____
87.	portly	cleaver	naturally	transferable	_____
88.	dramaticcal	drunken	unproductive	spasm	_____
89.	sharp	former	weep	fancy	_____
90.	defeatted	labor	cave	preserver	_____
91.	circle	modicum	exagerrate	branch	_____
92.	anger	pride	proclivity	merriment	_____
93.	detention	deception	vacume	conference	_____
94.	steal	sieze	worship	accumulated	_____
95.	lose	purify	exclude	immenent	_____
96.	negate	servile	displace	poligamous	_____
97.	swaying	deflection	lighten	dwelling	_____
98.	divorce	rudeness	posession	legacy	_____
99.	chasten	supplys	expand	polish	_____
100.	adress	omniscient	heavenly	earthly	_____

EXERCISE 53-2, SPELLING   (40)

Fill in each blank with the appropriate choice, either *ie* or *ei*. Don't guess. Use your dictionary.

1.	cash____r	7.	h____r	13.	f____nd	19.	conc____t
2.	f____gn	8.	f____rce	14.	misch____f	20.	sl____gh
3.	n____ce	9.	rec____ve	15.	br____f	21.	bel____ve
4.	c____ling	10.	w____gh	16.	hyg____ne	22.	w____rd
5.	l____sure	11.	n____ther	17.	perc____ve	23.	s____ze
6.	n____ghbor	12.	h____ght	18.	counterf____t	24.	th____ves

Write the correct spelling of each of the words formed by joining the given prefix or suffix to the given root. Remember that in some cases you will have to add, delete, or change a letter.

Examples   judge + ing   *judging*

swim + ing   *swimming*

busy + ness   *business*

weight + less   *weightless*

25.	run + ing	_____	34.	cancel + ed	_____
26.	brim + ing	_____	35.	continue + ance	_____
27.	marriage + able	_____	36.	renew + al	_____
28.	dis + taste	_____	37.	sever + ance	_____
29.	close + ure	_____	38.	bond + age	_____
30.	beauty + ful	_____	39.	intent + tion	_____
31.	judge + ment	_____	40.	disparage + ment	_____
32.	hope + less	_____	41.	pit + ance	_____
33.	lovely + ness	_____	42.	stop + er	_____

43. writhe + ing _____   59. swat + ed _____

44. rely + ance _____   60. petty + ness _____

45. carry + age _____   61. rid + ance _____

46. pun + ing _____   62. mere + ly _____

47. re + arrange _____   63. eighty + eth _____

48. debate + able _____   64. desire + able _____

49. strive + ing _____   65. label + ing _____

50. pre + existing _____   66. desire + ous _____

51. confer + ing _____   67. succeed + ing _____

52. consider + able _____ 68. tag + ing _____

53. icy + ness _____   69. intertwine + ing _____

54. exist + ence _____   70. flab + y _____

55. ninety + eth _____   71. mis + spell _____

56. value + able _____   72. witty + ness _____

57. incidental + ly _____ 73. tarry + ed _____

58. befit + ing _____   74. imbue + ing _____

To the right of each of the following sets of words, write the correct spelling of any misspelled word in the set. If no word in the set is misspelled, write *correct* in the space.

Example	adjacent	textured	temparate	infectious	*temperate*
75.	interested	enroll	laboratory	varous	_____
76.	clumsyly	driver	elephant	defamation	_____
77.	softened	generousity	extraordinary	wrong	_____
78.	whirlpool	poem	mold	licenseing	_____
79.	covered	grusome	authoritative	lazy	_____
80.	talkative	ridiculous	sad	supplementery	_____
81.	untrue	tax	prayerfull	supplement	_____
82.	portraial	established	prayer	riches	_____

83.	possible	text	nativaty	defamatory	_____
84.	dictionary	elf	dullard	satire	_____
85.	obviously	milky	briefly	cancealled	_____
86.	army	trickery	vegetable	wearyness	_____
87.	lewdness	fear	allowance	humorosly	_____
88.	blameing	weakening	burdensome	growth	_____
89.	tardiness	lewdness	fear	allowence	_____
90.	briefly	tearfuly	lewdly	envious	_____
91.	weariness	lazyly	tearfulness	drowsy	_____
92.	circular	milky	clearence	brief	_____
93.	tearing	stealling	stand	castilian	_____
94.	juvenile	legalaty	confusedly	bombastic	_____
95.	sinful	harmful	treacharous	carefree	_____
96.	bravery	orderring	essential	firm	_____
97.	turning	attacking	insertion	defendder	_____
98.	healthy	weakness	envyous	angrily	_____
99.	lamentation	confusion	lascivicious	lacerate	_____
100.	respectful	similiar	latent	humorous	_____

54
THE WRITING PROCESS   (41)

Sometimes when we have a writing assignment the words flow easily, and sometimes we spend hours before the blank sheets of paper, struggling to produce a few lines—filling the wastebasket with rejected efforts. All writers, including professionals, face dry spells; *Writer's Digest*, a magazine for freelance writers, periodically features articles about how to overcome "writer's block."

Although the ultimate goal of every writer is to create a well-crafted, effective product —whether it be an essay, a poem, a newspaper article, or a memo to the boss—that product is the result of a process. The writing process is the method a writer uses to create his or her essay, poem, or memo. When writers talk about writer's block, they are talking about ways to get the process rolling so the words will flow successfully.

We all use some process, some mental system for producing writing. One method may be more successful for you than another. Many people find that they most easily become involved in a subject if they just begin to fill pages with ideas, everything they can think of concerning their subject. Then they go back and pick and choose, order and shape, revise and edit, until they are satisfied with the result. Other people do this sort of "brainstorming" mentally and do not put words on paper until they have a fairly clear notion of what the contents and structure of the finished piece will be. Some people edit their sentences as they write them—correcting and revising as they go. Other writers edit and revise only after they have completed a first draft.

There is no one "best" or "right" writing process. You should observe your own methods and use the ones that work best for you. If your own system doesn't seem to be working, try some tactics others have found successful. One student, for example, felt dissatisfied with the "stuffy tone that just isn't 'me'" in a job application letter she had written. At her teacher's suggestion, she visualized what the letter's recipient might be like. Although she had never met the personnel officer to whom she was writing, she discovered that when she thought about her intended *audience,* a *real* reader, the tone of her letter became more forthright and better reflected her personality.

Another student found that *goals and purposes* were his stumbling block. In his application letter, he rehearsed his qualifications for the advertised job, his education and work experience, but still he felt the letter was unsatisfactory. In particular, it seemed to trail off ineffectively at the end. Once he realized that his goal in writing the letter was not just to apply for the job but also to secure an interview, the student was able to compose a strong, action ending that requested the interview.

The same assignment led another student to discover that her biggest problem was *organization.* Unhappy with the choppy, illogical structure of her letter, she decided that she needed to reorganize the paragraphs. Instead of using time order to present her education and employment experience ("first I worked here, then I went to school there"), she chose order of climax to present her skills, ending with those she believed her reader would find most important to the job she sought.

Although you may work best with a different or modified version of the writing process described next, its steps outline a method that many writers use successfully. The following sections and exercises enable you to try this method and see if it works for you.

PLANNING

1. Identify the goal(s) and purpose(s) of your writing task: What do you want to accomplish? What is your aim?

2. Select a subject appropriate to the writing task.

3. Think carefully about the kind of reader(s) to whom you are writing; the identity of the audience largely determines what you want to say and how you want to say it.

4. Begin to narrow and focus your subject to suit your purpose(s) and audience.

5. Make a list of ideas, assertions, facts, and examples that are related to your subject, and work this list into preliminary logical groupings.

6. Frame a specific thesis statement that will help you accomplish your writing goal(s) and purpose(s).

7. Choose those items from your preliminary list that fit your purpose(s) and support your thesis; add any new ones that are relevant. Then decide on the patterns of organization and methods of development that will best serve your purpose(s) and most effectively communicate your ideas to your readers. Now work these items into an outline that you can use as a guide while you write the first draft.

WRITING AND REVISING

8. Begin writing, and keep writing until you have completed a rough draft. Don't be overly concerned about wording, phrasing, grammar, or punctuation; at this stage pursue your thoughts rather than concentrate upon correctness.

9. Try to think of an illustration, an anecdote, or an example to use as an interesting introduction for your paper. Reread each paragraph to be sure it is clearly related to your thesis. Look at your ending paragraph: it should bring your essay to a *close* and not just *quit.*

10. Go over your first draft, checking it for correct spelling, punctuation, grammar, and effective sentences. Read it again for clarity, effective organization, and sound reasoning. Revise as necessary.

11. Give your paper a "cooling-off" period. Leave it for a while. When you reread it later, you may find rough spots that escaped your notice during the first writing and that you now want to rework or polish.

12. Prepare the final copy. Don't forget to create a title for your paper that indicates the topic and catches the readers' interest.

Practice: Brainstorming about topics   *Most people love a soapbox—a chance to stand up and speak their minds about a subject. A writing assignment is a readymade soapbox: You have decided, or someone has asked you, to "sound off." List at least three topics about which you'd like to sound off. Think about each one for a while. Then jot down some points that you think are especially important for each. Now imagine that you will be speaking from your soapbox to an audience. Compose an opening sentence for each of the topics, a sentence you could use to begin a speech.*

55
LIMITING TOPICS AND FORMING
THESIS STATEMENTS   (41–b,d)

Settling on a subject about which to write is usually not so much a matter of "finding" a topic as "creating" one. The Practice in Section 54 gave you some experience with this type of activity. Whether you are assigned a subject or choose one on your own, selecting a general subject area often involves simply deciding just which aspect of the subject to use as your **topic.**

While you were brainstorming for the Practice, you probably "found" quite a few subjects about which you had interest and opinions. But when you listed points about those subjects and composed the opening sentences for the speeches, you also probably discovered that you needed to narrow your focus—to limit the range of the subject. You were engaged in the process of creating the topic, defining its limits to make it interesting and effective for your audience. In other words, you were shaping the topic so that it was manageable.

The most manageable topics for short essays, such as those you write in English composition classes, are limited, specific topics. In order to do justice to a topic, you need one that is specific rather than general. Obviously, if you try to tackle freedom of speech in a short essay, you will either run out of space and time (after all, whole books have been written about it), or your treatment of the subject will be extremely superficial and loaded with unsupported generalizations. On the other hand, the high-school administrators' censorship of your student newspaper is a topic that would enable you to discuss the principle of free speech in some detail, using concrete examples in a manageable context. You would be exploring general truths through specific applications and illustrations of them.

If you examine magazine articles by professional writers, you will see that they use the same method. For example, an author writing about good ethnic restaurants may focus on one aspect of the subject—outstanding Greek restaurants in Chicago.

In the process of limiting your topic, you are already planning what you want to say about it just by choosing which aspect you want to focus on. When you jot down a list of points and then choose the pertinent, important ones, your brainstorming produces further "invention," further creation and development of the topic. As you arrange your points, deleting some and adding others, you are deciding in what direction you want to go with your topic. You are working out your purpose and preparing to compose the thesis statement for your paper.

The **thesis statement** presents the controlling idea you will develop in the body of your paper. Often it sets forth not only the main idea but also the important points, or **aspects**, that make up the idea. During the process of developing a thesis statement, you are thinking your topic through, determining what is relevant and what is not. You are deciding exactly what assertions you want to make about your topic and what points, examples, or illustrations you will need to support those assertions.

Usually the thesis statement can be expressed in one sentence, the subject identifying the topic and the predicate making an assertion about the topic:

SUBJECT
The golden years of retirement

PREDICATE
have become grim years of poverty for many senior citizens.

Mentioning the topic's major aspects will give you a good organizing statement for the development of the body of your paper and will also prepare your reader for what lies ahead:

> The golden years of retirement have become grim years of poverty for many senior citizens because their fixed incomes have left them defenseless against rising prices.

Just as a topic should be limited and specific, so should a thesis statement. If you are writing a 500-word essay on alcohol abuse, you know you can't say everything there is to be said about the subject, so you may decide to limit your discussion to alcohol abuse among teenagers or alcohol abuse among women. Even so, you can't say everything there is to be said about such a partially limited topic as alcohol abuse among women (causes, profile of abusers, physical and emotional effects on the drinker, effects on the family, various types of treatment and rehabilitation, recurring problems, life-long scars, etc.). So you won't want to compose a thesis that touches on all these points. Instead, you can focus in your thesis statement on one or two of them—for example, *Women who become alcoholics are often bored, lonely housewives who literally drink to "drown their sorrows."*

Notice how much more manageable this thesis statement is than *Lots of women are alcoholics.* or even *Lots of women drink because they are unhappy.* A good thesis statement restricts a topic to something you can reasonably discuss in some depth, focuses that topic on several specific aspects, and indicates the plan you intend to use in the rest of your paper to make the case you set up in the thesis statement.

Practice A: Limiting subjects   *Which of the following topics are too broad and general as stated to be manageable in a 500-word essay? The answers are listed at the end of this section.*

1. Ethnic groups
2. The Ulster Scots and eastern Richmond County
3. Difficulties faced by Vietnamese refugees
4. How "American" food became American
5. Immigration patterns in the nineteenth century

Practice B: Restricting and focusing thesis statements   *Which of the following thesis statements are too vague and imprecise to be effective? The answers are listed at the end of this section.*

1. American culture is a joke.
2. In this country, anyone can be a success.
3. Of all their contributions to the history of Georgia, the political contributions of the Ulster Scots may be the most important.
4. Immigrants coming to America now don't want to work as hard as earlier immigrants did.
5. Immigration into America is now less than one-hundredth of its highest level, which was at the turn of this century.

Answers to Practice A   1. Too general   2. Manageable   3. Manageable
4. Too general   5. Too general

Answers to Practice B   1. Too vague   2. Too vague   3. Manageable
4. Too vague   5. Manageable

Name _____ Date _____ Score _____

EXERCISE 55-1, LIMITING TOPICS   (41b)

For each general subject here, list three examples—each one more specific than the one that precedes it.

Examples   Automobiles   Contests

    A. The Sports Car   A. Athletic Competition
    B. The British Sports Car   B. Amateur Track Events
    C. The Jaguar XK 120   C. The Olympic Decathlon

1. Television   2. Education

  A. _____   A. _____

  B. _____   B. _____

  C. _____   C. _____

3. Leisure   4. Politics

  A. _____   A. _____

  B. _____   B. _____

  C. _____   C. _____

For each general subject here, list four specific essay topics. Each topic should be more specific than the one that precedes it.

Examples   Football   Weapons

    A. College football   A. Handguns
    B. The positions on a football   B. Small-caliber handguns
       team   C. "Saturday Night Specials"
    C. How to block   D. Recent gun-control legislation
    D. How to throw a "roll" block   aimed at limiting the sale of
                          small, inexpensive handguns

5. The space age   6. Energy

  A. _____   A. _____

  B. _____   B. _____

  C. _____   C. _____

  D. _____   D. _____

7. Popular fads

A. _____

B. _____

C. _____

D. _____

8. Studying

A. _____

B. _____

C. _____

D. _____

9. Choice of a career

A. _____

B. _____

C. _____

D. _____

10. Reading

A. _____

B. _____

C. _____

D. _____

11. Neighborhoods

A. _____

B. _____

C. _____

D. _____

12. Sports

A. _____

B. _____

C. _____

D. _____

13. Music

A. _____

B. _____

C. _____

D. _____

14. Family

A. _____

B. _____

C. _____

D. _____

15. Topic of your choice _____

_____

A. _____

B. _____

C. _____

D. _____

16. Topic of your choice _____

_____

A. _____

B. _____

C. _____

D. _____

EXERCISE 55-2, DEVELOPING A THESIS STATEMENT   (41d)

At each number here, list a general subject about which you would like to write.
You may use some of the subjects you listed in the previous exercise. Brainstorm
for a while, and then write down the specific topic you would explore in an essay.
Brainstorm some more, and then list six aspects of the topic that you might discuss
in your paper.

Example   *General subject:* Television
                      Specific topic: Music Videos
              A.   Offer a single visual interpretation of each song
              B.   Make the development of new talent even more expensive
              C.   Are frequently poorly done and trivial in content
              D.   Are sometimes violent
              E.   Become repetitive since there are too few to fill a day's
                   programming
              F.   Take important programming time from more worthwhile topics

1.   *General subject:* _____

     Specific topic: _____

         A.   _____

         B.   _____

         C.   _____

         D.   _____

         E.   _____

         F.   _____

2.   *General subject:* _____

     Specific topic: _____

         A.   _____

         B.   _____

         C.   _____

         D.   _____

         E.   _____

         F.   _____

3. *General subject:* _____

   Specific topic: _____

   A. _____

   B. _____

   C. _____

   D. _____

   E. _____

   F. _____

4. *General subject:* _____

   Specific topic: _____

   A. _____

   B. _____

   C. _____

   D. _____

   E. _____

   F. _____

5. *General subject:* _____

   Specific topic: _____

   A. _____

   B. _____

   C. _____

   D. _____

   E. _____

   F. _____

For each of your five topics, now select three of the aspects that would be manageable in a 500-word essay. List them. Then compose a focused thesis statement for the essay you would write on each topic.

Example   *Specific topic:* Music Videos
A. Offer a single visual interpretation of each song
B. Make the development of new talent even more expensive
C. Become repetitive since there are too few to fill a day's programming

Thesis statement: Music videos are an ill-advised development in the music industry, since they are repetitive, expensive to develop, and offer a single visual interpretation of each song.

Or   Music videos limit the audience's interpretation of each song, make the development of new talent even more expensive, and quickly become repetitive since there are too few music videos being made to fill a day's programming.

1. *Specific topic:* _____

   A. _____

   B. _____

   C. _____

   Thesis statement: _____

   _____

   _____

   _____

2. *Specific topic:* _____

   A. _____

   B. _____

   C. _____

   Thesis statement: _____

   _____

   _____

   _____

3. *Specific topic:* _____

   A. _____

   B. _____

   C. _____

   Thesis statement: _____

   _____

   _____

   _____

   _____

4. *Specific topic:* _____

   A. _____

   B. _____

   C. _____

   Thesis statement: _____

   _____

   _____

   _____

   _____

5. *Specific topic:* _____

   A. _____

   B. _____

   C. _____

   Thesis statement: _____

   _____

   _____

   _____

   _____

56
OUTLINING   (41h)

Outlining comprises an important part of the planning for the writing of a paper. Once you have identified the aspects you want to discuss in the composition, you must consider the order in which to present them. The outline provides a visible arrangement of aspects and subaspects and shows the logical sequence and rank of major and minor points.

The two types of outlines generally preferred in composition classes are sentence outlines and topic outlines. In the **sentence outline**, all headings and subheadings must be sentences. In the **topic outline,** headings and subheadings are not sentences; frequently they are composed of a few words or of phrases. Each type of outline has advantages. The sentence outline usually requires the outliner to think the subject through very thoroughly and also provides training in constructing short, to-the-point sentences. The topic outline usually requires less time to develop.

Outlines can have several levels. The first level is the main headings, designated by Roman numerals: I, II, III, etc. The second level is designated by capital letters: A, B, C, etc. The third level uses arabic numbers: 1, 2, 3, etc. The fourth and fifth levels, when used, are indicated by small letters: a, b, c, etc., and numbers in parentheses: (1), (2), (3), etc.

One important thing to remember about an outline is that when a heading or subheading is divided, it is always divided into at least two parts.

NOT	I.		BUT	I.
		A.		A.
				B.

Of course, headings or subheadings may be divided into more than two parts. Insofar as possible, all headings and subheadings of the same level of importance should be written in parallel form, with the same grammatical structure. Thus, if I is a noun phrase, II and III should also be noun phrases. If A begins with a gerund, B and C should too.

Following is a sentence outline that could provide the basis for the introduction of a composition "Finding a Summer Job."

I.   Students can choose among several ways to spend their time during summer vacation.
    A. They may take it easy.
        1. Loafing is a lot of fun.
        2. Doing nothing requires little effort.
    B. They may get summer jobs.
        1. Working includes many worthwhile experiences.
        2. Working enables them to make money.
        3. If they desire to work during the summer they must do the following.
            a. They must consult job sources.
            b. They must write letters of application for employment.
            c. They must make good appearances at their job interviews.

THESIS
STATEMENT IN
OUTLINE FORM

Once you have completed the outline for the introduction of the paper, you should develop the outline for the body and conclusion. If you have developed the introduction to provide for a thesis statement, you can now take the aspects of your thesis and use them for the main headings of the body of the outline.

The first aspect of the thesis statement contained in the outline on finding a summer job could be used for main heading II of the outline. This main heading would then be developed to three levels.

II. They must consult job sources.
   A. They can study the newspapers.
      1. The want ad sections list many job opportunities.
      2. They can acquaint themselves with firms through their advertising.
   B. They can use the college's employment service.
      1. Many employers advertise for help through this service.
      2. They can advertise their services through this function.

Part II of the outline has now been developed to three levels. A pertains to studying the newspapers. Subheadings 1 and 2 under A offer advice concerning the study of newspapers. B concerns the college's employment service. Subheadings 1 and 2 under B provide information concerning this service. A and B, in turn, by discussing the newspapers and using the college's employment service, pertain to the consulting of job sources mentioned in II.

Up to this point, the outline has continued to perform its basic functions:

1. It has provided details for development of this portion of the body of the composition.

2. Since each subheading relates to the subheading level preceding it, and level-two subheadings relate to the level-one main heading, the outline has continued to stick to the subject.

In the topic outline there are no sentences. Instead, each heading and subheading is followed by a noun or substantive or a phrase. You should avoid verbs in a topic outline since the resulting construction is often a sentence with an understood subject. To say *Follow the instructions carefully,* for example, is really to say *(You) follow the instructions carefully.* Also avoid constructions that are not sentences only because they lack verbs. For example, *Schools not as good as they used to be* is really only an incomplete sentence; all it needs to qualify as a sentence is the verb *are.*

CRITERIA FOR TOPIC OUTLINES

The topic outline should, of course, follow the basic requirements of all outlines: each heading and subheading, when divided, should be broken down into at least two parts, and each level should relate to the level preceding it. In addition, keep the following points in mind:

1. Use no verbs.

2. Use no expressions that would be sentences if only a verb or subject were added.

3. Strive for phrases that contain a noun (substantive) with modifiers—for example, *Progress in testing* or *Testing progress.* Generally, a noun by itself may be insufficient. Enough should be said in the outline to provide a definite guide to the writer. The outline should indicate not only the aspect, but also the particular point to be discussed concerning that aspect. *Testing,* for example, provides much less guidance to the writer than does *Progress in testing.*

EXERCISE 56-1, OUTLINING   (41h)

Following is part I of a sentence outline for a paper titled "What a Family Must Do If It Adopts a Pet." To the right of each entry of the outline, insert the appropriate letter or letters of items *A* to *D*, which describe the possible flaws in the outline. Errors in the outline include the following:

A. Subheading is not a sentence.
B. Subheading is not broken into a minimum of two parts.
C. Subheading does not relate to the subhead level preceding it.
D. Subheading does not provide the basis for a thesis statement with three aspects.

I.   Although owning a pet can have advantages, it also involves responsibilities   _____

   A.   It brings a lot of pleasure   _____

      1.   Children can romp with it   _____

   B.   Instilling of a sense of responsibility   _____

      1.   It helps children to mature   _____

      2.   It need not cost much   _____

   C.   If a family decides to get one   _____

      1.   It must pay veterinarian bills   _____

      2.   It must give it the proper food   _____

Complete the following sentence outline for the introduction of a paper titled "The Advantages of Going to College." Be sure that you write a complete sentence after each subheading.

I.   High school students have two choices after graduation.

   A.   They may go to work.

      1. _____

      2. _____

   B.   They may go to college.

      1. _____

      2. _____

      3.   If they go to college, they will profit in three ways.

         a. _____

         b. _____

         c. _____

Develop main headings III and IV of the outline for a paper about finding a summer job. Go to three levels, and make sure that each subheading is a full sentence. Also be sure that each subheading relates to the subheading or heading preceding it. The main headings, of course, relate to the other two aspects of the thesis statement. In developing III, you may wish to consider the parts of a letter of application for employment: the introductory covering statement and the resume. You may also wish to consider what the letter will and will not do for the applicant.

III. Students must write letters of application for employment.

    A. _____

        1. _____

        2. _____

    B. _____

        1. _____

        2. _____

In the main heading IV, you may want to consider the impression the job interviewee's appearance makes on the employer and how important appearance may be to the employer's customers.

IV. They must make good appearances at job interviews.

    A. _____

        1. _____

        2. _____

    B. _____

        1. _____

        2. _____

Develop main heading V of the outline for the paper "Finding a Summer Job." Since this will be the conclusion of the essay, suitable development might include advice to students concerning the basis on which they would select their jobs. Be sure that each subheading is a sentence and that it relates to the outline level preceding it.

V. Students should consider two factors in selecting jobs.

    A. _____

        1. _____

        2. _____

B. _____

    1. _____

    2. _____

Portions of the outline for the paper "Finding a Summer Job" are reproduced here as a topic outline. Certain parts, however, are incorrect according to the criteria we have discussed throughout Section 56. Study each outline heading and subheading carefully. Then, to the right of each entry, either rewrite the entry correctly or insert *correct*. (The sentence outline forms of I and II are given in Section 56.)

I.   Option of student concerning summer activity

    A.   Take it easy

        1.   Fun of loafing

        2.   Doing nothing little effort

    B.   Getting a summer job

        1.   Worthwhile experiences of working

        2.   Make money

II.   Methods of finding a job

    A.   Newspapers

        1.   Job opportunities in classified ad sections

        2.   Advertising of firms

    B.   Use college's employment service

        1.   Employers

        2.   Advertise student's own services

Change the following portion of a sentence outline to a topic outline, using the criteria discussed in Section 56.

II.   One of the most important uses of a dictionary is looking up the meanings of words.

    A.   An individual should understand the significance of the order in which meanings are given.

        1.   Some dictionaries give the most common meanings first.

        2.   Others give the definition with the centralized meaning first.

        3.   Still others give definitions in chronological order, with the original meanings before the ones in current use.

B.   The consulter should notice if the definition is labeled as a special or technical meaning.

      1.   Some words have both a general and a special meaning.

      2.   Some words are used only in a technical field.

II. _____

    A. _____

      1. _____

      2. _____

      3. _____

    B. _____

      1. _____

      2. _____

Using your own paper, choose one of the topics for which you composed a thesis statement in Exercise 55–2 and develop a three-level outline for it. You may develop either a sentence outline or a topic outline; your instructor may specify one or the other.

57
EFFECTIVE BEGINNINGS AND ENDINGS   (41i)

BEGINNINGS

Oddly enough, the best time to think about the beginning of your essay is usually after you have finished the first draft. Occasionally an interesting opening may come to mind as soon as you decide on a specific topic. If that happens, fine. Write it down so you won't forget it. But more frequently the process of writing the paper will clarify your purpose, and composing a beginning will be easier after your first draft is completed.

Journalists and other professional writers talk about creating a "lead" or a "hook" for their stories. They want an opening that will grab the readers' interest—get them "hooked" in the opening paragraph so they will want to read the whole article. You want strong, direct, compelling openings for your own papers too.

An effective beginning attracts the readers' interests and introduces them to the topic. Although the beginning should not be too long in proportion to the rest of the paper (it is only the introduction, after all), it should be long enough to achieve some rapport with the readers and to establish a clear statement of purpose before you launch into the development of your topic's aspects. Other points to remember in beginning your paper include the following:

1. Try to get the readers' attention with a suitable anecdote, a justification of the subject, a startling statement, or a statement of the relevance of the subject to some local issue or happening.

2. Discuss briefly the general area or the subject matter, or supply background information as appropriate.

3. Indicate the purpose of the paper. A good way of doing this is to insert the thesis statement as the last sentence of the introduction.

4. Do not ramble. Make what is said in the introduction relevant either to the specific subject or to the background information.

5. Do not launch immediately into the principal topic of discussion without first providing some indication as to what the topic is going to be.

6. Do not comment upon the title without first introducing the idea in the title as a basis for discussion.

7. Do not insert material that has nothing to do with the topic.

Consider the following introduction written by a student in an English composition class:

> As we cruised down the moonlit country road, my ancient Volkswagen Beetle began to sputter. Throwing my date a worried glance, I steered to the berm, where the car finally died. "We're out of gas," I said. "Sure, sure," she replied in exasperation. "What a cheap, corny old trick. Now start this car and take me home." We really were out of gas; the fuel gauge on my VW hadn't worked in ten years, and since the car guzzled gas one minute and sipped it the next, I never knew for certain how much was in the tank. My date would not believe me. That night I learned the first of many lessons in how young women thoroughly accept stereotypes about male dating behavior.

The student's beginning paragraph accomplishes several things. First, it shows he has a sense of humor; it invites the readers to join the student as he laughs ruefully at himself and at human nature. The anecdotal opening engages the readers' interest and holds it by turning the tables on a stereotyped dating scene. Both male and female readers will identify with the characters in the anecdote and enjoy the turn of events. And finally, the student author introduces his topic—one that is quite specific. His general subject is human behavior, but he has narrowed it to dating behavior. His thesis statement focuses the topic even more tightly: women's stereotypes of their dates.

In this fairly long introduction, the author has used each sentence purposefully to get his paper on the stereotypes of dating off to a good start. He might have begun his paper in a number of other equally successful ways, but the method he chose is effective.

ENDINGS

A well-crafted paper needs an effective ending as well as good introductory and body paragraphs. Nothing detracts more from an otherwise appealing paper than to have it end abruptly or trail off into a weak or meaningless conclusion. Two things to avoid are apologizing for any weaknesses in the paper or introducing another aspect of the topic at the last moment. The first type of ending will pique readers' impatience and make them wonder why you didn't get rid of weaknesses rather than apologize for them. They will be left with a negative impression instead of a positive one. The second type of ending causes readers to feel cheated. No one likes to be left hanging at the end of an essay, wondering what you might have said if you had gone on to explore the topic's new aspect.

The ending of your paper should make the reader feel the discussion has been tied up, no loose ends, and rounded off in a satisfying way. A good ending can be compared to the bow tied on a birthday package or the icing on a cake—something good finished off with a flourish that makes the whole experience of reading your paper especially satisfying. Your reader should feel that without the conclusion the paper would have been incomplete. Some things you may do to achieve such a satisfactory ending include the following:

1. Restate briefly (not repeat word for word) the thesis statement of your paper.
2. Summarize briefly the major points of the paper.
3. Use a short anecdote or quotation that illustrates and supports your viewpoint.
4. Draw a conclusion from the discussion that shows the meaning of the facts and information you have presented.

The student who wrote the essay about dating behavior ended his paper by combining the second and fourth methods just listed.

> Each of my youthful episodes contributed greatly to my understanding of female stereotypes about male dating behavior. I learned that running out of gas is always deliberate, that taking a girl to a fancy restaurant means you'll try to attack her later, and that you invite a homely girl to the prom *only* because ten other cute girls turned you down—*never* because you happen to find her more interesting to talk to. I also learned another valuable lesson: as a stereotype, I'm a complete failure.

Practice: Identifying effective beginnings and endings   *Look through several popular magazines and select two or three articles that you think have especially good beginnings and/or endings. Bring them to class, ready to explain why you find them effective.*

EXERCISE 57-1, EFFECTIVE BEGINNINGS   (41i)

Questions 1 to 10 give the titles and introductions of compositions. In the blanks, write the letters of the characteristics listed in items *A* to *F* that best describe each introduction.

A. No clear purpose
B. Too short
C. Rambles
D. Discusses topic without first indicating what the topic is
E. Comments upon the title without first introducing the title into the discussion
F. Satisfactory

Example   Wild Foods

Wild foods grow almost everywhere, even in cities. Almost everyone can recognize a cattail. Dandelions grow wild in many lawns, and wisteria are often planted as a decorative addition around other shrubs.   *A, C*

1.   Minorities at the Top

Experts on organizational behavior cite several reasons for the lack of minorities at top executive levels in business. First, there are simply fewer minorities than others in management. Second, minorities are not easily accepted by majority-dominated management. Finally, many minority managers are just beginning to learn to play promotion politics.   _____

2.   Nontraditional Dentists' Offices

Fully one-half the population will not see one. The reason is fear. So dentists are designing offices in new ways, and they are learning relaxation techniques. This is all to make patients less frightened.   _____

3.   Gypsy Marriage Customs

Gypsy marriages are almost all arranged marriages. It's not that they don't understand romantic love. A Gypsy marriage is just much more than one person's marrying another person. Other things have to be considered.   _____

4. Community Watch

Community watch groups can help reduce crime. These groups can warn people and educate them about home security. Members of neighborhood watches will keep an eye on your house while you are out of town. The organization of community groups is one step toward the reduction of crime in the U.S.

_____

5. Recruiting Police Recruits

There are shortages of police officers in many states. If there were more police officers on the job, they could control and protect their jurisdictions better. Many big cities with high crime rates are understaffed and not able to enforce every law. If there were more police, they would be able to reduce the crime rate.

_____

6. Lowering the Crime Rate

The crime rate in the U.S. is unequaled by any other industrialized nation. Crime runs rampant in the streets of America. But the problem could be solved if a little decisive action were taken.

_____

7. The U.S. Crime Rate

The crime rate in the United States is about normal for a country this size. Many other countries have a much worse crime rate than ours. The U.S. needs to drastically change its penalties against these crimes. Otherwise, crime against the person will continue to soar in the U.S.

_____

8. Computer World

Computers are revolutionizing the business world. The largest computer company, appropriately named International Business Machines Corporation (IBM), has sales of over $26 million.

_____

9. Status Symbols on the Job

On Friday afternoon you leave your large, carpeted office with the nice view of the park. On Monday morning you discover you've been moved to an office with no windows and with linoleum on the floor. Is the boss trying to tell you something? In many companies, office location and furnishings are clear indications of status—who is on the way up, and who is on the way down or out.

_____

10. Keeping Fit

This is particularly difficult to do if you don't have a daily exercise routine. Students, working women and men with high-pressure jobs, senior citizens, almost everybody has an excuse to put it off until tomorrow, but tomorrow may be too late.

_____

After each of the following titles, write an introductory sentence or two using the specific technique for effective beginnings called for.

Example   Be Prepared—For Career Changes

Repeat the title: *Be prepared to change careers at some point in your life. That's what career counselors are telling students these days.*

Paraphrase the title: *Career counselors are advising students not to expect to work in one field for the rest of their lives. Instead, their education should prepare them to change to related fields if necessary.*

Start with a statement of fact: *The majority of working Americans have changed careers at least twice. As technology affects the job market, that figure is likely to grow.*

Use a startling statement or anecdote: *Leslie Richards has a master's degree in political science, but today you'll find her tending bar. "I like bartending," she says. "I didn't like my government job."*

11.   If I Could Choose Anywhere in the World to Live

Repeat the title: _____

_____

_____

Paraphrase the title: _____

_____

_____

Start with a statement of fact: _____

_____

_____

Use a startling statement or anecdote: _____

_____

_____

12.   Why Video Games Are Losing Popularity

Repeat the title: _____

_____

_____

Paraphrase the title: _____

_____

_____

Start with a statement of fact: _____

_____

_____

Use a startling statement or anecdote: _____

_____

_____

13. Title for a topic you developed in Section 55 or 56:

_____

Repeat the title: _____

_____

_____

Paraphrase the title: _____

_____

_____

Start with a statement of fact: _____

_____

_____

Use a startling statement or anecdote: _____

_____

_____

EXERCISE 57-2, EFFECTIVE ENDINGS   (41i)

Using your own paper, develop thesis statements for the given composition titles. Then, for each of the approaches indicated, write at least four sentences that would end the composition suitably.

Example   Be Prepared—For Career Changes

Thesis statement: The evidence shows that most people change careers several times, so college students would be wise to choose courses that give them some career flexibility.

Restate thesis statement: Many college students choose their majors with one career goal in mind and resent having to take courses that do not fit their short-term employment plans. A few years after graduation, they may find themselves out of work, a narrowly focused education having locked them into a dead-end career path.

Summarize briefly major points of paper: Although it's not easy to take a long-range view when one is primarily concerned about landing that first job after graduation, wise students consider the variety of career options their education will provide. They take courses that will give them a well-rounded, general education as well as those that train them for a specific job. They also choose extracurricular activities that offer a range of experiences. In short, they develop flexible skills that have several career applications.

Use an anecdote or quotation: *Chicago Tribune* columnist Dan Dorfman writes of "society's growing disenchantment with the so-called 'specialist' or 'professional'—not only in supply-demand factors, but in changing public attitudes." The point is, today's specialist may be on tomorrow's unemployment line, because technological, economic, or social change can make a profession overcrowded or obsolete. Career changes, increasingly, are not only possible but probable. The graduates with the most flexible career skills are the best prepared to meet them.

Draw conclusion from paper: Whether he or she is aware of it, today's college student faces the likelihood of an eventual career change. Consequently, educational institutions and their career counselors have an obligation. They must help students develop a long-range perspective; they must stress that, although training for the first job is important, an interdisciplinary education—featuring a working knowledge of different specialties—is more serviceable over the long haul.

1.   If I Could Choose Anywhere in the World to Live

Thesis statement:

Restate thesis statement:

Briefly summarize major points of paper:

Use supporting anecdote or quotation:

Draw conclusion from paper:

2. Why Video Games Are Losing Popularity

Thesis statement:

Restate thesis statement:

Briefly summarize major points of paper:

Use supporting anecdote or quotation:

Draw conclusion from paper:

3. Drunk Drivers

Thesis statement:

Restate thesis statement:

Briefly summarize major points of paper:

Use supporting anecdote or quotation:

Draw conclusion from paper:

4. Schools Fail to Educate Students—Whose Fault?

Thesis statement:

Restate thesis statement:

Briefly summarize major points of paper:

Use supporting anecdote or quotation:

Draw conclusion from paper:

5. Title for the topic of your choice

Thesis statement:

Restate thesis statement:

Briefly summarize major points of paper:

Use supporting anecdote or quotation:

Draw conclusion from paper:

6. Title for a topic you developed in Section 55 or 56

    Thesis statement:

    Restate thesis statement:

    Briefly summarize major points of paper:

    Use supporting anecdote or quotation:

    Draw conclusion from paper:

7. What Can Schools Do to Discourage Cheating?

    Thesis statement:

    Restate thesis statement:

    Briefly summarize major points of paper:

    Use supporting anecdote or quotation:

    Draw conclusion from paper:

8. Do Extracurricular Activities Harm Students?

    Thesis statement:

    Restate thesis statement:

    Briefly summarize major points of paper:

    Use supporting anecdote or quotation:

    Draw conclusion from paper:

9. Coping with Academic Stress

    Thesis statement:

    Restate thesis statement:

    Briefly summarize major points of paper:

Use supporting anecdote or quotation:

Draw conclusion from paper:

10. Why Are So Many Americans Overweight?

Thesis statement:

Restate thesis statement:

Briefly summarize major points of paper:

Use supporting anecdote or quotation:

Draw conclusion from paper:

58
PARAGRAPH UNITY   (42a)

Paragraphs are the building blocks of essays. As noted in the process outlined in Section 54, every paragraph should be related to the thesis of your essay. Each paragraph furthers your purpose, supports your thesis, and explains your thinking about the topic.

The aspects of your topic thus become the paragraphs of your paper. Sometimes an aspect can be handled in a single paragraph; sometimes more than one paragraph are necessary because an aspect of your topic may contain subaspects that need explaining.

No matter how many paragraphs your finished essay contains, each one should be unified, coherent, and adequately developed. (The next several sections define and explain those rather abstract terms.) A good paragraph needs all three of these characteristics to be effective. A good essay needs them as well. In fact, you may find it helpful to think of a paragraph as a mini essay.

A paragraph is **unified** if it has a clear, controlling idea and if all the sentences in the paragraph relate to that idea. Most paragraphs use a **topic sentence** to state the paragraph's controlling idea. The topic sentence in a paragraph functions in the same way as the thesis statement in an essay: both express a central idea. The topic sentence of a paragraph focuses on one of the aspects or subaspects of the topic encompassed by the thesis. For example, if your thesis statement mentions three aspects (let's say, stripping, sanding, and varnishing) of a topic (refinishing furniture), then your essay will probably have three body paragraphs with corresponding topic sentences: one on stripping furniture, one on sanding it, and one on varnishing it.

The topic sentence may be the first sentence of a paragraph, it may be the last sentence of a paragraph, or it may appear in slightly different form in both places—particularly if the paragraph is long, involved, and needs summing up at the end.

Some paragraphs have implied topic sentences; but even when the topic sentence is unstated, the reader should be able to tell from the paragraph's details that a central idea is controlling the discussion. If your reader cannot formulate a topic sentence from the paragraph's discussion, then your paragraph is not controlled or unified. A paragraph that lacks a clear focus and contains irrelevant statements will cause your reader to wonder where you are headed and what the information has to do with your topic.

Practice A: Identifying topic sentences   *Underline the topic sentence in each of the following paragraphs. If a paragraph has an implied topic sentence, compose your version of what the topic sentence might be. The answers are listed at the end of this section.*

A.   [1] Chile con carne was not invented in Mexico, and the Mexicans don't want credit for it. [2] Food historians say that chile first appeared around 1880 in San Antonio, Texas. [3] A German from New Braunfels, Texas, invented chili powder—a spice previously unknown, of course, in Mexico or anywhere else. [4] Six years later, the inventor's canning company was turning out canned chile con carne. [5] One Mexican dictionary defines chile con carne as "detestable food with a false Mexican title."

B.   [1] Caesar salad was first served by Caesar Cardini, who owned and ran a small hotel in Tijuana. [2] Originally the salad contained only lettuce, croutons, Romano cheese, a coddled egg, lemon juice, and vinegar. [3] The anchovies were added somewhere else, as the fame of the salad spread. [4] The Caesar salad is one Mexican dish that found a home on the tables of many different cultures and on the menus of continental restaurants.

C.   [1] California is one of the largest producers of sweet potatoes in the United States today. [2] The state produces almost 800 million pounds of sweet potatoes each year. [3] John B. Avila, a native of the Portuguese Azores, planted the first twenty acres of sweet potatoes in California in 1888 and helped teach local farmers to cultivate the new crop, perfect for California's climate.

Practice B: Identifying irrelevant statements   *Circle the letters of the sentences in each group that are not closely related to that group's topic sentence. The answers are listed at the end of this section.*

1.   Some of the most famous department stores in America were begun by immigrants anxious to make their marks in America's economic system.

A.   Brentano's, the bookstore chain, was founded by an Austrian immigrant.

B.   William Filene, originally from Poland, started the stores in Boston that bear his name.

C.   Hammacher Schlemmer, the world-famous gadget store, was started when German immigrant William Schlemmer convinced Alfred Hammacher to invest in his hardware store.

D.   There is only one Hammacher Schlemmer store, on East 57th Street in New York.

E.   The oldest retail store in New York is Lord and Taylor, started in 1826 by two Englishmen.

F.   Rich's was begun by Morris Rich, an immigrant from Hungary.

G.   Rich's has its headquarters in Atlanta and stores in most major cities in the Southeast.

2.   Americans learned the custom of sending greetings on Valentine's Day from the English and French.

A.   In the fourteenth century, British villagers drew the names of unmarried men and women and wrote love notes to their choice on February 14.

B.   A Frenchman imprisoned in the Tower of London sent a love note to his wife in 1415.

C.   Gradually the custom changed until notes were sent to loved ones rather than strangers, following this lead by the Duke of Orleans.

D.   Valentine's Day was originally meant to honor St. Valentine, but his festival was held on the Lupercalia, the Roman fertility feast.

E.   St. Valentine was an Italian priest who was martyred in 270.

Answers to Practice A   A. First sentence   B. Fourth sentence   C. Implied topic sentence; one possibility: *A Portuguese immigrant introduced the American West to what later became one of its major crops.*

Answers to Practice B   1. D, G   2. D, E

EXERCISE 58, PARAGRAPH UNITY   (42a)

Some sentences in the following paragraphs are irrelevant to the central ideas of the paragraphs. Write the letters of such irrelevant sentences in the blank to the right of each paragraph.

1.   (A) That most American garment, a pair of blue jeans, was developed by a Bavarian immigrant, Levi Strauss. (B) In 1850 Strauss discovered a market for canvas trousers among California miners who needed sturdy work pants. (C) Canvas was used to make sails. (D) Pioneers used it for Conestoga wagon coverings. (F) Levi's pants were neither blue nor denim, but today's blue denims are their direct descendants.

_____

2.   (A) Among the refugees of the Vietnam War are slightly more than 1,000 people who once earned their living fishing the South China Sea. (B) Now they are located half a world away, fishing the Gulf of Mexico off Mississippi. (C) Years ago they lived in North Vietnam, but they fled to the south when the Communists took over in 1954. (D) With the fall of South Vietnam in 1975, they fled again and were picked up by American ships. (E) To many of these fishing families, the whale is sacred and signifies good luck.

_____

3.   (A) The French Foreign Legion was regarded as one of the world's greatest fighting forces. (B) In an ill-fated attempt to conquer Mexico in 1863, its members fought so bravely in Camerone that the legion thereafter celebrated Camerone Day. (C) Interestingly, the legion had more Germans in its membership than French. (D) The white cap of the legionnaire was the only one to which the U.S. Marines, another great fighting group, would doff their own. (E) Gary Cooper glamorized the legion by his romantic portrayal of Beau Geste. (F) There were many ex-criminals in the legion. (G) In their training, the legionnaires were taught to be utterly cold-blooded and fearless in combat.

_____

4.   (A) New York's Fifth Avenue is perhaps the nation's most famous parade route. (B) It is the address of Tiffany's, Saks, and many other expensive, fashionable shops. (C) When the country wants to honor a hero, it schedules a parade on Fifth Avenue. (D) Astronauts, presidents, baseball teams, and returning political hostages have ridden up Fifth Avenue amid confetti and ticker tape. (E) Each year Irish, Jews, Italians, Greeks, Germans, Puerto Ricans, and Poles celebrate their ethnic heritages with parades on Fifth Avenue. (F) There is even a well-known song about Fifth Avenue's Easter Parade.

_____

5.   (A) The Smithsonian is the world's largest museum. (B) Over 78 million items fill the shelves and storage rooms of the Smithsonian buildings, which sprawl across the entire center of Washington. (C) Even with all this room, the collection is so large that at any given time, 95 percent of the museum's collection is in storage, on loan to other museums, or in traveling exhibits. (D) No one knows why James Smithson, who had never even seen America, left his entire fortune to start this museum. (E) The collection fills thirteen huge buildings and the Washington Zoo.

_____

6. (A) Charles Curtis was America's first senator and Vice President to be of American Indian ancestry. (B) Curtis, who was one-eighth Kaw Indian, served as Senator from Kansas for 25 years. (C) He was also descended from French frontierspeople. (D) Under Herbert Hoover, Curtis served as Vice President. (E) During his career, Curtis helped protect the rights of Indians. (F) The Curtis Bill allowed Indians to incorporate their own towns and elect their own officials.

———————

7. (A) Bad luck comes in many forms. (B) Japanese believe that trimming one's nails before a trip brings bad luck. (C) Ashes flying into the room from a fireplace bring bad luck, according to Greek superstition. (D) In Denmark, spilling damp salt is an evil omen. (E) Spilling dry salt brings good luck, though. (F) Sneezing while tying one's shoes is bad luck for a German. (G) Scots never mail letters on Christmas Day, February 29, or September 1—all unlucky days for letters and packages.

———————

8. (A) Most American workers are classified as either "exempt" or "nonexempt" employees under the terms of the Fair Labor Standards Act of 1938, which established minimum-wage, overtime-pay, equal-pay, record-keeping, and child-labor standards for employees unless a specific exemption applies. (B) The law established four exempt job categories: bona fide "executives," "administrative employees," "professionals," and "outside sales people." (C) Legal regulations define the criteria that must be met in full before an employee is classified as exempt. (D) Most of the criteria have to do with job duties and responsibilities, not with job titles or whether an employee is paid a salary or an hourly wage. (E) Generally speaking, if an employee is exempt, his or her employer is not required to pay for overtime work. (F) It seems rather ironic that "exempt," which usually implies that someone benefits, is free from an obligation or duty, in this case means that the employee loses the right to overtime pay. (G) The employer is the one who gains if an exempt employee takes work home or stays late at the office. (H) The Fair Labor Standards Act has been amended several times since 1938.

———————

9. (A) Dr. Percy Julian was an award-winning Black chemist. (B) When Julian died, he held over 130 chemical patents. (C) Julian's work with soybeans helped create low-cost foods, waterproofing agents, fire-extinguishing chemicals, and synthetic hormones. (D) Millions of arthritis sufferers can thank Percy Julian for synthetic cortisone, which made relief from pain affordable. (E) Who knows what other uses may be found for the chemicals produced by the soybean?

———————

10. (A) The bagel was introduced to America by Jewish immigrants. (B) Until the 1960's, the bagel was popular only in Jewish neighborhoods or in cities with large Jewish populations. (C) In 1960, there were only forty bagel bakeries in the U.S., and thirty of these were in New York. (D) Soon, however, the chewy roll caught on with Americans. (E) By 1977, there were over 360 bagel bakeries, and they were distributed all across America. (F) Bagels are first boiled, then baked. (G) This is the process that makes them so chewy. (H) The popularity that bagels suddenly enjoyed after 1963 may be traced to Harry Lender, a Polish immigrant who first opened a bagel shop in 1927 and who introduced a line of frozen bagels in 1963.

———————

Using your own paper, write four topic sentences on subjects of your choice. Underneath each topic sentence, write four sentences related to that topic sentence. Be sure that every sentence you write directly concerns the subject matter introduced in your topic sentence.

59
PARAGRAPH COHERENCE   (42b)

A paragraph is **coherent** if the sentences convey a smooth, logical flow of thought from one idea to the next. Each sentence should show an evident relationship to the one that precedes it and a clear connection to the one that follows it, as well as a bearing on the paragraph's controlling idea.

Whereas unity depends upon your selecting ideas that are relevant to the topic of your paragraph, coherence depends upon your ability to show how the ideas are relevant by presenting them in a smooth, orderly, well-knit arrangement. Smoothness in a paragraph is achieved partially by using transitional elements; these are discussed more fully in Section 60. Orderliness can be achieved by using one of several organizational patterns for your sentences. The patterns you choose for your paragraphs depend upon your topic and purpose; each is a means for creating coherence in your writing.

Descriptions and examples of common organizational patterns follow. In some of the example paragraphs, transitional links are italicized.

1. **Time order (chronological order)** is the order in which events occur: one thing happens after another.

> My visit to Professor Crump's office for help with an astronomy problem *at first* seemed more like a social call than a tutorial. *After* I knocked and entered the room, he invited me to be seated in one of his overstuffed chairs. We spent *the next several* minutes of our conference discussing my work in other courses, and I *began* to realize he was trying to put me at ease. *Then* he offered me a cup of tea, which he poured into china cups. *Only when* I was settled comfortably with my tea cup *did he* spread his astronomical models on the desk and ask, *"Now,* which aspect of retrograde motion would you like me to explain?"

2. **Space order (spatial order)** is sentence arrangement according to physical layout, such as top to bottom, left to right, back to front, east to west, and so forth.

> The astronomy professor's office was unlike any other faculty office in the science building. Visitors noticed first the enormous antique desk *against the far wall. On the right* were heavy, glass-fronted bookcases. *On the left* were several overstuffed chairs. The *overhead* fluorescent lights had been turned off. *Instead,* Tiffany lamps cast a warm glow through their colorful glass shades. The Victorian decor was completed by the oriental rug *underfoot.*

3. **Order of climax** is order by increasing importance: minor details lead to the main point.

> *Sometimes* Professor Crump digressed from his class lectures on astronomy and *told anecdotes about his life. On various occasions he told about* helping to build one of the nation's first big reflecting telescopes, about his transcendental religious experience on a mountaintop in Kashmir, *about* a picnic lunch with an attractive stranger who turned out to be Mussolini's mistress. *Most of these stories* had little if anything to do with astronomy. We gradually realized, *however,* that for Dr. Crump the mysteries of the stars were just one aspect of life's rich, diverse mystery.

4. **General to particular** or **particular to general order** is a general statement followed by (1) supporting evidence and illustrations or (2) particular evidence and illustrations

leading to a concluding generalization. When either of these arrangements is used, the generalization usually appears in the topic sentence—at the beginning of the paragraph in the first case, at the end of the paragraph in the second. The previous paragraph illustrating order of climax is also an example of particular to general order. The following paragraph shows general to particular order.

> To the students on our small college campus, Professor Crump *was more than an elderly astronomer:* he *was a chunk of civilization.* At nearly eighty years of age, *he had seen* astronomy grow from relative infancy; *he had worked* with many of the century's greatest scientists. *He had witnessed* two world wars, *taught* at five colleges and universities, *and led* a full—even exotic—life. *Yet he chose* to end his long career with us. We were flattered.

5. **Comparison** and **contrast** are natural methods of organization for many topics. Comparison stresses similarities between items. Contrast explains their differences. Sometimes you will develop an entire paragraph using just one method or just the other; sometimes you will want both to compare and to contrast in the same paragraph. The following paragraph principally uses contrast to develop its controlling idea. Notice how the transitional words provide the reader with clear connections between ideas.

> *Except for* the fact that dogs and cats are both four-legged, furry mammals, they are distinctly different types of pets. Dogs are very loyal and subservient to their masters. Cats, *on the other hand,* never totally commit their allegiance to anyone, *but instead* maintain their independence. Cats are relatively self-sufficient and can be left alone if their owners go away for the weekend. All they need is a supply of food and fresh water and a clean litter box. Dogs, *however,* wolf all their food immediately and have to be taken out every few hours. Woe to owners whose dogs get lonely while they are gone; upon returning they will find chewed shoes, hats, gloves, and furniture.

6. **Definition** is useful for clarifying terms or concepts the reader may not know or understand in just the way you want them understood. Sometimes you need not go into much detail as you define. In this case, you will be employing an informal definition, which can involve as little as a word or a phrase.

The eosin (dye) was smeared all over the page.
The kibitzer (an onlooker who offers advice) infuriated the card players.

At other times, though, you may choose or need to be more detailed or explicit when you define. Then you may employ a **formal definition**, which consists of a term to be defined; a genus (class), which is a general category in which the term can logically be included; and a differentia, which is a statement of the way the term differs from other members of the genus. The following is a formal definition:

TERM TO BE DEFINED	GENUS (CLASS)	DIFFERENTIA
Introductory Composition is a	communicative process	in which students convey their thoughts in writing, often in compositions about 500 words long.

Often a formal definition will be expanded into an **extended definition**. The extended definition may use examples, comparison and contrast, and any of the other forms of organization and development to explain its subject more fully.

PARAGRAPH CONTAINING AN EXTENDED DEFINITION
BEGINNING WITH A FORMAL DEFINITION

A door is a movable structure contained within a framework that separates two areas by covering an opening and whose principal purpose is to facilitate entrances and exits. There are all kinds of doors. There are hanging doors, swinging doors, overhead doors, trap doors, and sliding doors. As a matter of fact, even strings of beads or sheets of canvas or leather have been used as doors. Doors come in all sizes and shapes. Although they can be made of beads or canvas, they more customarily are made of wood, steel, aluminum, or glass. However we describe them, we have to conclude that they are pretty handy devices. Without them, our living wouldn't be nearly as comfortable or as secure as it is.

7. **Organization** by **cause** and **effect** works in one of two ways. You can list the effect, condition, or result first and then discuss the causes or reasons why the effect has come about. Or you can reverse the process, first investigating the causes or reasons and then discussing what effects, conditions, or results they have produced. Like comparisons and contrasts, causes and effects may be handled in the same paragraph, or you may want to divide them among several paragraphs—one or more on causes, one or more on effects—depending on the nature and complexity of your topic. The following paragraphs first detail effects and then explore the causes of those effects.

My mother could not understand why her left arm was swollen, itching, and covered with a red rash. When the rash turned to blisters that broke and suppurated, and when the itching kept her awake at night, she went to the doctor. His diagnosis was poison ivy.

She protested that she had not come in contact with any poison ivy plants, although the salve the doctor gave her healed the blisters. A few days later my father mentioned that the highway department had sprayed the poison ivy along our road. The mystery of the rash was solved. While driving with her arm out the car window, my mother had come in contact with the oily fumes of the dying poison ivy plants.

8. **Analysis** and **classification** take things apart and put them together again. When you **analyze** something, you break it down into its various parts and look at the characteristics of those parts and at how they fit together to comprise the whole. For example, if you analyze the time you spend doing homework, you are likely to find you spend so many minutes on getting your books and cup of coffee; so many minutes on daydreaming, petting the dog, and rereading the assignment; and so many minutes actually studying productively.

When you **classify**, you put items into groups according to their common characteristics. Suppose you want to classify fruit. First you have to establish a basis for classification: natural fruits. Once you have established this basis, you must be sure that the classifications are mutually exclusive, that the items being classified are comparable, and that you do not shift the basis of classification (an error known as **cross-classification**). These points are illustrated here:

BASIS OF CLASSIFICATION
FRUITS IN THEIR NATURAL STATE

(1)	(2)	(3)	(4)	(5)
citrus fruit	oranges	oranges	oranges	oranges
noncitrus fruit	apples	apples	winesaps	apples
	grapefruit	grapefruit	grapefruit	grapefruit
	pears	winesaps	pears	potatoes
	peaches	peaches	peaches	peaches

In list (1) are broad groupings of fruit. In (2) are listed various species of fruit. Both (1) and (2) classify fruit in accordance with the stated basis of classification. In (3), however, both apples and winesaps are listed. This classification is not **mutually exclusive**—that is, it lists a subcategory as a separate aspect of discussion. If the subcategory is to be discussed, it must be discussed under the category of which it is a member. In (4), by contrast, winesaps, a subcategory of apples, are listed as being comparable to the categories oranges, grapefruit, pears, and peaches. Hence, the classification is not **comparable** because the subcategory is classified at the same level as the main category. Finally, list (5) departs altogether from the basis of classification, which was fruits, by listing potatoes, which are, of course, vegetables. The result is a **cross-classification**.

PARAGRAPH USING CLASSIFICATION AND ANALYSIS

We can communicate in three basic ways. Each way has its advantages. One way is by speaking. When we speak we have a chance to judge our audience's reactions. If they don't understand, we can reword as necessary to make our points. We can also invite additional questions and clarify additional aspects for our listeners. Another way of communicating is by writing. When we write, we have more time. We can think our subject through thoroughly. We can modify our development and polish our phraseology until we get it the way we want it. The third way of communicating is nonverbal. Communication of this type can involve such actions as a look, a nod of the head, or a shake of the hand. Nonverbal communication can be quite effective in a very noisy atmosphere or when we don't want to dignify a response with actual words.

The preceding paragraph establishes as the basis for classification the ways of communication. Its classification is mutually exclusive since it analyzes subaspects of speaking, writing, and nonverbal communication only under the aspects to which they pertain. The aspects in its classification are comparable, and no cross-classification occurs since speaking, writing, and nonverbal communication are all methods of communication.

EXERCISE 59, PARAGRAPH COHERENCE   (42b)

In the blank following each set of sentences, write the numbers of the sentences in the order that would develop a coherent paragraph.

A.

1. At fifteen, King entered Morehouse College in Atlanta, where he was a high-ranking student.
2. It was in his work with the Council that King first came into contact with whites on a regular basis.
3. Martin Luther King studied at two high schools, University High and Booker Washington High, and graduated in two years.
4. At Morehouse, he worked with the City Intercollegiate Council, a group of students from all the colleges in Atlanta who worked on college social problems.
5. "As I got to see more of white people," King later said, "my resentment softened and a spirit of cooperation took its place."

_____

B.

1. Nevertheless, he was impressed by the way the students all worked closely together.
2. In Gandhi, King discovered a man, a member of an oppressed group, who had met that opposition with a new weapon, nonviolent resistance.
3. King attended Crozier Theological Seminary in Chester, Pennsylvania.
4. Most of all, King admired the writings of Gandhi.
5. He worked as hard as the rest, reading all the works of the great social philosophers.
6. This was King's first experience in an integrated school and his first time in the North.
7. In reading Gandhi and the other philosophers, King thought he saw a way to ease racial tension and begin a struggle for civil rights.
8. At Crozier, he was one of only six Blacks in a group of a hundred graduate students.

_____

C.

1. He was the first to link scientifically certain diseases such as rickets, pellagra, and scurvy with nutritional deficiencies.
2. Vitamins were discovered by Casimir Funk in Warsaw, Poland.
3. When it was later determined that not all vitamins contained an amino group, the *e* was dropped from the word.
4. Three years before he immigrated to the United States in 1915, Funk published his research findings on the connection between disease and the lack of what he dubbed *vitamines*.

5. He created the word *vitamine* from *vita,* meaning life, and *amino.*
6. Hence the word became *vitamin,* as we spell it today.
7. *Amino* stood for the nitrogen group he thought was a chemical component of all vitamines.
8. Sailors long ago discovered that citrus fruits such as oranges prevent and cure scurvy.
9. It took a Polish-American scientist to learn the reason and give it a name.

D.

1. If sweets weren't enough, pushcarts sold dill pickles and pickled tomatoes.
2. But the favorite of all, according to Harry Golden, who has written about this fantastic open-air market, was the good old hot dog with mustard.
3. The best of all the old candies was halvah or "buckser" from Palestine.
4. In the old immigrant neighborhoods in New York, pushcart vendors and other sidewalk salespeople sold every kind of ethnic food imaginable.
5. Imagine being sent out onto those teeming streets with a whole dime!
6. First there were all sorts of confections.
7. Schoolchildren could sample candy from Turkey, the Orient, or eastern Europe.
8. Baked sweet potatoes, nuts, hot corn-on-the-cob, and hot chickpeas were among the more substantial foods offered for sale.
9. Other vendors sold all sorts of fruits, exotic and common, as the seasons allowed.
10. In those days, according to Golden, a hot dog was three cents and the accompanying drink was two cents.

Using your own paper, first list five different paragraph topics. You may want to choose some of the topics you developed in earlier exercises. Then write a coherent paragraph for each topic, using a different organizational pattern each time. The organizational patterns are *chronological order, spatial order, order of climax, general to particular order, particular to general order, comparison and contrast, definition, cause and effect,* and *analysis and classification.*

60
TRANSITIONS WITHIN PARAGRAPHS   (42d,g)

Sentence arrangement helps to achieve coherence in paragraphs, but to establish the relationships between ideas clearly, you need to guide your reader smoothly from one thought to the next. Doing so involves the effective use of transitional elements. These are: (1) a consistent point of view; (2) parallel grammatical structure; (3) repeated words and phrases, synonyms, or repeated ideas; and (4) transitional words and phrases.

1. **Consistent point of view** is maintained if you avoid unnecessary shifts in person, verb tense, or number within a paragraph (see Section 21). The following paragraph shows how such unnecessary shifts can ruin continuity and confuse the reader:

> Many fanciful beliefs have surrounded the moon. People at one time or another believed the moon was a goddess, it is a map's face, or it was thought to be the cause of various diseases. You know, strange creatures even had been thought to live on the moon. After decades of space flights, we find the moon much less mysterious.

Notice how much smoother the revision is:

> People have believed many fanciful things about the moon. At one time or another they have believed the moon to be a goddess, a man's face, or the cause of various diseases. People have even thought strange creatures lived on the moon. After decades of space flights, the moon has become much less mysterious.

2. **Parallel grammatical structure in successive sentences** emphasizes the relationship between them and the relationship between them and the relationship to the paragraph's main idea. The sentences in the general-to-particular paragraph in Section 59 use parallel structure to reinforce their relationship. Notice that the subject-verb arrangement of the clauses beginning *he had seen, he had worked, he had witnessed . . . taught . . . and led* echo the structure and support with examples the controlling idea in the topic sentence *He was a chunk of civilization.* In the following paragraph, written by the college president after the death of the astronomy professor described in Section 59, the parallel grammatical structures are italicized.

> His gentle presence will be sorely missed from this campus. *It is clear that he loved* the college and its students deeply, and *it is a challenge to live* up to his high standards of character and academic excellence. *Clifford Crump believed in the life of the mind; he believed in the life of the spirit,* and his own life proved that the two can be one in daily practice.

3. **Repeated key words or phrases, synonyms, or repeated ideas** indicate to the reader that relationships exist between thoughts in a paragraph. Something as simple as using a pronoun to refer to a clearly established antecedent or inserting a synonym can provide coherence for a paragraph. The preceding example paragraph not only uses parallel structure but also repeats words and phrases to cement relationships between ideas and to provide a smooth flow. The three crucial repetitions in that paragraph are *it is, believed in,* and *life of.* The pronouns *his* and *he,* referring to Professor Crump, remind the reader that the same individual is the subject throughout the paragraph. The following paragraph relies even more heavily on repetition to achieve coherence:

Star gazing on a winter night *is not necessarily a romantic pastime.* Even when *your* boyfriend is the instructor, *learning constellations* for *your* astronomy midterm *is not necessarily* a *heart-warming experience. All you* can think about is *your cold* feet, *your cold* hands, *your cold* nose. *All you* want to do is *get someplace* warm, and *get there* as quickly as possible.

4. **Transitional words and phrases** that appear at or near the beginning of a sentence indicate a relationship between that sentence and the one preceding it. Coordinating conjunctions such as *and, but, or, nor, so,* and *yet* are often used in informal writing to provide bridges between sentences. However, you can use many other words and phrases to establish connections in more formal writing. A number of them are listed here:

ADDITION	again, also, and, and then, besides, equally important, finally, first, furthermore, in addition, last, likewise, moreover, next, second, third, too
CAUSE AND EFFECT	accordingly, as a result, because, consequently, hence, otherwise, since, so, then, therefore, thus
COMPARISON	by the same token, in a like manner, likewise, similarly
CONCESSION	after all, at the same time, even though, of course
CONTRAST	although, at the same time, but, by contrast, for all that, however, in spite of, nevertheless, on the contrary, on the other hand, still, yet
EXAMPLE OR ILLUSTRATIONS	for example, for instance, in fact, in other words, specifically, such as, that is, to illustrate
SUMMARY	in brief, in conclusion, in essence, in short, on the whole, to conclude, to sum up
TIME RELATIONS	after, afterwards, as long as, as soon as, at last, at that time, before, immediately, in the meantime, later, meanwhile, next, presently, soon, then, thereafter, thereupon, until, when, while

Use transitional elements appropriately. Remember what these words mean, and do not simply throw them into your sentences without regard for sense.

Be aware, too, that transitional words can become extremely tiresome if they are overused. If every sentence in a paragraph begins with one of these words, the paragraph can become very choppy, as the following example shows:

Many of the constellations were named by the Greeks. *However,* the Greeks were not the first people to name configurations of stars. *In fact,* 5,000 years ago the Mesopotamians saw patterns or pictures in the stars and named them after animals and occupations. *Moreover,* today we still use many of the ancient names for constellations. *For example,* the constellation containing the Big Dipper is called Ursa Major, the Great Bear. *Furthermore,* we call the constellation that looked to some ancients like a bowman, Sagittarius, the Archer.

Learn to use a variety of means to show relationships between your ideas. Notice how much smoother the revision of the preceding example paragraph becomes when several types of transitions are used to replace some of the transitional words at the beginnings of sentences. Also notice how combining some of the sentences smooths the flow of ideas.

Although the Greeks named many of the constellations, they were not the first people to name configurations of stars. In fact, 5,000 years ago the Mesopotamians saw patterns or pictures in the stars and named them for animals and occupations. Today we see the same heavenly patterns and call them by many of the same ancient names: Ursa Major, the Great Bear, the constellation containing the Big Dipper; Sagittarius, the Archer, the constellation that looks like a bowman.

332

EXERCISE 60, TRANSITIONS FOR UNITY AND COHERENCE   (42d, g)

Using your own paper, revise the following paragraphs, eliminating unnecessary shifts in point of view and providing transitional elements where they are needed. You may combine or rearrange sentences to achieve a smooth, coherent paragraph.

1. Friday the thirteenth has a bad reputation as a day of bad luck. Fridays were reserved for hangings and public executions. Many evil events in the Bible, such as the temptation of Eve, occurred on Friday. According to superstition, thirteen guests at a party is a bad omen. Thirteen people were present at the last supper in the New Testament. When Loki, the Norse god of mischief, showed up at a banquet for twelve other gods, the result was the death of Baldur, one of the favored gods.

2. American history and Scandinavian folklore show no such fear of the number thirteen or of Fridays. There were thirteen original American colonies. The Revolutionary Army was taken over by Washington on Friday the thirteenth. On Friday the thirteenth construction began on the White House. The American dollar has thirteen stars. They have thirteen arrows. There are thirteen leaves and thirteen olives in the eagle's right claw. Each pyramid has one side with thirteen rows of building blocks. Scandinavians consider Friday a lucky day. People born on the thirteenth are considered lucky. Friday the thirteenth is their lucky day.

3. The government of England once decided to prove that all the superstitions associated with Friday were simply superstitions. A naval yard began construction of a new ship on Friday. The ship was named on a Friday. As its name, it bore *HMS Friday.* On a Friday, the ship was launched. Its first voyage began on a Friday. They have never been seen or heard from again.

4. Some of the most common superstitions are "immigrants" from other countries. The Dutch were the first to knock on wood for good luck. He has to knock on unpainted wood for it to work, so we knock on the unvarnished underside of a table. A Dane believes that breaking a mirror can bring either good or bad luck for seven years. Unfortunately, they can't predict which it will be. An American tied shoes to the car of a couple going on a honeymoon in imitation of an Irish custom of throwing shoes after a person starting on a long journey. Many cultures preserved the custom of throwing rice, salt, or flowers at a newlywed couple. These objects all represented fertility and prosperity in many European cultures.

5. The Romans believed June was the best month for marriage. The bridal veil was introduced by the Romans. Veils shielded the bride from evil spirits. A wedding cake was prepared and served to assure prosperity. The French introduced the custom of throwing the bride's bouquet to her maids. Ancient Hebrews considered blue the color of love and purity. He urges a bride to wear "something blue." Egyptians first used the ring as a symbol of eternity for weddings. Romans and early Christians made the rings the size of fingers. The custom of wearing wedding bands was introduced to America by early German settlers.

6. Various cultures set the entry into adulthood at different times. Jewish children enter adulthood on their thirteenth birthdays. A traditional ceremony, a Bar (for boys) or Bat (for girls) Mitzvah, marks the passage. Japanese celebrated the passage into adulthood at the age of 15 or 16. A ceremony in which a boy is given an adult's cap marks the change to adult ways of dressing. "Sweet 16" parties or debutante balls celebrate the fact that an American girl was ready to enter society or to start dating. The *quince* is a celebration of a girl's fifteenth birthday. A *quince* was the Hispanic equivalent of a debutante ball. *Quinces* can be very elaborate and expensive; it signified not only that the young girl was ready to begin dating, but also that she was ready to start dating seriously.

Using your own paper, write paragraphs at least four sentences long that illustrate the use of the transitional elements called for in items 7 through 10. Underline and label the transitional elements you use.

Example comparison, contrast, concession, example, summary

A sentence outline and a topic outline are alike in some respects. The sentence outline uses headings and subheadings. The topic outline proceeds similarly in this respect. Likewise, both outlines, if they are properly developed, will be unified—that is, all subheadings will relate to the subheadings or headings preceding them. In turn, the main headings will pertain to the subject of the paper. The two papers differ, on the other hand, in that whereas the sentence outline contains only sentences, the topic outline has none. Of course, both outlines are good. In essence, the one should be used which best fits the needs of the occasion.

7. comparison, contrast, examples, parallel structure

8. cause and effect, addition, summary, synonyms

9. time relations, concession, contrast, summary

10. word repetition, addition, examples

61
PARAGRAPH DEVELOPMENT   (42e–f)

A paragraph is adequately **developed** if it has enough evidence, examples, supporting facts, details, and reasons for your readers to understand your topic sentence fully and be persuaded of its validity. Just as all the paragraphs in your essay should explain and support your thesis statement, so the sentences in your paragraphs should clarify and support the topic sentences.

Details, examples, and illustrations are the most common types of support for a paragraph's controlling idea. In fact, most methods of development rely on details and examples. Details are a catalog of particulars, usually presented without much explanation. Examples, on the other hand, require some explanation to show their relevance to the paragraph's main topic. Development by illustration is the same as development by example, except that instead of using several examples to support the main point, you use one example that you explain at considerable length. The following paragraph is developed with details. It makes use of a chronological arrangement to ensure the coherence of these details. The second paragraph is developed with examples.

PARAGRAPH DEVELOPED WITH DETAILS

Getting ready to write a composition is quite an ordeal. First, you have to find a quiet place where you can concentrate. Then you have to make sure you have a good pen, plenty of paper, a dictionary, a handbook, and plenty of hot coffee. When you are finally settled and ready to go, you next have to think of a subject, construct a thesis statement, and make up an outline with the right number of headings and subheadings. If you are still with it after having done all of the preceding, then you write a rough draft. The next to the last step is to revise the composition, making sure that it is coherent, unified, properly developed with good sentences and paragraphs, and that there are no errors in spelling, mechanics, punctuation, and diction. The last step is to endorse it, say a short prayer, and collapse on your bed. As you do, you hope you will have no nightmares in which English instructors are chasing you with gigantic red pens and waving papers you have written which have more red marks on them than anything else.

PARAGRAPH DEVELOPED WITH EXAMPLES

One can meet all kinds of drivers on the road. First, there is Obnoxious Oscar. Oscar careens down the street with the throttle wide open, poisoning the atmosphere with noxious smoke, waking up everyone within miles with his noisy muffler, and honking insistently at anyone who happens to be driving ahead of him. Second, there is Cautious Chauncey. Chauncey putters along at only ten miles per hour. He slows down to two miles per hour at each driveway and displays massive indifference to the immense traffic jam behind him. Third, there is Slippery Sam. Sam writhes in and out of traffic like an eel among coral. Nothing ever seems to happen to him, but such is not true of the other drivers who have been around him. Most of them are basket cases with thoroughly jangled nerves and with hips that have been hopelessly dislocated by jamming down on the brakes in trying to avoid him.

How much paragraph development is enough? That is a hard question to answer. Only your readers know for sure. If readers are not given enough examples or explanations to understand or accept your topic sentence, your paragraph is not sufficiently developed and, hence, one of the aspects of your thesis will be weakened.

Put yourself in the readers' position. If you were seeing the essay for the first time, would you find enough information in the body paragraphs to follow the author's ideas and understand the essay's generalizations and conclusions?

EXERCISE 61, PARAGRAPH DEVELOPMENT   (42e–f)

Read the following paragraphs and decide if they are sufficiently developed with supporting evidence. If a paragraph is sufficiently developed, write *yes* in the upper blank at the right; if it is not, write *no*. For each paragraph you have labeled *no*, on your own paper develop the paragraph adequately by adding appropriate supporting evidence.

Example   Pets can be a lot like children.   _no_

                         Both enjoy being spoiled and fussed over.

1.   The drive-up window at McDonald's is the direct descendant of the   _____
      hot-dog vendor's cart on the nineteenth-century street corner.
      Those pushcarts were the beginning of the fast-food business in
      America.

2.   Washing a car requires hard work if you do the job right. Not   _____
      only do you have to assemble the proper equipment—hose, bucket,
      soap, sponge, towels—usually from all over the house, but you have
      to use the proper method. Wetting the car, soaping and scrubbing
      it, scraping off road tar and squashed bugs is a messy, tiring
      procedure. Then you have to dry all the nooks and crannies
      carefully so the body doesn't rust. If you have any energy left,
      you can spend the rest of the afternoon waxing and buffing so
      the neighbors will actually be able to tell the car has been washed
      and not just caught in a rainstorm.

3.   Although the common cold results from viral infection, you are   _____
      more likely to catch a cold under certain circumstances. If you
      have not been taking good care of yourself, you may come down
      with a cold caused by weakened resistance to infection.

4.   In 1854, when Commodore Matthew Perry's Yankee warships   _____
      arrived in Edo (Tokyo) Bay, Japan was almost totally secluded.
      The nation had no interaction with the West. Things are quite
      different today.

5.   Ethnic foods from countries with hot climates often tend to taste   _____
      hot or spicy. Is the correspondence between climate and taste just
      an accident? One clue is food preservation against spoilage.

6.   Football is a game played by two teams of men. They move the   _____
      ball up and down the field, trying to cross one another's goal line
      and score points.

7. One student's preferred study habits may be another student's nightmare. My roommate likes to study on her bed while listening to records through her stereo earphones. If I tried that method, I would either be asleep in five minutes or writing song lyrics instead of chemistry problems. On the other hand, she thinks my study routine must be torture. I put my feet on the desk, prop the book on my knees, and chew gum furiously when I concentrate. My roommate says this can only lead to curvature of the spine, sore jaws, and cavities.

8. Sometimes people are reluctant to spend a lot of money on dinner in an ethnic restaurant, especially if they are unfamiliar with the cuisine. Visiting a festival sponsored by an ethnic group may be a good idea.

9. Choose a topic. Then, on your own paper, write a paragraph of at least four sentences, using details to develop the topic.

10. Choose a topic. Then, on your own paper, write a paragraph of at least six sentences, using examples and explanatory remarks concerning those examples to develop the topic.

11. Choose a topic that involves a question. Then, on your own paper, write a paragraph of at least five sentences, using reasons and explanations to develop the answer.

62

CONSISTENCY OF PARAGRAPH TONE   (42g)

A paragraph is **consistent** if its tone does not change unexpectedly for no apparent reason. The tone of your writing should be appropriate—both for your assumed audience and for your purpose and subject matter. Readers are unlikely to find your ideas and point of view credible if the language is sarcastic in one sentence, light and humorous in the next, and very solemn in the next. They will not trust you if the tone keeps shifting, because tone is an indication of attitude.

That is not to say that an essay may not shift among lighter moments and more serious ones; good writing often does that deliberately, to further the purpose and achieve desired effects. But unnecessary changes in tone will disconcert the reader, an experience you have probably had yourself. Imagine reading a paragraph that has a fairly serious tone when suddenly the author seems to find the subject very funny. You may become uncomfortable, even rather embarrassed, and begin to wonder if you've somehow overlooked the punch line or missed the point.

Tone is a cue to readers about the attitude you are taking toward the subject—and the attitude you want them to take. It is also a cue about your attitude toward the readers. If the level or type of vocabulary is inappropriate and inconsistent, not only will readers be confused and unsettled, they are likely to become irritated or even insulted.

The type and level of vocabulary used in a paragraph give it its tone. Notice how the tone of the following two paragraphs differs, although the subject is the same in both:

> Last night I had a blind date with one of the most attractive but least popular women in the class. She has a very superior attitude and makes men feel that they are not good enough for her. In view of her attitude toward the opposite sex, few men date her twice.

> Last night I was set up with one of our class's real losers. She's a knockout as far as looks go, but as for personality—a drag for sure. Talk about stuck up! She made it plain that on a scale of one to ten, I was a minus two. No wonder none of the guys are beating down her door.

The tone in each paragraph is consistent. In the first paragraph it is fairly formal, impersonal, and unemotional. The tone in the second paragraph is very informal. The use of slang emphasizes the writer's intensely personal feelings. The word choice conveys a sarcastic, somewhat angry attitude.

The tone of the second paragraph would be appropriate for a letter written to one of the author's close friends. The tone of the first paragraph is appropriate for a broader, more general audience. Imagine how inappropriate the second paragraph would be for that audience. Furthermore, imagine how inappropriate a mixture of the two tones would be.

> Last night I had a blind date with a real knockout as far as looks go, but she is one of the least popular women in the class. A real drag for sure, she has a very superior attitude and makes men feel like a minus two. In view of her attitude toward the opposite sex, none of the guys are beating down her door for dates.

Tone is one way of telling the reader how you want the meaning of a paragraph to be understood. If the tone is inconsistent, readers may dismiss your writing as amateurish, uncontrolled, and immature.

EXERCISE 62, CONSISTENCY OF PARAGRAPH TONE   (42g)

Using your own paper, revise the following paragraphs so that they reflect a consistent tone appropriate for a thoughtful, college-level audience.

1. The nation's immigration laws have not undergone reform since 1952. Recently, however, members of the U.S. House and Senate as well as other politicos have been horse trading, favor swapping, and jaw boning over proposals to stem the tide of illegal aliens flooding into the good ol' U.S. of A.

2. Mediterranean fruit flies are a menace sure to strike fear in the heart of any citrus grower. These pesky varmints can devastate an orange crop, costing the agriculture industry big bucks. Eradication programs involving aerial spraying and quarantines of infested areas can do the trick if a "medfly" invasion isn't too far along.

3. If icky, fishy, slimy stuff is your thing, you will probably go for the cuisine of Japan. Unlike Chinese food, many Japanese dishes are composed of raw ingredients, particularly seafood. Sushi is a good example. Sushi bars really pack 'em in in the San Francisco Bay area.

4. One special Japanese delicacy is sashimi prepared with "fugu"—the raw flesh of the poisonous puffer fish. When you eat fugu, you really have to be into living dangerously, because puffer toxin is 275 times more deadly than cyanide. Fugu chefs—guys who are up on how to detoxify the fish—have apprenticed for at least two years and have taken exams to become licensed in fugu preparation.

5. Awhile back I returned to the old country to visit Norway, the home of my ancestors more than a century ago. They hailed from around Bergen, an area on the west coast of Norway that is noted for its fjords. The way the mountainous cliffs rose majestically from the sea really knocked my socks off. That was some scenery, well worth the hassle of the long flight from the States and the lack of shut-eye on the train ride from Oslo.

63
WRITING PERSUASIVELY   (43d)

To be effective, writing must not only be unified, coherent, developed, and consistent, it must also be persuasive. An essay with a clear, manageable thesis that is sufficiently supported with well-organized, well-developed paragraphs will not be successful unless the reasoning used in the paragraphs is logical and fair.

That means that the generalizations presented in the thesis statement, topic sentences, and conclusions should not be so broad or overstated that they cannot be supported adequately by evidence. Judgments should be fair and soundly based in facts, not emotions or prejudices. The reasoning used to draw conclusions about the topic and to show the truth of a point of view should be logical, not filled with fallacies and errors. If you want to convince your readers, your writing must be credible. Credibility is built on supportable generalizations, fair judgments, and sound reasoning.

An unqualified **generalization** asserts that what is sometimes true is always true.

I know two members of the varsity football team and they are very poor students.
It's too bad that football players are so stupid.

In this example, a sweeping statement has been made based upon very limited evidence. Checking the scholastic records of all members of the team, however, very likely would have shown that on an overall basis, football players make about the same grades as other students. Some may be poor students, but others are good students and the majority, like the majority of all students, are probably average in their studies.

The point is, of course, that generalizations should be based upon a scrutiny of representative samples of actual, verifiable evidence. If, for example, the scholastic records of an entire football team were examined and it was determined that the scholastic average of these players was below average, it could be stated with authority, in this particular instance, at that particular school, that football players were below-average performers in the classroom. But to go further and state that all football players are below average would be making a generalization that had not been substantiated.

Unless you are certain about the absolute truth of a generalization and certain your readers are aware of its truth, you need to qualify the generalization to conform to the evidence. For example, the assertion about football players would have been more accurate and acceptable if the author had written, "It's too bad some football players are so stupid." If the reader can think of exceptions to the "rule" asserted in your generalization, then the generalization is "hasty." It is too broad, and making it weakens the credibility of your argument.

Fair judgments, like generalizations, must be based on facts. Making a judgment on what you want to believe is rarely as good as making a judgment on what you know. You should be particularly careful to avoid prejudice. Prejudiced statements can be not only those based on your own prejudices but those that appeal to the prejudices of others. Another tactic you should avoid is making your argument against an individual instead of against the issue; this type of argument is known as *argumentum ad hominem,* "argument to the man."

For example, one politician may say of an opponent, "Candidate Robbins will not represent working people's interests in the legislature. He inherited all his money. What could he know about the problems of average, working people?" This argument attacks Robbins personally because he has inherited wealth. It does not deal with the issue of his abilities as a state legislator. Robbins certainly does not necessarily have to be poor or even middle class to understand his constituents' problems or to speak on their behalf.

If a judgment cannot be supported by hard evidence, no amount of name calling or appealing to readers' personal biases will make it legitimate. Even if your prejudices are shared by readers, you are still responsible for presenting a fair and truthful point of view. Besides, thoughtful, questioning readers, unlikely to be fooled by prejudicial judgments derived from sketchy, loaded, or manipulated evidence, will respond negatively to arguments so constructed.

Various forms of unsound reasoning are known as **logical fallacies.** Some of the more common types of fallacious reasoning can be broadly categorized as fallacies of oversimplification or fallacies of distortion. Two fallacies have already been mentioned: hasty, broad generalization, a fallacy of oversimplification; and "argument to the man," a fallacy of distortion. Following is a discussion of some other fallacies included in these two categories.

FALLACIES OF OVERSIMPLIFICATION

1. *Post hoc, ergo propter hoc* ("after this, therefore because of this") is an inappropriate assumption that a cause-and-effect relationship exists.

> I knew when that black cat crossed my path last week I would have some bad luck. Sure enough, today I broke my leg. [It's very doubtful the cat was a contributing cause.]

2. *False analogy* occurs when the arguer assumes that because two things are alike in some respects, they are alike in all respects.

> Children are like fragile spring flowers. To be properly raised, both need lots of tender, loving care and plenty of protection from life's cold winds. [Children and flowers do benefit from loving care, but as many parents will testify, children are also resilient and suffer if they are overprotected from learning to deal with life's disappointments.]

3. *Either/or* (also known as *"all or nothing"*) *fallacy* is a statement that assumes only two alternatives when more than two are involved. This fallacy is sometimes called a "false dilemma."

> I know she isn't a Republican so she must be a Democrat. [The woman may be an Independent, a Communist, a Libertarian, unaffiliated, and so on.]

FALLACIES OF DISTORTION

4. *Argumentum ad verecundiam* (transfer fallacy) is an attempt to transfer characteristics, knowledge, or authority from one area of expertise to an unrelated area. This fallacy is commonly used in political campaigns and consumer advertisements such as endorsements by celebrities.

> Indianapolis 500-winner Ralph Racer says Super-Slick Oil is best. I'd better get some for my car. [There aren't many similarities between a race car and the family station wagon; Ralph's testimony may be less "expert" than it is being made to seem.]

5. *Argumentum ad populum* ("argument to the people") is an appeal to readers' emotions and biases, usually playing on beliefs that are widely held to be sacred (such as family values or patriotism) or on deeply ingrained distrust and fear (such as threats of Communist

invasion or nuclear war). A related fallacy is known as "bandwagon"; it appeals to people's instincts to "join the crowd."

> Every right-thinking citizen believes the federal government interferes too much in Americans' lives—except for Nicholas, but then he's an admitted socialist. [The "glitter" words "right-thinking citizen" and the "scare" word "socialist" play upon the crowd's desire to belong to an in-group.]

6. *Non sequitur* ("it does not follow") is a wrong inference instead of a logically sound conclusion, usually a leap in logic that omits proof.

> He is the person the class voted to be most successful. He is bound to be a company president. [Success has many definitions, and it's a long way to the executive suite.]

7. *Begging the question* is an assumption of the truth of a statement when, in fact, the truth has to be proven.

> Since she's rich, she must have done something illegal to get all that money. [Wealth is assumed to be evil or at least the result of evil doings. The writer assumes but does not prove that wealth cannot be acquired honestly. The fact is, many fortunes are built on honest labor and sound, legal investments.]

8. *Red herring* is a false "scent" or "trail," an attempt to distract the reader from the real issue needing proof by changing the subject to something else. A red herring often introduces an emotional subject intended to divert the reader's attention.

> I didn't deserve a D on the French test. Besides, the instructor doesn't like me. [Personal dislike, whether true or not, is beside the point. The issue is the quality of the student's work.]

Practice: Identifying unqualified generalizations   Some of the following statements contain qualifying words that make them acceptable generalizations. Other statements do not contain qualifiers, are too sweeping, and are thus unacceptable generalizations. Underline the qualifying words in the acceptable generalizations. Write unacceptable after those generalizations that are unqualified and too sweeping. The answers are listed next.

[1] Anybody who can make money in this business must be crooked. [2] College professors are all so liberal they will support any cause. [3] Some Italians talk very fast and wave their hands while they talk. [4] Beautiful women usually turn out to be stupid. [5] Swedes are big, blonde, and dumb. [6] Because of the Southerners' record of racial prejudice, some people are concerned that Blacks occasionally cannot get a square deal in parts of the South. [7] Orientals sometimes have trouble learning English because the linguistic systems of the Indo-European languages and Oriental languages are so different. [8] Environmentalists will oppose his nomination for Secretary of the Interior. He voted against environmental issues when he was in Congress. [9] A person who has taken three writing courses will generally write better than the person who has taken none. [10] Almost everyone enjoys professional football, but a few people become fanatical football fans.

Answers to the Practice   [1]unacceptable [*anybody* is too sweeping and all-inclusive] [2]unacceptable [*all* and *any* are too all-inclusive]   [3]*some*   [4]unacceptable [*beautiful women* and *usually* are too all-inclusive]   [5]unacceptable [*Swedes* is too sweeping, implying that *all Swedes* are big, blonde, and dumb.]   [6]*Some, occasionally, parts*   [7]*sometimes*   [8]unacceptable [*Environmentalists* is too all-inclusive; some environmentalists might approve the nomination. The second sentence needs no qualification because it is a matter of record.]   [9]*generally* [10]*almost, few*

Name _____ Date _____ Score _____

EXERCISE 63-1, GENERALIZATIONS AND FAIRNESS   (43)

For each of the following statements, insert an X in the blank at the right if the statement is a faulty generalization; write *OK* if the statement is not faulty.

Examples	There's no doubt about it: Latins are very warmhearted and outgoing, whereas Swedish people are cold and reserved.

_____X_____

It almost never snows in Miami.

_____OK_____

1. All politicians are dishonest.   _____

2. Jones is a well-liked instructor. In student evaluations, over 90 percent of his students give him the highest possible rating.   _____

3. A barometer's dropping sharply indicates that rain or some kind of inclement weather is probable.   _____

4. College graduates are more intelligent than anyone else.   _____

5. If you go out with wet hair, you are bound to catch a cold.   _____

6. Women make poor business managers; they're too emotional.   _____

7. Fat people don't care about their looks or they would lose weight.   _____

8. We sold twice as many Lee jeans in our store as all other brands combined. Our customers obviously prefer Lees.   _____

9. Sales in district A have dropped. We need a new district manager.   _____

10. Statistics show that over 50,000 people die and over 2 million others are injured in automobile accidents every year in the U.S.A. You take your life in your hands every time you get into a car.   _____

11. Less than half the people in the 18 to 21 age group voted last year. Obviously, young people don't care about their country.   _____

12. O'Malley flunked biology, chemistry, anatomy, and physiology. I think she should give up trying to be a doctor.   _____

13. Some high school students are not college material.   _____

14. Since Americans are law-abiding citizens, they obey the 55-mile-per-hour speed limit.   _____

15. He voted against the school bond issue. I wonder why he is against children.   _____

16. Hemingway is regarded as one of the great writers of this century. Everyone who reads him likes him. _____

17. On our campus, engineering students take only one semester of the English composition sequence. Obviously, they are good writers and don't need the second writing course. _____

18. You can't play tackle in professional football unless you weigh over 200 pounds. _____

19. All of Professor Simpkin's students get A's and B's. This proves he is a good teacher. _____

20. Every time I go to the doctor, he finds something wrong with me. Doctors are certainly out after the money. _____

21. Capital punishment involves the destruction of a human being. Consequently, everyone who favors it is a murderer at heart. _____

22. College entrance scores have gone down considerably over the past ten years. This proves that young people are not as smart as they used to be. _____

23. Grades are bad because they give some students an inferiority complex. Consequently, we should do away with grades. _____

24. We know we have a good coach because our team has won the championship six years in a row. _____

25. Prices at the grocery store keep going up. Farmers must be making a nice profit. _____

For each of the following statements, insert an *X* in the blank to the right if the statement is unfair, unethical, prejudiced, or based on apparent wishful thinking rather than on a straightforward examination of the evidence. If the statement is correct, write *OK*.

Example   My neighbor Jack says Ann Jones hates children; no wonder she's a lousy teacher.   X

26. They made their money in the liquor business so they are obviously an immoral lot. _____

27. I know that they have a much better record than we do, but our team has spirit and will win. _____

28. Hudson County would vote for the devil himself if he were on the Democratic ticket. _____

29. My son says he saw the minister's daughter shoplifting at the discount store. He must have been mistaken. _____

30. He has been convicted twice for graft. I can't see voting for him for county treasurer. _____

31. There must be something wrong with their merchandise since the prices are so low. _____

32. College professors are smart in the classroom, but they don't have enough common sense to walk across the street. _____

33. Teenagers pay more for insurance because statistics show that a greater percentage of that age group is involved in accidents than are other groups. _____

EXERCISE 63-2, UNSOUND REASONING: FALLACIES   (43)

For each of the following statements, write an *X* in the blank to the right if the statement contains any of the fallacies discussed in Section 63. If the statement is logical, write *OK*.

Example   The poor are not industrious; if they were, they   _____X_____
                wouldn't be poor.

1. All twentieth-century wars in which the United States has been
    involved were started under Democratic administrations. So if
    you want war, vote Democratic.   _____

2. If *The New York Times* says so, it's probably true.   _____

3. Senator Millstrom says the Russians will never attack us, so let's
    do away with our ICBM's.   _____

4. They pull their pants on one leg at a time just as we do, so they
    can't be any better than we are.   _____

5. The rain came because the Indians staged their rain dance.   _____

6. I'm sure she isn't Catholic, so she must be Protestant.   _____

7. I have had trouble with botany, so I'll probably have trouble
    with zoology.   _____

8. Since he was a Heisman Trophy winner, his chances of being
    a starter for the Cowboys are good.   _____

9. Professor Stillwell kicked the demonstrators out of his class.
    He certainly doesn't believe in free speech.   _____

10. Joe worked twenty hours a week this term and flunked out.
    It just goes to prove you can't go to school and work at the
    same time.   _____

11. She is a very inconsistent person because she does one thing
    one time and just the opposite the next.   _____

12. Flu shots work only about three-fourths of the time. But it's
    still a good idea to take them if a flu epidemic is suspected.   _____

13. They won the national championship last year and have most
    of their personnel back. So they're bound to win again this year. _____

14. Twenty movie stars have endorsed this brand of cosmetics. If
    it's good enough for them, it's good enough for you.   _____

15. American auto workers have sabotaged several cars on automobile
    production lines. You're better off buying a foreign automobile. _____

16. When you have insomnia, you can either toss and turn or take a sleeping pill. _____

17. Since he received nothing but A's in accounting, he should be a good accountant. _____

18. To become a successful person, one must be successful in what he or she attempts. _____

19. Buying stock in our company is a good investment. We are planning to expand our market and the value of your shares will skyrocket. _____

20. Professor Jones is one of the top psychologists in the country; so when she says that nuclear power is dangerous, we should listen to her. _____

21. Cleenzo must be the best detergent or it wouldn't be the leading brand. _____

22. I said you're too young to drive 400 miles to your grandmother's by yourself. Since I'm your parent, I know what's best. _____

23. Television programs that portray homosexuality and extramarital affairs are a threat to American family values. _____

24. A prison can be a lot like a pressure cooker. If the prisoners' anger and frustration reach the boiling point and find no safe release, the lid can blow off. _____

25. After Marcia dyed her hair, she had many more dates. It is true that blondes have more fun. _____

64
BUSINESS CORRESPONDENCE   (48)

All the skills you have practiced throughout this workbook are applicable to the writing tasks you will face on the job. Both academic and business writing require attention to the same elements of composition: purpose, audience, tone, style, grammar, spelling, punctuation, and organization. If anything, your business associates will be *less* tolerant of poor writing than your college teachers have been. The purpose of business correspondence is to get things done. Consequently, good business writing does not waste a reader's time. It is clear, straightforward, and, above all, efficient.

When you compare business correspondence with academic writing such as essays or term papers, you first might think of the visual differences. College papers are usually composed of uninterrupted paragraphs headed by a title. They also tend to run for a number of pages, frequently three or more. On the other hand, business correspondence uses various kinds of headings, routing instructions, and visual cues to assist the reader. With the exception of reports, most business correspondence is much shorter than college papers: letters are usually no more than a page or two, memos rarely more than three pages long.

Visual cues are important in business correspondence. Paragraphs tend to be shorter than in an essay, research paper, or novel. Lists are sometimes presented vertically, and series may include bullets (dots, asterisks, or dashes preceding listed items) or numbers that would be omitted in an essay.

These stylistic differences between academic and business writing have to do with the way business letters and memos are used. As part of its function of getting a job done, business correspondence often serves as a reference document. Consequently, the reader must be able to find items quickly. By dividing the discussion more frequently into subtopics and by providing more visual cues, the writer aids not only the reader's understanding but also provides a fast, easy reference to specific portions of the document. (For a full discussion of business correspondence types and formats, see Section 48 of the *Prentice-Hall Handbook for Writers,* Ninth Edition.)

The following examples illustrate how the same topic might be treated in the opening paragraphs of a college essay and in a business memo. Notice the differences in the looks of the two examples.

Those Vital Volunteers

ESSAY

Volunteers comprise a vital part of the staff behind a city's efforts to help its disadvantaged citizens. Volunteers assist the professional personnel in many social service agencies by answering telephones, providing transportation, raising funds, and meeting clients when appropriate. Locally, volunteers serve many programs such as Legal Advocates for the Poor, Crisis Hot-Line, the Job Training Center, and the Battered Wives and Children Shelter. In recent years, the number of volunteers has decreased. Our city's Chamber of Commerce is developing a Leadership Academy to attract and train large numbers of volunteers for this important work.

To:	Barbara Swift, Mayor
From:	Stan Cox, Councilman
Date:	July 26, 198___
Subject:	Local Volunteer Leadership

The Chamber of Commerce on July 22 approved a plan for a Leadership Academy. The purpose of the academy would be to train leaders for local volunteer work. Having attended that meeting, I recommend that the City Council endorse the Chamber's plan.

Program Priorities

The Chamber members believe our city must enlarge its dwindling corps of volunteers to assist local social service agencies. A recent Chamber survey shows that programs in great need include

- Legal Advocates for the Poor
- Crisis Hot-Line
- Job Training Center
- Battered Wives and Children Shelter

Besides using routine instructions—usual in the memo format—and short paragraphs, a list with bullets, and a heading, this memo shows two other features common to effective business correspondence: a summary beginning and streamlined sentences.

Section 57 discusses various types of beginnings for essays. Although any of these may occasionally be effective in business correspondence, most businesspeople prefer an opening that gets right to the point—as Stan Cox does when he states his recommendation in the first paragraph. Remember, recipients of business correspondence are not reading for pleasure or for edification. They are reading because they need information to make decisions, to take action. If your letter or memo takes too long to get to the point, you will have wasted your reader's time and tried his or her patience. As a result, you are less likely to achieve the response you want from the reader.

This same principle of efficiency should be carried out in the sentence structure you use. Try to give your readers the greatest amount of necessary information in the fewest number of words. For instance, compare

The Chamber members believe our city must enlarge its dwindling corps of volunteers to assist local social service agencies.

It is believed by the members of the Chamber of Commerce that the corps of volunteers, whose numbers have decreased in recent years, needs to be enlarged by our city so that they can give assistance to social service agencies in the local area.

Obviously, the second example is much more long-winded than the first. The extra words are caused by unnecessary nominals, weak verbs, passive voice verbs, expletives, and phrases. Although none of these are grammatically incorrect, they can be time wasters in business correspondence.

Nominals are nouns formed from verbs: *assistance* from *assist; opposition* from *oppose; statement* from *state.* Common suffixes added to verbs in forming nominals are *-ment, -tion, -ance,* and sometimes *-ity, ize, -ness.*

Weak verbs such as *give, make,* or *take* often appear with nominals because strong verbs have been changed into nouns, so that new verbs must be found for the sentences. The previous sample contains just such a combination of nominal and weak verb: "so that they can *give assistance.*" Notice how restoring a strong verb adds power and brevity to the sentence: "so that they can *assist.*"

Passive voice verbs tend to drain energy from sentences while adding extra words. (Passive constructions are discussed thoroughly in Sections 13 and 45.) For instance, the phrases "It *is believed* by the members" and "the corps . . . *needs to be enlarged* by our city" become more forceful when revised: "The members *believe*" and "our city *needs to enlarge* the corps . . . ."

Expletives (*it is, there were,* etc.) can also be great time wasters. The previous example shows that "It is" adds nothing important to its sentence. An expletive often occurs with a relative pronoun clause containing a sentence's real subject: "*It is* clear *that we* need volunteers." Replacing the expletive with the subject of the relative pronoun clause streamlines the sentence: "Clearly, *we* need volunteers."

Unnecessary phrases can clog writing, too. Frequently, relative pronouns can be "understood" and thus dropped from a sentence: "The Chamber of Commerce believes (*that*) our city must . . . ." Often a prepositional phrase can be rewritten as a single-word modifier: "social service agencies *in the local area*" becomes "*local* social service agencies"; "the members *of the Chamber of Commerce*" becomes "the *Chamber* members." Using the *'s* possessive form can sometimes eliminate a phrase: instead of "the decision *of the mayor*" write "the *mayor's* decision." Verbals (root verb + *ing*) can also be substituted for prepositional phrases into one short, smooth verbal phrase: *with regard to the meeting on Tuesday* becomes *regarding Tuesday's meeting.*

Nominals, passive voice verbs, expletives, relative pronoun and prepositional phrases all have their place in good writing, including good business writing. The point is, we often use more of them than we need; as a result, we use more words than we need or our readers want. Besides lengthening sentences, these constructions can add a ponderous, pompous tone to writing, creating stuffy-sounding business correspondence. Letters and memos should sound cordial and natural. You don't want a chummy, overly casual tone, but neither do you want to sound like a stuffed shirt. Avoid **business jargon**: rather than creating a businesslike tone, it simply makes your writing sound stiff and old-fashioned, even cold and unfriendly. Instead of "as per your request" say "as you requested"; instead of "at the time of this writing" say "now" or "today." The following list contrasts jargon phrases to more natural, often shorter equivalents preferred in modern business correspondence:

JARGON	PREFERRED
at all times	always
due to the fact that	because
in the amount of [referring to money]	for
in the event that	if
please find enclosed	enclosed is
pursuant to	concerning

EXERCISE 64-1, SUMMARY BEGINNINGS AND ACTION ENDINGS   (48)

Much business correspondence wastes a reader's time because its subject, purpose, and main point are unclear or buried in a mass of detail. Furthermore, the ending of a business letter or memo should not leave the reader wondering what happens next. The writer should supply an "action ending" that clearly indicates the action the writer desires from the reader.

Read the following memo, paying careful attention to its organization as well as to its contents. Then write a new subject line that more accurately and specifically identifies what you believe to be the memo's true topic. Second, write a new opening paragraph that clearly expresses what you believe to be the memo's main point and purpose. Finally, write a concluding paragraph that contains an action ending.

To: Bob Jones, district supervisor

From: Melanie Harper, sales representative

Date: August 3, 198__

Subject: Sales visits

This week I called on my customers to obtain their holiday toy orders. I was able to see buyers at all but two of the sixteen stores in my territory.

Mr. Hobson at Brown's Department Store placed orders for our full line of existing toys. He increased his order for Outdoor Andy, our male doll, noting that it sold very well during the last holiday season. Outdoor Andy seems to have done well at other stores in my territory too. I showed Mr. Hobson Sprinkle, the plastic puppy that drinks from its own dish and then wets. I explained that this new toy would be available next month in time for holiday ordering. Mr. Hobson wasn't interested.

Only three buyers in my territory showed any interest in Sprinkle. Two said they would order a dozen in September. Can you suggest ways that I might make this toy more attractive to buyers? I think we're going to have a hard time selling it.

The promotional strategy we discussed at the district sales meeting in July focused on Sprinkle's cuteness. Most of my customers pointed out that while children may think the puppy cute, parents will object to a toy that could leave water marks on rugs and furniture. Pardon the expression, but Sprinkle is likely to be a real "dog" in terms of new sales for the company.

I plan to spend next Monday and Tuesday revisiting Toy Palace and Murphy's Play Shop to talk with the buyers I missed last week. So far, holiday orders in my territory are about the same or slightly lower than last year.

To: Bob Jones

From: Melanie Harper

Date: August 3, 198___

Subject: _____

Opening paragraph: _____

_____

_____

_____

_____

_____

_____

_____

_____

Concluding paragraph: _____

_____

_____

_____

_____

_____

_____

_____

_____

_____

_____

_____

EXERCISE 64-2, STREAMLINING SENTENCES
AND ELIMINATING JARGON   (48)

The following job application letter is set out in correct business form and is well organized. However, its style is poor. The letter contains long-winded sentences and stuffy business jargon that give it an impersonal, unpleasing tone sure to create a negative impression of the job applicant. Revise the letter, eliminating ~minals, weak verbs, passive voice verbs, expletives, and unnecessary phrases wh ~ doing so improves the letter's tone and readability. Substitute more cordial, natu ~sounding expressions for the jargon.

329 Maple Cou
Stanton, Texas
May 14, 198__

Ms. Josephine Yeager
Director, User Systems
Data Processing Services, Inc.
Industrial Park, Texas

Dear Ms. Yeager:

Pursuant to your advertisement posted in the placement office at our college, I see that you have a position open for a computer programmer. It is my hope that you will give consideration to my application for that job.

My qualifications include a bachelor's degree in computer science which will be received on June 10 from Mesa College. During the past summer I gained experience in data processing at Software Specialists, a company in the local area. This year I was also given employment on a part-time basis by Mesa College in the business office where I helped with the maintenance of the computer files of the college. I was chosen over four other students who were majoring in computer science who applied for the job.

In accordance with your request, please find enclosed a resume, which gives further details of my educational and work experience. You will see that my initiative and reliability are evidenced by the fact that most of my college education has been paid for by myself.

Due to the fact that I will be making a visit to the home of my parents soon, I would like to pay Data Processing Services a visit and discuss your job opening with you. You will get a call from me early next week to make arrangements for an interview. In the event that you have questions in the meantime, please do not hesitate to contact me.

Sincerely,

Martin Burgess

Martin Burgess

_____

_____

_____

_____

_____

_____

_____

_____

_____

_____

_____

_____

_____

_____

_____

_____

Using your own paper, write an application letter for a job you would like. Further discussion of employment letters and resumes can be found in Section 48 of the *Prentice-Hall Handbook for Writers,* Ninth Edition.

PRENTICE-HALL DIAGNOSTIC TEST REVIEW I

The purpose of this section and the next one is to provide practice for the *Prentice-Hall Diagnostic Test for Writers.* The instructions are similar to those on the *Diagnostic* test. This section reviews punctuation, basic grammar, and sentence recognition.

Some of the following sentences require additional punctuation. Decide if any punctuation is needed immediately *before* the italicized word, and then write the corresponding number in the blank at the right.

1. The sentence needs a comma.
2. The sentence needs a semicolon.
3. The sentence needs a colon.
4. The sentence is correctly punctuated.

Example   The book had been ordered *however* it had not arrived.   _2_

1. In his new book about immigrants *Julian* L. Simon discussed myths about immigrants. _____
2. As a matter of fact *Nine Myths About Immigration* is the title of Simon's book. _____
3. When immigrant families and native families are matched by age and education *the* results show that neither category tends to use welfare services more than the other. _____
4. The average immigrant family is younger *than* the average native family. _____
5. Because immigrant families are younger and tend to have younger children *they* do in fact spend more money on education. _____
6. When a family spends money on public education *the* government is also paying to provide that service. _____
7. The higher education cost is offset *however,* by lower payments from Social Security, Medicare, and Medicaid. _____
8. In 1975 *the* base year used for Simon's study, the average native family received more money from these sources than did immigrant families. _____
9. The average native family received $922 from these sources *the* average immigrant family received only one-tenth this amount. _____
10. Some studies show that *even* illegal immigrants do not place excessive burdens on the country's social agencies. _____
11. Only four percent of illegal immigrants go to school free *and* only one percent receive food stamps or welfare payments. _____
12. Seventy-seven percent of all illegal immigrants pay Social Security taxes *but* almost none of them receives these funds back from Social Security. _____
13. Within three to five years after legal entry into the United States *immigrant* family earnings are higher than those of native families. _____

14. Immigrant wage earners are, of course, subject to the same income taxes, sales taxes *and* excise taxes everyone else pays. _____

15. Clearly, immigrants continue to *improve* the tax base in the United States. _____

Read the following sentences carefully for errors in standard English. Circle any errors, and then revise the sentences specifically to correct the errors you have circled.

Example   Do immigrants actually take jobs away from native workers who (wants) work?

Do immigrants actually take jobs away from native workers who want work?

16. That immigrants actually increase unemployment are one of the most common myths.

_____

17. In a few cases these charge may be true.

_____

18. There have been a large influx of foreign physicians into the U.S.

_____

19. Native physician may earn less since this influx has increase the number of available physicians.

_____

20. However, in the restaurant, agriculture, and hotel industries immigrants take jobs that they won't take.

_____

21. A study in San Diego concluded that recent immigrants often take jobs that "were not appealing to the local residents."

_____

22. The wages was too low, the hours was too long, and the work was too difficult.

_____

23. Four out of five legal immigrants under the age of forty.

_____

24. Immigrants starts their own businesses more rapidly than do natives.

_____

25. The current image of immigrants as a burden on the country are in sharp contrast with the economic reality.

_____

PRENTICE-HALL DIAGNOSTIC TEST REVIEW II

This section reviews sentence, paragraph, and composition elements in a manner similar to the *Prentice-Hall Diagnostic Test for Writers*.

Each of the following three groups contains four sentences expressing the same general thought. Select the most precise, clear, and effective sentence, and write its number in the blank at the right.

A.

1. Immigrants are not a burden on the economy and are often blamed for it.
2. Immigrants are people who are not a burden on the economy and blamed for it.
3. Immigrants are not a burden on the economy and are people who are blamed for being so.
4. Although they are not a burden on the economy, immigrants are sometimes blamed for being so.   _____

B.

1. In the modern world of today we desire the world of tomorrow with impatience, but looking back from tomorrow, we may want today back again.
2. Today we await the future impatiently, but tomorrow we may long for the past.
3. We may be impatient for the future, but tomorrow we may long for the past.
4. Today impatient, the past may be longed for by us tomorrow.   _____

C.

1. Immigrants as a whole contain uneducated and educated.
2. The entire population of immigrants has some dummies and some really sharp types.
3. With respect to the attainment of various levels of education, the immigrant population exhibits a remarkably high standard deviation.
4. The immigrant population in this country includes a high percentage of unskilled workers, but it also includes a very high percentage of highly skilled, highly educated professionals.   _____

Each of the following two groups contains a topic sentence for a paragraph and five supporting sentences. Read the sentences and then decide how the supporting sentences would best form a well-organized paragraph. You may decide to omit some sentences entirely. In the blank following each exercise, list the numbers of the supporting sentences in the order you believe they should appear in the paragraph.

A.   Topic sentence: Being overqualified for a job can affect
                                            an employee's performance.

1. This dissatisfaction may result in several kinds of behavior.
2. Others try to change the nature of the job, actually putting in extra effort to make their jobs more interesting.
3. A person who is overqualified for his or her job is often a dissatisfied employee.
4. Some employees react to job dissatisfaction by being absent from work frequently or by loafing while at work.
5. More than 35 percent of the workers in the United States believe they are overqualified for their jobs.   _____

B.   Topic sentence: Changing careers in middle age takes special
                                            preparation.

1. To help people deal with these negative feelings, counselors and educators are developing courses in changing careers.
2. Sometimes they believe themselves to be weird or different— or believe that they have failed—if they no longer like their old jobs.
3. At first people considering career changes may experience overwhelming fear at the thought of leaving their old job's security.
4. For some people, a change of career can be the best thing that ever happened to them.
5. Such courses enable participants to share their fears and receive professional advice.   _____

The following two groups list ideas that might be used for a 500-word essay. Read each essay assignment and choose the answer you think would be the most suitable. Write its number in the blank at the right of the exercise.

A.   For an assignment requiring a 500-word essay on *popular music,* which of the following topics has the best focus?

1. The influence of Scots Border Ballads on American Country Music
2. The Modern Symphony
3. The Appeal of Black Gospel Songs
4. Protest Music and the 1960's   _____

B.   For a 500-word essay on *recent immigrants,* which of the following topics has the best focus?

1. Recent Immigrants
2. Recent Immigrants to the United States
3. Problems Faced by Vietnamese Immigrants to the United States
4. Immigrants: Myths and Realities   _____

INDEX